A SystemC™ Primer

Second Edition

A SystemC™ Primer

Second Edition

J. BHASKER
eSilicon Corporation

BSP **BS Publications**
An Imprint of **BSP Books Pvt. Ltd.**
4-4-309/316, Giriraj Lane,
Sultan Bazar, Hyderabad - 500 095

A System C™ Primer, Second Edition *by* J. Bhasker
First Indian Ed. 2008
Fifth Reprint 2025

Published by :

BS Publications
An Imprint of **BSP Books Pvt. Ltd.**
4-4-309/316, Giriraj Lane, Sultan Bazar,
Hyderabad - 500 095
Phone: 040 - 23445688
e-mail: info@bspbooks.net
website: www.bspbooks.net

In arrangement with
Star Galaxy Publishing
1058 Treeline Drive, Allentown, PA 18103
Phone : 610-391-7296

For sale in India, Pakistan, Srilanka, Bangladesh, Nepal, Maldives and Maynmar only.

WARNING - DISCLAIMER

The author and publisher have used their best efforts in preparing this book and the examples contained in it. They make no representation, however, that the examples are error-free or are suitable for every application to which a reader may attempt to apply them. The author and the publisher make no warranty of any kind, expressed or implied, with regard to these examples, documentation or theory contained in this book, all of which is provided "as is". The author and the publisher shall not be liable for any direct or indirect damages arising from any use, direct or indirect, of the examples provided in this book.

Price: Rs. 795.00

ISBN: 978-81-7800-141-8 (Paperback)

Other books by the same author:

- A VHDL Synthesis Primer, Second Edition, BS Publications, ISBN 81-7800-014-8, Indian Reprint 2001 **(for Indian subcontinent)**.
- A Verilog HDL Primer, Third Edition, BS Publications, ISBN 978-81-7800-142-5, Indian Reprint 2008 **(for Indian subcontinent)**.
- Verilog HDL Synthesis, A Practical Primer, BS Publications, ISBN 81-7800-011-3, Indian Reprint 2001 **(for Indian subcontinent)**.

To my theses advisors:

Prof. J. Vasi
Prof. S.N. Maheshwari
Prof. Sartaj Sahni

who have been a great source of inspiration for me.

Contents

❑

Foreword

SystemC is the by-product of the confluence of multiple interrelated "stress points" occurring in the electronic design world. Two of the most interesting stress points are:

- The increasingly shortened time to market requirements for electronic devices.
- The growing complexity of electronic devices and the coming of platform-based design methodologies.

SystemC is designed to help address these and other stress points, as I shall briefly discuss.

The increasingly shortened time to market requirements for electronic devices.

Customers of electronic devices have become pampered by the way they are treated by manufacturers of electronic devices. Discount stores are filled with devices that until recently could have been (and often were) props in a science fiction novel. One need only look at the size and features of cellular phones or portable computers to see this point.

Moreover, because profit margins for both producers and sellers are so narrow, there is extreme motivation to repeatedly introduce even more advanced products into the market in the hope that consumers will replace last year's wonder device with this year's winner. This spiral of rapid introduction of new electronics with enhanced features at cheaper prices is exacerbated by the intense competition between manufacturer and lack of customer loyalty: if you don't give the consumer what they want when they want it, someone else will.

There are multiple ways that manufacturers can cut time to market. One fundamental way to speed design ideas to reality is to shorten the design cycle. This shortening will undoubtedly involve methodologies for finding bugs as early in the design process as possible, thereby eliminating or reducing the need to 'cycle back' to correct those bugs. However, an even more fundamental way to shorten the time needed to produce an integrated circuit is to shorten the time required for each step of the design process.

As it turns out, functional verification, i.e., (broadly speaking) the validation that the device does what it was designed to do, is not only a key portion of every design process, but also a substantial bottleneck. Such functional verification may involve a check regarding quality — will my pocket PC continue to play my MP3 files when I start up a word processing application, or will I hear an annoying audio glitch? Alternatively, there may be a need to make sure that the electronic device conforms to an agreed upon standard, e.g., a wireless networking standard such as the 802.11b. Finally, there may be a need to determine as much as is feasible that the device will not fail when an unusual combination of events happen, e.g., the simultaneous pushing of the 'start' and 'stop' buttons.

This type of functional verification is obviously crucial if product quality is to be maintained. Unfortunately, the very act of modeling a complex circuit in software, and executing this model on a software verification system is inherently very slow. Indeed, if the model is designed to represent every state of the device under design right down to each clock cycle, the time needed to exhaustively verify performance may easily run into centuries!

Use of SystemC can help speed up this functional verification in that it allows designs to be initially written in an untimed manner, i.e., without regard to the clocking scheme that will be actually implemented in the device. This provides a significant speedup in that changes in clock signals make up a large portion of the events that an event-driven simulator must process during the verification process. Indeed, this desire to be able to simulate a design independent of the system clock(s) was the motivation behind the introduction of variable assignments into VHDL. Unfortunately, so-called 'behavioral VHDL' proved fairly limited in its expressive power, a limitation avoided in SystemC due to its basis in the quite general C++.

One point to be made here is that use of C++, even SystemC, by itself does not provide significant additional speed. If all clock transitions in a design are represented in SystemC, the resulting speed of simulation will more than likely be very close to that of the corresponding VHDL or Verilog model. Any additional speed gained in this case will be the result of optimizations made by the simulator developer. However, such optimizations will be much more modest than those attained by simulating at a higher level of abstraction.

The growing complexity of electronic devices and platform based design.

Great interest is often paid to the number of transistors able to be placed on a single piece of working silicon — even popular publications have references to "Moore's Law". However, the number of possible transistors is less interesting in this context than the increased functional devices that can be put on a single functioning piece of silicon. Today, the notion of 'System on Chip' is a reality, and full functioning systems that include complex processors (and their peripherals), digital signal processors, multi-layer buses, multiple memories and other blocks that might have been separate ASICs in the past, e.g., MPEG blocks, are actually being fabricated.

This is tremendous progress, since it allows multiple devices to "talk" to each other without incurring the inherent cost in speed degradation that comes when communication must flow between chips. Moreover, putting an entire system on a single piece of silicon allows for the sort of product miniaturization that is required given the ever-shrinking size of (especially) consumer products.

This advent of true systems on chip together with increasing time to market has begun to give rise to the notion of 'platform-based design'. The basic notion in platform-based systems envisions a new kind of division of labor: silicon producers develop a basic silicon platform, complete with processors (control and DSPs), memory hierarchy and possibly specialized application specific blocks. Systems companies, who have no incentive (or, often, capability) to develop this basic silicon platform, add their value on top of it by leveraging the programmable portions of the platform, i.e., either by adding software on one of the processors or by programming specialized hardware in the platform's FPGA area (if the platform has one).

Thus, in a simplified scenario, a silicon manufacturer may develop a platform that can be used as the core processing center for a third generation cellular phone. A systems company, who is in the business of selling such phones, takes this base platform and "programs" it (either in software or in hardware via FPGAs) to give it an identity specific to the systems company. For example, the systems company may add user interface software that will make the cell phone extremely easy to use. It may also program some energy saving IP into the FPGA blocks of the platform to allow for extended battery life. After such programming, the enhanced platform is returned to the silicon provider, who then fabricates it.

This is a win-win for both parties to the transaction, since the silicon manufacturer keeps its fabrication facilities filled, while the systems company can concentrate on adding those features that will differentiate its product. Indeed, the systems company may decide to create an entire product family, by programming the platform differently for different members of that product family. The chip in the low cost product may not have the power monitoring facility, while the chip in the high end product may have a myriad of features programmed into it -- with family members between high and low end having some subset of those features. Underlying this product family would be the same silicon platform.

A problem, however, lurks in this scenario: how to communicate the nature of the platform to the systems designers who shall be customizing it? It is a silicon platform, but the traditional ways that have been used to represent designs in silicon, e.g., layouts, gate descriptions and so forth, will most likely not be understood very well by systems designers. Similarly, a description in a language such as VHDL or Verilog at the register transfer level will probably not be very understandable. Indeed, even a textual description in a natural language such as English by itself will be of limited use — it will be just too voluminous.

Clearly, what is needed is an "executable specification". The executable specification will be a simulation model of the platform that its recipients can execute using input test benches (their own and/or that given by the platform provider). Observing the behavior of the various parts of the platform for different input stimuli, and looking at the source code for various portions of the platform, can give the systems engineering team knowledge of the platform that they are to customize.

This will work, however, only if the performance of the executable specification will be quick enough to make observation of its behavior practical. Further, since the system design team will read it, this specification should be written in terms understood by them, i.e., it should be written at the right level of abstraction. Thus, in a network design, communication between blocks may be best described in terms of the transport of packets, rather than by the underlying changing of signals.

These dual needs to have a speedy execution model and one in which lower level constructs are represented at a higher level of abstraction points to use of an untimed C++ description to represent the platform. As noted above, untimed models written in C++ will execute quickly, and C++ is a language well suited to the definition of those abstract data types that will be recognizable to systems designers.

Moreover, use of C++ as an executable specification has an additional advantage in that it can naturally interface with the C++ software models written by systems design teams to customize the platform. This allows creation of an even larger executable specification — original silicon platform plus software customization — that can be used by both the systems company and the silicon platform provider to understand the behavior of the customized platform. In fact, given that EDA vendors are starting to develop tools that can synthesize C++ to FPGAs, even models that are used to customize the platform in hardware can be easily interfaced to the original specification of the platform.

Given the above, it is not surprising that both producers and consumers of silicon platforms are adopting design styles that include SystemC modeling.

Why SystemC?

If one accepts the above, then the increasing need for design methodologies that include modeling in C++ should be clear. This does not, however, by itself argue for SystemC as defined by the Open SystemC Initiative (OSCI). C++ is an open and quite malleable language. Given the right level of manpower, any company can define a style of using C++ that can meet the requirements laid out above. Indeed, a large number of companies have already done so.

Therein lies the rationale for SystemC as defined by OSCI. If each company (or even small groups of companies) defines their own methodology for using C++ to do design, then the ability for companies to easily interact with each other is greatly diminished. As designs are shared between companies, it will be incumbent for the recipient of the design to first understand the dialect of C++ that the producer has used. Clearly, this will be an impediment for the sort of design exchange required between silicon platform provider and consumer.

Further, this also impairs the ability of third party intellectual property (IP) providers, e.g., developers of models of processors, to develop models that can be adapted by a wide range of companies. Having to cope with multiple dialects of C++ will require developers of complete systems to either develop all of their own models for sub-systems, or else to adapt a third parties' models to its own C++ standards. Neither of these options looks attractive in a marketplace where speed of design is a key.

This leaves two options, either allow a *de facto* C++ usage model to emerge or else develop a use model that is agreed upon by all of users of C++: silicon providers, systems companies, developers of IP and EDA tool providers. The former option is not out of the question: Verilog emerged as a *de facto* HDL standard as Cadence Design Systems, its originator, became successful. A parallel to this in the C++ arena is a possibility. On the other hand, VHDL emerged as an industry-developed standard precisely due to the perceived need for a *lingua franca* that could be used uniformly throughout the industry. OSCI represents more of an effort along the VHDL model. It just is too risky to wait for an adequate *de facto* standard to emerge.

The bottom line is that there really is no time to wait for a possible *de facto* standard to emerge. The needs of the electronic industry dictate that a standard methodology for using C++ be available as soon as possible, and that such a standard meet the needs of as many potential users as possible. With this in mind, OSCI was formed and continues to grow with a healthy mixture of members representing semiconductor companies, systems companies, IP providers and EDA companies.

Why this book?

I have known Bhasker for almost 20 years, since he joined my group at Honeywell Labs after getting his Ph.D. at the University of Minnesota. Even then he had the excellent ability to see through dense technical issues and clarify them for more junior team members. This ability to explain difficult technical material has only deepened over the years, as Bhasker has published numerous texts on VHDL, Verilog, Logic Synthesis etc. that have become mainstays at universities around the world. These texts have helped prepare a generation of engineering students by exposing them in a rigorous but understandable way to the "raw materials" of the electronic design world.

This particular text *A SystemC Primer* promises to have the same impact in the SystemC area as Bhasker's earlier books. In this book, he is not aiming at the advanced researcher or language guru, but rather, has written a primer that gradually introduces the reader to the complexities of SystemC by reference to common digital design concepts. His usual easy-to-read style facilitates rapid understanding of the underpinnings of SystemC, and will prepare the reader to both begin using SystemC as a design language and perhaps, to do further research into even more advanced features of the language.

At the end of the day, SystemC will become a truly useful standard only when it becomes as ubiquitous a part of the design landscape as VHDL and Verilog are today. *A SystemC Primer* is an excellent catalyst for making that happen.

Stanley J. Krolikoski
Chairman, Open SystemC Initiative
San Jose, California
March 2002

Preface

Why did you pick this book? To learn about SystemC, I presume. Well, you made the right choice. So jump right in, as this book introduces you to the world of SystemC. Just by reading Chapter 2 and Appendix A, you can start writing SystemC models and simulating them in a short time.

RTL: Register Transfer Level.

SystemC is both a system level and hardware description language. It is a single language for modeling hardware and software systems. It is a hardware description language because it allows you to model the design at the register transfer level (RTL). It is a system level specification language because it allows you to model your design at the algorithmic level. You can also model your complete system using SystemC and describe its behavior as a software program. Even though it can describe gate level netlists, it is not intended to be used as such. It is cumbersome and inefficient to use and model a gate-level netlist.

SystemC is based on the C++ programming language. It extends the capabilities of C++ to enable hardware description. SystemC adds such important concepts as concurrency, events and data types. This capability is provided via a class library that provides powerful new mechanisms to model system architecture with hardware elements, concurrency and reactive behavior. These mechanisms are simply built on top of the class construct of the C++ programming language. SystemC provides a simulation kernel that allows you to simulate an executable specification of the design or system.

This book describes the SystemC 2.0 standard. This standard is maintained by the Language Working Group of the Open SystemC Initiative (OSCI) organization. The intent is to make it into an IEEE standard in the near future. You can obtain more information on SystemC and OSCI from the web site:

IEEE: Institute of Electrical and Electronics Engineers.

http://www.systemc.org

The complete SystemC 2.0 standard is described in a functional specification and a users guide available as part of the SystemC 2.0 software package available for download at the above mentioned web site.

OSCI: Open SystemC Initiative.

The Open SystemC Initiative (OSCI) was formed in 1999 with the cooperative collaboration of a number of companies, and in September 1999, the first version of SystemC, SystemC 0.9, was released as open source and made freely available. SystemC 1.0 was released in March 2000. This version of the language was limited to the behavioral and register transfer level of modeling and it lacked many system level modeling features.

SystemC 2.0, released in October 2001, contains many system level modeling features. These new features included, amongst others, channels, interfaces and events. This edition of the book is based on SystemC 2.0.

This book mainly introduces you to the hardware modeling aspects of SystemC, that is, the RTL synthesizable subset of SystemC. Models written using this subset can be synthesized into logic gates and then into a hardware implementation of the model. The reason to focus on the hardware modeling aspects is threefold.

Verilog HDL: Verilog Hardware Description Language, IEEE Std 1364.

VHDL: VHSIC Hardware Description Language, IEEE Std 1076.

- First, today's hardware designers who know VHDL and Verilog HDL would like to know and learn SystemC. As the abstraction level moves from the register transfer level to higher levels, design engineers currently modeling in RTL will have to learn system level modeling. This book helps bridge the gap by introducing SystemC in a very natural way to these designers.

- Second, system designers who are writing high-level algorithmic software models will need to understand the RTL synthesizable level so that they can iteratively refine their models down to the register transfer level to enable synthesis of their models to gates.

IP: Intellectual Property.

- Third, model writers can develop SystemC Intellectual Property (IP) models using the RTL synthesizable subset. This will allow for the IP blocks to be reusable and synthesizable.

This book is specifically targeted for design engineers and system engineers who want to learn and get introduced to the world of SystemC.

This is a beginner's book. So some of the advanced SystemC topics are left out. For example, a master slave communication library that is defined in SystemC as a methodology specific library is beyond the scope of this book.

The book can be used in a college or a university course as part of an architecture class or a digital design or a system design class. SystemC concepts can be introduced using this book. One big advantage of using SystemC as part of an university curriculum is that a simulator for SystemC and all the class libraries of SystemC are open source and freely available for anyone to use. This appeals to many university professors as no new monetary investment needs to be made to teach and understand this new system level design language. The fact that it is open source allows ambitious students at universities to extend the capabilities of SystemC beyond what is available, by directly modifying the source code, both in terms of features and optimizations.

The RTL synthesizable subset of SystemC described in this book is based on my understanding of the subset of SystemC that can be synthesized. This subset closely matches the IEEE standard Verilog and VHDL RTL synthesizable subsets, both of which were (are being) standardized under my chairmanship. Currently available synthesis tools may or may not support this synthesizable subset. For details on specific features supported by a synthesis tool, the reader is urged to consult the respective tool's documentation.

IEEE Standard for VHDL RTL Synthesis, IEEE Std 1076.6.

Draft Standard for Verilog RTL Synthesis, IEEE P1364.1.

What background do you need to read this book and understand SystemC? You have to know the basics of C++ programming language. That is a must. You should also have a background in logic design. If you already know either of the two popular hardware description languages, VHDL or Verilog HDL, learning SystemC will be very easy using this book (I purposely don't equate VHDL and Verilog HDL models with SystemC models anywhere in this book). If you know the C++ programming language very well, you will find yourself very comfortable in writing advanced system level models using SystemC - you will also be able to understand the internals of SystemC. However, knowing VHDL or Verilog HDL is not a prerequisite to read this book! If you want to harness the full power of SystemC, you will need to be an advanced C++ user. However to model hardware and understand the RTL synthesizable subset, you need only know the basics of the C++ programming language. A good book to learn the C++ programming language is "C++ Primer, Third Edition" by Stanley B. Lippman and Josee Lajoie, Addison-Wesley, 1998.

All models described in this book have been tested and simulated on a Solaris machine. Synthesized logic shown in the figures have been obtained by manually translating the SystemC model into its equivalent Verilog representation and then synthesizing the Verilog model using the Ambit BuildGates synthesis tool.

The future of SystemC

The language is still undergoing changes - this will continue at a rapid rate until it becomes an IEEE standard. Even then I expect a useful standard to continually evolve. There are plans to develop a 2.X, 3.0 and a 4.0 release. Version 2.X plans to include fork and join, interrupt/abort for behavioral hierarchy, performance modeling support, and timing specification support. Version 3.0 plans to support abstract RTOS modeling and scheduler modeling. Version 4.0 plans to support analog mixed signal systems modeling.

RTOS: Real Time Operating System.

Acknowledgments

It is with deep gratitude that I acknowledge the contributions made by the following individuals in reviewing a draft copy of this book and for providing constructive feedback and new ideas that has resulted in a significantly improved book.

Mike Baird
Abhijit Ghosh
Thorsten Groetker
Jeff Hantgen
Kurt Heinz
Sven Heithecker
Xiaoyan Huang
Martin Janssen
M.N.V. Satya Kiran
David Long
Grant Martin
Dale Mehl
Sanjiv Narayan
Smail Niar
Bernhard Niemann
Stuart Swan
Kartik Talsania
Punitha Thandapani
Yves Vanderperren
Jean Witinski

Thank you very much!

Finally, yes, it's true. This book would not be possible without the continued support of my wife Geetha and my three Rajahs, Arvind, Vinay and Vishnu.

I welcome any corrections or suggestions that you may have about the book. Send these via email to jbhasker@cadence.com or through my publisher.

J. Bhasker

April 2002

Preface to Second Edition

Since the first edition was published, an updated version of SystemC, v2.0.1 has been released, including an updated master slave library. The SystemC verification working group has developed a SystemC verification library. It is an open source C++ library that provides a standard way to construct advanced verification components and testbenches in SystemC. The verification library supports transaction-based verification, transaction monitoring and recording, and weighted and constrained randomization.

This edition includes a CD with all example code in the book. A *README.txt* file on the CD provides links to some available SystemC trial software. The edition also expands on many of the features described with additional examples to make the concepts more clear. New exercises have been added.

All examples in this edition have been verified using SystemC 2.0.1.

Please continue to provide feedback directly to me at *jbhasker@esilicon.com* or through my publisher.

J. Bhasker

November 2003

1

Introduction

This chapter describes the "what" and "why" of SystemC, and describes a methodology for its use. The chapter also provides a high-level view of the SystemC capabilities.

1.1 What is SystemC?

SystemC is based on the C++ programming language. C++ is an extensible object oriented modeling language. SystemC extends the capabilities of C++ by enabling modeling of hardware descriptions. SystemC adds such important concepts to C++ as concurrency (multiple processes executing concurrently), timed events and data types. SystemC adds a class library to C++ to extend the capabilities of C++. The class library is not a modification of C++, but a library of functions, data types and other language constructs that are legal C++ code.

SystemC is C++.

The class library provides powerful new mechanisms to model system architecture with hardware timing, concurrency and reactive behavior. The mechanisms are simply built on top of the class construct in the C++ programming language that allows for extensibility of the language.

The SystemC library provides constructs that describe concepts that are familiar to a hardware designer such as signals, modules and ports. Additionally, the library provides familiar capabilities such as processes and waiting for a negative edge of a clock.

SystemC does not add new syntax to the C++ programming language. It simply defines a new C++ class library, and thus it is C++. These classes enable the user to define modules, processes, and communication through ports and signals that can handle a range of data types ranging from bits, bit vectors to standard C++ types to user-defined data types such as enumeration types and structure types.

SystemC also provides a simulation kernel that allows you to simulate the executable specification of the design or system that you write in SystemC. The simulation semantics are defined by SystemC.

An executable specification is a model of a system written in SystemC.

Since SystemC is C++, you can use the standard C++ programming language development tools available to create, simulate, debug and explore various architectural and algorithmic descriptions of your design. Also since it is C++, a SystemC model can be compiled on a multitude of C++ compilers on several platforms. Figure 1-1 shows you how to use a SystemC model in a standard C++ development environment. You can use exactly the same set of tools to write and debug SystemC models (after all, it is C++). The SystemC model is often called the *executable specification*; this is because you can compile and execute the SystemC model to understand the behavior of the system.

You can effectively use SystemC to describe a cycle-accurate model of your design. SystemC also provides a methodology for describing:

- system level design
- software algorithms
- hardware architecture

SystemC provides a single language to define hardware and software components, it provides a single language to facilitate seamless hardware software cosimulation, and provides a single language to facilitate step-by-step refinement of a system design down to the register transfer level for synthesis.

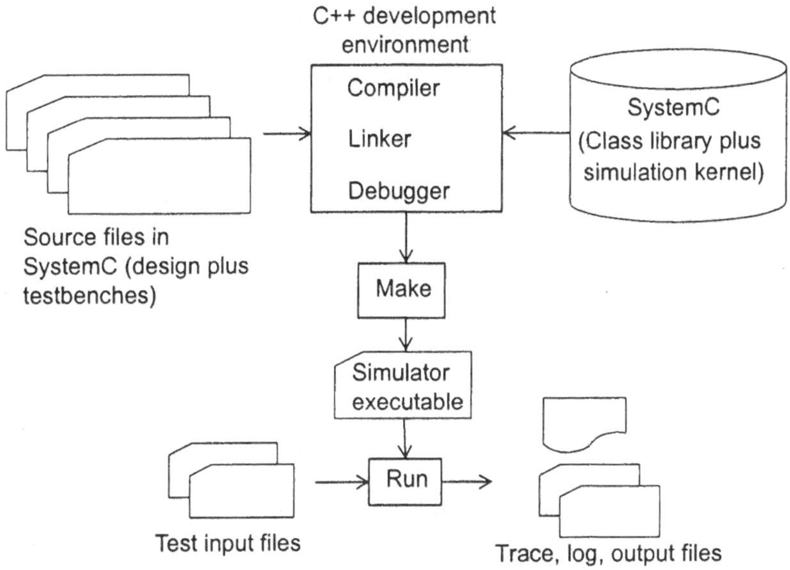

Figure 1-1 SystemC in a C++ development environment.

You can use the standard C++ environment to create a system level model, quickly simulate to validate and optimize the design, explore various algorithms, and provide the hardware and software teams with an executable specification, a C++ program with the same behavior.

More importantly, SystemC is open source. This means that it is freely available under an open source license agreement. There is no licensing fee for using it, either for internal or for commercial purposes. It is being developed and maintained under the OSCI organization which is a non-profit organization. In fact, tools can be built on top of SystemC and made available on a commercial basis while including SystemC as part of the product.

1.2 Why SystemC?

Designs are getting bigger and bigger in size and faster in speed and larger in complexity. This makes it necessary to describe designs at higher levels of abstraction so as to enable:

- Faster simulation
- Hardware / software cosimulation
- Architectural exploration

Expressing designs at the system level becomes important to manage the complexity of large designs so that all design optimizations and explorations can be performed at the system level. In addition, hardware and software complexity is also growing. This means a lot more of the design is being incorporated into software as opposed to hardware. So critical partitioning needs to be performed in order to figure out what should go into hardware and what part of the design ought to be in software.

System level design offers a way to have a fast executable specification of the design that can be used to validate the system concepts. The behavioral specification enables you to have a specification of the design before implementation starts and to ensure that it correctly interacts with its environment (all blocks external to the system design). System design enables early verification by having bus-cycle accurate models for faster simulation early in the development process.

When a design is expressed at the system level, it is easier to iterate and explore various algorithms and alternate architectures quickly, as compared to exploring at the register transfer level or the gate level. Figure 1-2 shows the size of a design is rather large at the chip level and trying to explore various design changes or structures is rather time-consuming if not too difficult. However at the system level, the size of the system level model is manageable enough such that different architectures, changes, etc. can be quickly made.

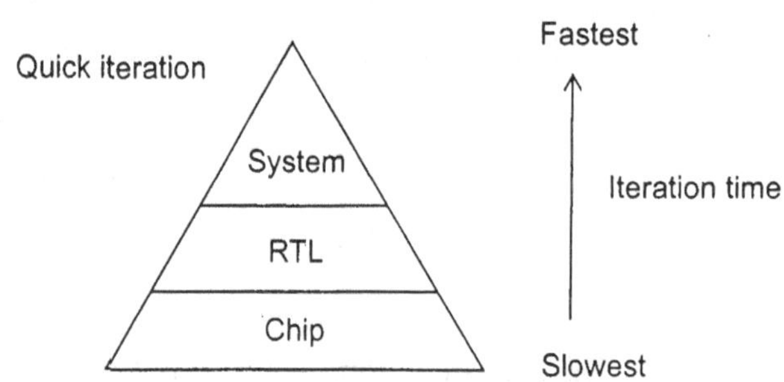

Figure 1-2 Exploring alternate architectures at different levels.

The key factors driving the development and standardization of SystemC as one language are for:

- System level design
- Describing hardware architectures
- Describing software algorithms
- Verification
- IP exchange

The unique thing that SystemC provides is that the same language (a single language) can be used for all the above described capabilities. You can write the design in one language, verify the design using the same language, and further refine it all the way to the implementation level (typically the register transfer level). From this point onwards, synthesis tools can take over. A system can be modeled at the behavioral or architectural level and then iteratively refined to the register transfer level. The same testbench can be used for all refinements of the design.

You can describe the overall system using SystemC. The system level model becomes the executable model for the hardware design team which iteratively refines the system model from the higher level down to the register transfer level to enable synthesis and subsequent implementation. The hardware design process becomes a refinement of the specification.

The same SystemC system model also drives the hardware software exploration, and co-design techniques can be used at this level. It is much easier to trade-off in SystemC (at this level) because both the software and the hardware part is described and refined using a single language. The single language also is much faster to simulate than a multi-language simulation.

SystemC is based on C++ and hence is powerful enough to describe all kinds of verification environments from the signal level to the transaction level. SystemC also allows for testbench generation and testing. It can serve as a verification language as well. Assertions can be described in a SystemC model and verified either using traditional verification techniques such as simulation, or by using formal techniques such as formal verification. Since it is C++ based, complex assertions about the design can be specified easily. Typically designers and verification engineers have to learn a second language, a high-level verification language (HVL), to verify a design. This is not the case with SystemC, which can be used as an HVL. Having a single language helps make verification

HVL: High-level Verification Language.

faster as compared to a multi-language environment which may cause slower verification.

SystemC provides a single unique language for IP creation as well - either at the register transfer level or at the algorithmic level or at the system level, including the test environment (instead of having to describe in two or three different languages). In addition, the SystemC framework allows for a full standard simulation environment that the user can immediately use to verify the IP.

SystemC has direct support for modeling at high levels of abstraction. It can be refined to the behavioral level or the register transfer level using the same language. Behavioral and RTL designs become refinement paths in the methodology.

1.3 Design Methodology

To write a SystemC model, the designer writes a model in C++ using functions and data types defined in the SystemC class library following the methodology of describing a design in SystemC. The model, which is the executable specification, can then be compiled and linked in with the SystemC simulation kernel and SystemC library to create an executable.

Having an executable specification provides for many advantages:

- Understand the design/system specification.
- Validate the functionality of the system before implementation.
- Create performance models of the system and validate the system performance.
- Refine and reuse testbench at the higher level down to the implementation level.

In the past, system designers have written executable specifications in their language of choice (typically C or C++), debugged and verified the functionality and when satisfied, handed over the executable specification to the RTL design group. The RTL design group would then rewrite the design at the register transfer level to synthesize it to gates. Figure 1-3 shows this process. This methodology has a major problem in that the "hand over" can cause the functionality of the RTL description to differ from the executable specification and consequently become prone to error. Debugging the resultant differences is quite difficult, challenging, time consuming and error prone. Another problem is that getting to the RTL design and then discovering that something in the conceptual model cannot be implemented is a real problem when there is no common environment between the system design and design implementation.

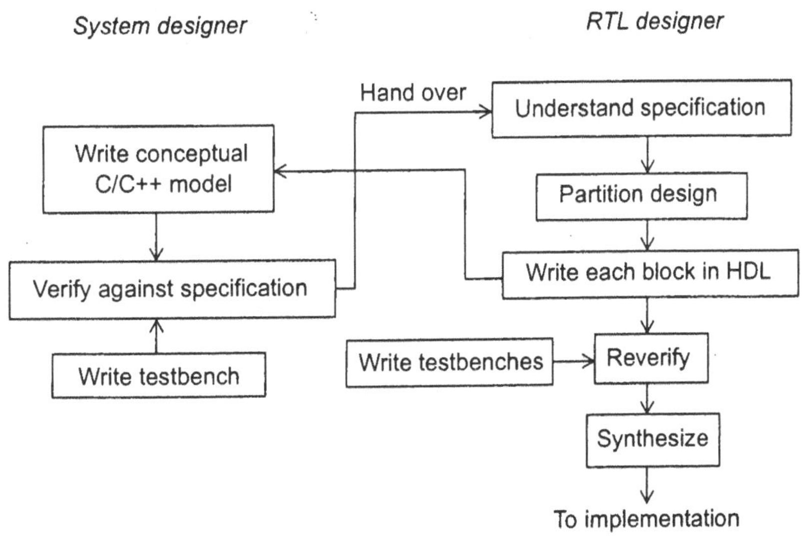

Figure 1-3 Non-SystemC methodology.

With SystemC supporting modeling at both the hardware level and the software level, a system designer need only write a SystemC model. The designer can iteratively refine the executable specification down to the register transfer level, which is still in SystemC, prior to synthesis. The testbench, which is also written in SystemC, can be reused to ensure that the iterative refinements of the SystemC model did not introduce any errors. Figure 1-4 shows this process. Thus modeling in SystemC potentially avoids the drawback of the methodology shown in Figure 1-3. Notice that the "understand" step can be skipped if the same system designer refines the design down to SystemC RTL, ensuring that the final SystemC model is synthesizable before handing it over to an RTL designer for synthesis and implementation. If during the RTL implementation, it is discovered that something in the conceptual model cannot be implemented, it is much easier to go back to the conceptual model, rewrite it and get back to the RTL design since now there is a common environment for system design and design implementation.

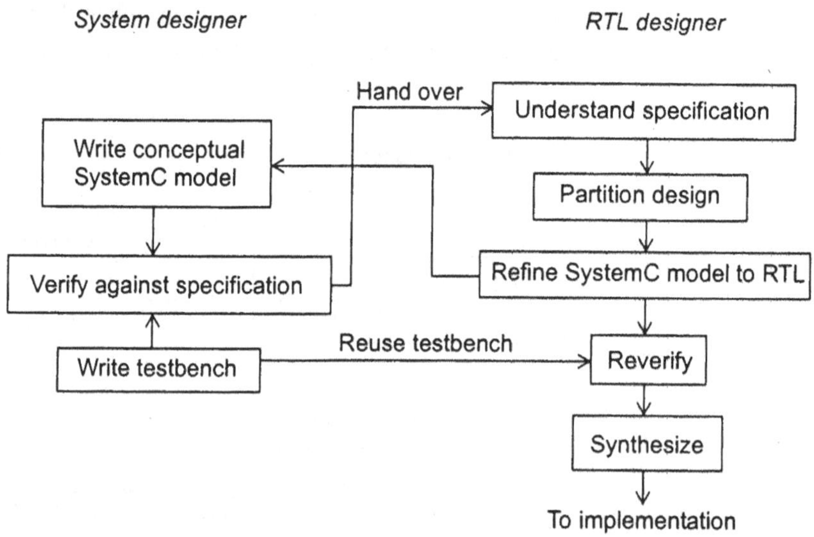

Figure 1-4 SystemC methodology.

Figure 1-5 shows the design flow in a system level design process. A system level model is first written in SystemC. The first conceptual model is typically not synthesizable, it is event driven, uses abstract communication, for example, semaphores, has abstract data types, such as classes, and finally it is typically an untimed model, that is, only the behavior of the system is captured without regards to its timing behavior. At this level, various algorithms can be explored and the specifications of the system under design can be understood and verified.

Next, the model may be refined to a timed system level model, that is, the notion of timing is introduced into the model, maybe by assigning run times to processes or by introducing the notion of a clock cycle. The model behavior may also be described at this level using transactions. Once having obtained the timed model, various architectures of hardware and software can be explored, performance analysis done to determine the best scenario for hardware and software partitioning and thence partitioning done. The next step in implementing the software part is the selection of the real time operating system and from there, to develop the target code. The hardware implementation consists of refining the hardware part of the timed model to generate a behavioral model of the design, which is still in SystemC. Such a behavioral model may be synthesizable, it may be at the algorithmic level, and demonstrates input-output cycle-accurate behavior. If a behavioral synthesis tool is not available, the behavioral model may further be refined to the register transfer level, with the model still being in SystemC. The RTL model is synthesizable and describes the finite state machine behavior of the design. This RTL model can then be used for synthesis and implementation.

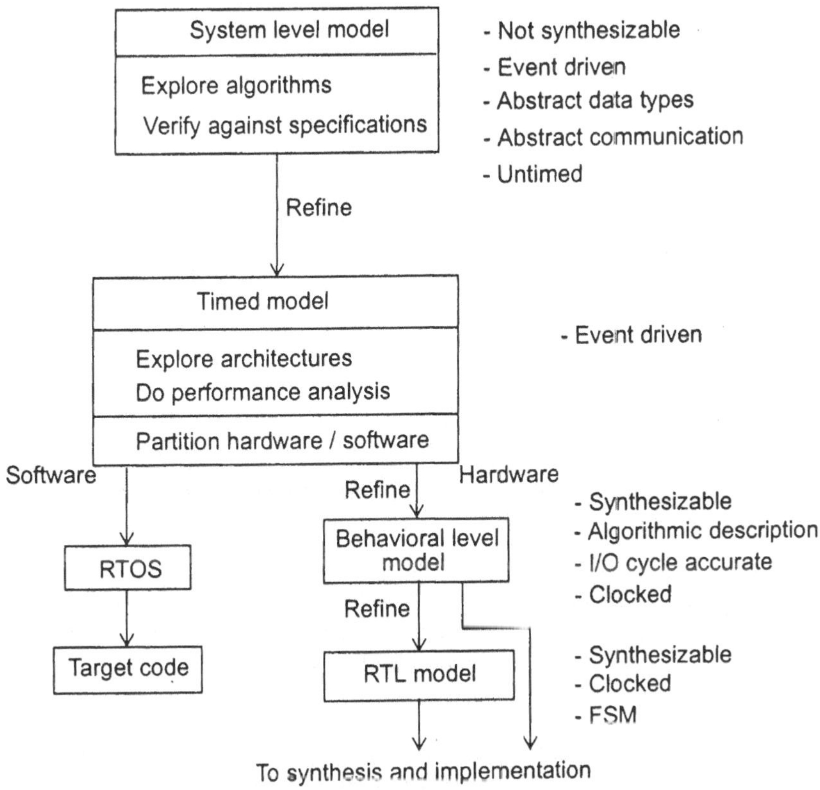

Figure 1-5 System level design process.

1.4 Capabilities

SystemC offers the following capabilities.

- *Modules*: A module can be described via a module class SC_MODULE. A module can be hierarchical in that it can have processes and other modules instantiated within it.
- *Processes*: A process is used to describe functionality. Processes appear inside modules. There are two kinds of processes that can model different process abstractions: SC_METHOD and SC_THREAD. Processes define concurrent behavior. Furthermore, processes are not hierarchical.
- *Ports*: A module has ports through which it communicates with other modules. There are three kinds of signal ports: input, output and inout ports. There is also the capability to describe a new kind of port with a user-defined interface.
- *Signals*: A signal can carry a value. It is used to connect multiple processes and module instances. There are two kinds of signals: resolved and unresolved signals. A resolved signal can have multiple drivers (all assignments to a signal from one process constitutes a single driver). A signal also updates after a delta delay as in classical HDL simulators.

HDL: Hardware Description Language.

- *Rich set of data types*: Supports multiple design domains and abstraction levels. There is fixed precision for fast simulation, arbitrary precision for large numbers and fixed point data types for DSP applications. There is support for both 2-value and 4-value logic. Also any type from C++ programming language may be used.

DSP: Digital Signal Processing.

- *Clocks*: Built-in notion of clocks.
- *Event-based simulation*: Provides an ultra lightweight event-based simulation kernel that allows for high speed simulation.
- *Multiple abstraction levels*: Supports modeling of untimed models at different levels of abstraction, from high-level functional models to detailed clock cycle-accurate RTL models. Also supports iterative refinement from a high level model to a lower level down to a RTL model.

- *Communication protocols*: Provides multi-level communication semantics that allow one to describe protocol and interfaces at different levels of abstraction.
- *Debugging support*: Runtime error checking can be turned on with a compilation flag. Supports debugging using standard C++ debugging tools.

VCD: Value Change Dump (Described in IEEE Std 1364).

WIF: Waveform Interchange Format.

ISDB: Integrated Signal Data Base.

- *Waveform tracing*: Supports saving of results in three different waveform formats: VCD, WIF, ISDB.
- Can model *concurrency* and *process interactions*.
- Can link to *IP* written in C/C++.
- Supports *RTL synthesis* flow.
- Supports *generation of embedded processor code.*
- Is an *OSCI standard.*
- *Ease of modeling*: Based on a standard programming language C++.
- Support for describing *both hardware and software* using a single language.
- *Communication* between modules and processes via channels, interfaces and events.
- *System level design*: Facilitates system level design tasks such as communication refinement and mapping of design specifications to hardware and software. Allows a wide range of design models of computation, design abstraction levels and design methodologies for system design. Provides a general purpose modeling foundation for this such that additional features can be added and adopted cleanly.
- *Models of computation*: Supports various models of computation based on the model of time, kind of process activations, and the method of communication between processes. Examples of these include Kahn process networks, static multi-rate dataflow, dynamic multi-rate dataflow, and communicating sequential processes.
- Develop and verify complex system specification.
- Supports system specification refinement to mixed software and hardware implementations.

- Can reuse extensive knowledge and infrastructure and code base around C++.

1.5 SystemC RTL

SystemC is C++. Thus it is complex and very flexible. The flexibility allows the language to be used to describe any behavior including hardware behavior but the same behavior allows the designer to write legal SystemC code that cannot be possibly be implemented in hardware.

SystemC RTL is the subset of SystemC that can be used to describe models at the register transfer level. Such models can be automatically synthesized to gates using RTL synthesis tools. The majority of this book describes SystemC at the register transfer level. Only the last two chapters describe SystemC features beyond SystemC RTL.

1.6 Book Organization

The next chapter quickly gets you started in modeling using SystemC. It is a tutorial that explains how to write a module with ports and processes. Additionally, it shows how to test a module using a simple testbench.

Chapter 3 describes the various SystemC data types supported by SystemC RTL. Examples of these are bit vector, logic vector, variable length vectors, and signed and unsigned integer types. The chapter also lists the C++ data types that are supported for synthesis in SystemC RTL. A section therein describes the recommended data types.

Modeling combinational logic is the focus of Chapter 4. It explains, through numerous examples, how various constructs in SystemC (and C++) can be used to model combinational logic. Synthesized logic for many of the examples are also shown.

Chapter 5 shows how to model synchronous logic, the basic elements being a flip-flop and a latch. Chapter 5 also presents modeling of asynchronous set and reset logic for such synchronous devices. A section provides highlights on how to avoid inadvertently created latches.

Chapter 6 focuses on modeling of three-state drivers, handling don't-cares and describing parameterized modules.

Chapter 7 presents a number of example models of common design functions. All the descriptions presented are synthesizable. The synthesized logic for most of them are also shown.

Chapter 8 and beyond begins looking at SystemC features beyond RTL modeling. Chapter 8 focuses on testbenches. Aspects such as clock generation, application of stimulus and how to write monitors for testbenches are presented. The chapter also describes how to write reactive and non-reactive testbenches. These include the ability to generate waveforms and the ability to create your own ASCII text output.

Chapter 9 describes system level modeling features. This includes the concept of channels, interfaces and events, dynamic sensitivity and fixed point types.

Solaris platform: A machine running the SUN Solaris operating system.

Appendix A provides a sample scenario of how to download a SystemC release from the web site and how to install the release on a Solaris platform. It also shows how to compile, simulate and debug SystemC models on a Solaris machine. As you can see, this appendix is very specific on how SystemC works on a Solaris machine. You can, however, read the appropriate README files that are part of the installation to better understand how to install SystemC on other platforms.

Finally, Appendix B provides a summary of SystemC RTL, a subset of SystemC that can be used to describe a design at the register transfer level and can be synthesized into logic gates.

1.7 Exercises

1. Can a function written using the C programming language be called from within a SystemC program?
2. Describe five important hardware modeling attributes of SystemC.
3. How does SystemC help in IP reuse?
4. Describe two areas of challenges with the SystemC design methodology.

❑

2

Getting Started

This chapter provides a quick introduction to SystemC modeling. It shows the structure of a module, how to declare ports and their types and how to describe the behavior of the module. The last section provides a quick tutorial on what a testbench looks like and describes a small example.

2.1 Basics

A module is the basic unit for describing structure in SystemC. A module can have any number of input, output or inout ports. A module can have any number of processes. A process is used to describe the functionality of the system and allows the expression of concurrent behavior. Each process is sensitive to a specified set of signals and ports and executes whenever a change occurs on the signals and ports specified in the

A process is a method (member function) in C++.

sensitivity list. Signals are used for interprocess communication. In addition, an assignment of a value to a signal (and a port) always occurs after a delta delay; a delta delay is an infinitesimally small delay used to model the cause and effect relationships of logic; more on this is described in Chapter 9. A module also allows for expressing hierarchy. In other words, you can instantiate a module within another module.

Figure 2-1 shows a simplified view of a module. It has two input ports identified with `sc_in`, and two output ports identified with `sc_out`, and one inout port identified with `sc_inout`. The module has two processes that are of kind SC_METHOD and contains an instantiation of another module. Signals, identified with `sc_signal`, are used to interconnect the two processes and the child module.

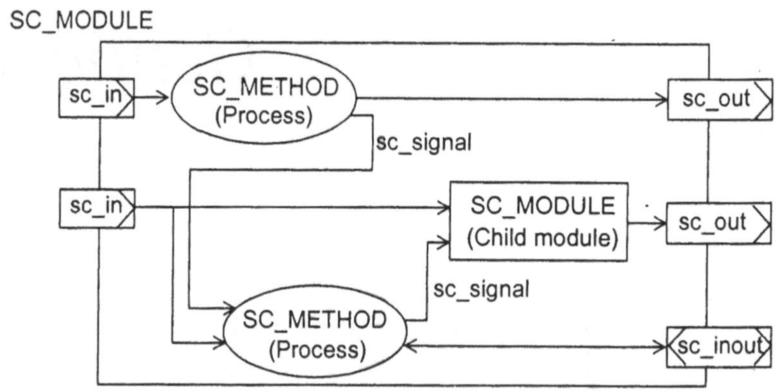

Figure 2-1 A module, ports, processes and signals.

Figure 2-2 shows a half-adder circuit. Its SystemC model follows.

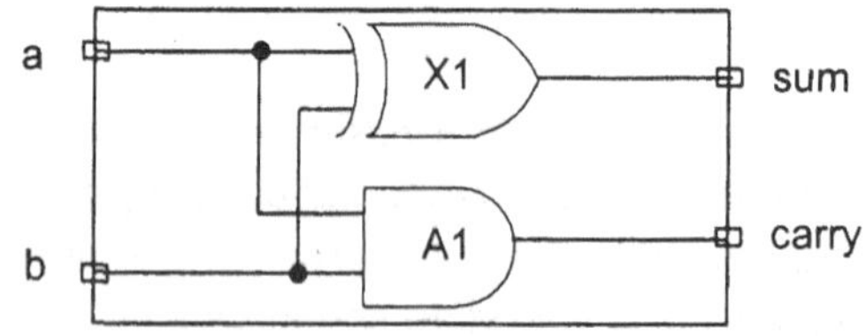

Figure 2-2 A half-adder circuit.

```
// File: half_adder.h                        // Line 1
#include "systemc.h"                          // Line 2

SC_MODULE (half_adder) {                      // Line 3
  sc_in<bool> a, b;                           // Line 4
  sc_out<bool> sum, carry;                    // Line 5

  void prc_half_adder ();                     // Line 6

  SC_CTOR (half_adder) {                      // Line 7
    SC_METHOD (prc_half_adder);               // Line 8
    sensitive << a << b;                      // Line 9
  }                                           // Line 10
};                                            // Line 11
```

```
// File: half_adder.cpp                       // Line 1
#include "half_adder.h"                       // Line 2

void half_adder::prc_half_adder () {          // Line 3
  sum = a ^ b;                                // Line 4
  carry = a & b;                              // Line 5
}
```

The half-adder circuit is described in two files, `half_adder.h` and `half_adder.cpp`. The `half_adder.h` (a header file) contains the module description and the declaration for the process, while the `half_adder.cpp` (C++ program text file) contains the definition of the process. This is common C++ programming style - to specify the declarations and definitions in separate files.

Line 2 of the file `half_adder.h` specifies an include directive to include the file `systemc.h`. This directive must appear in all SystemC models. The include file contains the definitions of the SystemC class libraries.

SC_MODULE is a C++ macro - it starts the definition of a module class.

The keyword SC_MODULE starts the declaration of a SystemC module. The name of the module is specified as `half_adder`. The module has two input ports: `a` and `b`. The ports are declared to be of type `bool` (bool is a standard type in C++). The module has two output ports: `sum` and `carry`. These are also of type `bool`.

The SC_CTOR block at line 7 declares the processes, and the kind of processes, used to describe the behavior of the module. In the module half_adder, the SC_CTOR block declares one process of kind SC_METHOD. The name associated with the SC_CTOR block must be identical to the name of the module. An SC_METHOD process is sensitive to a specified set of signals and ports and cannot suspend due to a wait statement; wait statements are not allowed in SC_METHOD processes. The other kind of process SC_THREAD is described in more detail in Chapter 9. The name of the process is specified in the SC_METHOD declaration. In this case, the name of the process is prc_half_adder. It is declared on line 6. The process, which is a member function, must return void and not have any arguments. The sensitive statement that appears on line 9 is used to specify the set of signals and ports that the SC_METHOD process is sensitive to. It shows that the process prc_half_adder is sensitive to the input ports a and b. This implies that whenever there is a change of value on ports a or b, the process prc_half_adder is executed in its entirety, and upon return waits for another event to occur on its sensitivity list. Notice the SC_MODULE declaration ends in a semicolon.

In C++ terminology, the SC_CTOR defines the constructor for the module class.

SC_CTOR is a C++ macro.

SC_MODULE declaration ends with a semicolon.

The second file half_adder.cpp contains the definition of the process. The two assignment statements on lines 4 and 5 compute the values of the output ports sum and carry. An assignment to a port always occurs after a delta delay. The same is true for a signal assignment. What this means is, if port a had a change of value at time 5ns, then sum and carry get their new updated values at time 5+Δns.

2.2 Another Example

Let us look at another example. This one is a 2-by-4 decoder circuit as shown in Figure 2-3.

```
// File: decoder2by4.h
#include "systemc.h"

SC_MODULE (decoder2by4) {
  sc_in<bool> enable;
  sc_in<sc_uint<2> > select;
  sc_out<sc_uint<4> > z;
```

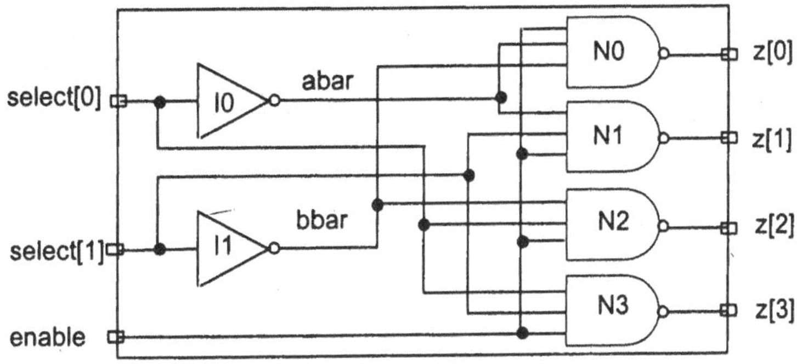

Figure 2-3 A 2-by-4 decoder circuit.

```
  void prc_decoder2by4();

  SC_CTOR (decoder2by4) {
    SC_METHOD (prc_decoder2by4);
    sensitive(enable);
    sensitive(select);
  }                                    // Note: No semicolon.
};

// File: decoder2by4.cpp
#include "decoder2by4.h"

void decoder2by4::prc_decoder2by4() {
  if (enable) {
    switch (select.read()) {
      case 0: z = 0xE; break;
      case 1: z = 0xD; break;
      case 2: z = 0xB; break;
      case 3: z = 0x7; break;
    }
  }
  else
    z = 0xF;
}
```

The `read()` method can be used when reading the value of a port or a signal when the C++ compiler has trouble disambiguating the types (C++ is strongly typed) or has trouble performing implicit conversion.

The decoder module with the name `decoder2by4` is defined in the file `decoder2by4.h`. It has two input ports and one output port. The input port select is of type sc_uint<2 >. This means it is a two-bit unsigned integer. The output port is declared to be of type sc_uint<4>. This means it is a four-bit unsigned integer. sc_uint is a SystemC predefined type. Note that a space character is required between the size <2> and the following character '>' for the model to be a legal C++ model.

```
sc_in<sc_uint<2> > select; // Space
// required here ^ for legal C++.
```

The constructor block, starting with SC_CTOR, declares an SC_METHOD process with name prc_decoder2by4. This process is sensitive to the ports select and enable. Notice that the list of sensitive signals for the SC_METHOD process is specified using a different style; this is the *function notation style.*

```
sensitive (enable);
sensitive (select);
```

In the module half_adder described in the previous section, we used the *stream notation style* to specify the sensitivity list. The stream notation style, if applied to the process prc_decoder2by4, would appear as:

```
sensitive << select << enable;
```

We prefer using the stream notation style for specifying the sensitivity list which is what we have used elsewhere throughout this book.

When using the stream notation style, it is possible to write each signal or port sensitivity using multiple statements, such as:

```
sensitive << select;
sensitive << enable;
```

In the process definition appearing in the file decoder2by4.cpp, the behavior of the decoder is specified using an *if* and a *switch* statement. The read() method has to be used to read the value of the input port select (else a compile error occurs; this is because the C++ compiler has trouble performing the implicit conversion from the sc_in<sc_uint<>> type to the integer type that it is expecting in the switch expression). Once again the output assignment to port z occurs after a delta delay. If select changes value at time 7ns, then z would change its value at time 7+Δns.

2.3 Describing Hierarchy

The hierarchy of a design can be specified using the same SC_MODULE construct. Here is an example of a full-adder circuit, shown in Figure 2-4, that instantiates the half-adder circuit described earlier in a previous section.

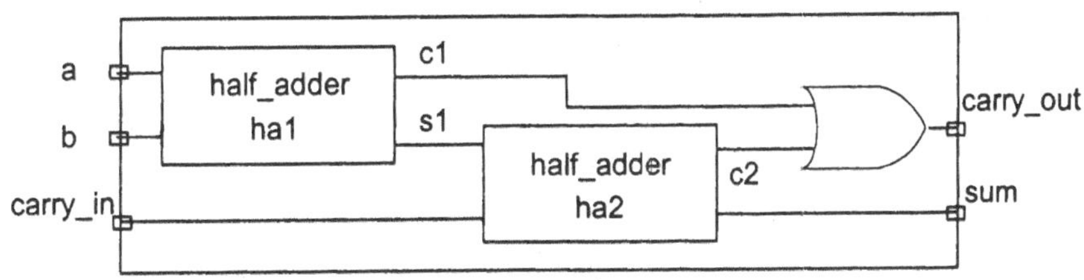

Figure 2-4 A full-adder circuit.

```
// File: full_adder.h
#include "half_adder.h"

SC_MODULE (full_adder) {
  sc_in<bool> a, b, carry_in;
  sc_out<bool> sum, carry_out;

  sc_signal<bool> c1, s1, c2;
  void prc_or ();
  half_adder *ha1_ptr, *ha2_ptr;

  SC_CTOR (full_adder) {
    ha1_ptr = new half_adder ("ha1");
    // Named association:
    ha1_ptr->a (a);
    ha1_ptr->b (b);
    ha1_ptr->sum (s1);
    ha1_ptr->carry (c1);

    ha2_ptr = new half_adder ("ha2");
    // Positional association:
    (*ha2_ptr) (s1, carry_in, sum, c2);
```

```
    SC_METHOD (prc_or);
    sensitive << c1 << c2;
  }

  // A destructor:
  ~ full_adder() {
    delete ha1_ptr;
    delete ha2_ptr;
  }
};
```

A destructor is typically used to deallocate any acquired memory automatically when the class is no longer used.

```
// File: full_adder.cpp
#include "full_adder.h"

void full_adder::prc_or () {
  carry_out = c1 | c2;
}
```

The module `full_adder` has three input ports and two output ports. All are of type `bool`. Also appearing prior to the declaration is an include directive that includes the declaration of the half-adder module. No include is necessary for the SystemC include file `systemc.h`. It automatically gets included via the include of the file `half_adder.h`.

The line:

```
sc_signal<bool> c1, s1, c2;
```

declares signals that are local to the module. In addition, they are declared to be of type `bool`. Signals are used to communicate between and amongst processes and module instances. The line:

```
half_adder *ha1_ptr, *ha2_ptr;
```

declares two pointers to the module `half_adder`, one for each instance.

The SC_CTOR block for the module `full_adder` contains two module instantiations and one SC_METHOD process declaration. The first instantiation:

```
ha1_ptr = new half_adder ("ha1");
```

creates a new instance of module half_adder with instance name ha1. The pointer returned is saved in ha1_ptr which is used to connect external signals or ports to the ports of the instance. There are two forms of specifying such interconnections:

i. Using *positional association.*

ii. Using *named association.*

A recommendation is to always use named association as it is more readable and the interconnections are clear.

In instance ha1, named association is used for the interconnection. Port a of instance ha1 is connected to port a of the module full_adder. Port b of ha1 is connected to port b of the module full_adder. Port sum of ha1 is connected to the signal s1 while port carry is connected to the signal c1.

The second instantiation of the module half_adder has instance name ha2 and a pointer ha2_ptr. In this case, positional association is used for specifying the interconnection. The order in which the instance ports are connected in the association is very important. Connections are made in the order of the ports declared in the module. Port a of instance ha2 is connected to signal s1, port b of ha2 is connected to port carry_in of full_adder, and so on.

The SC_CTOR block also declares an SC_METHOD process called prc_or that is sensitive to signals c1 and c2, the behavior of which is described in full_adder.cpp. This process computes the logical-or of the two intermediate carry signals to create the output carry_out.

This module has a destructor. The destructor deletes the memory that was created using the new operator in the SC_CTOR (constructor) block. This is important so as to avoid memory leaks. For non-C++ users, here is the format of what a destructor looks like in our context.

A destructor is ignored from a synthesis perspective but is important for simulation.

```
~ module_name () {
  delete ptr1;
  delete ptr2;
  . . .
  // ptr1, ptr2, ... are all pointers that were allocated
  // memory in the SC_CTOR block using the new operator.
}
```

Note that the destructor is required only when memory is acquired via the new operator in the SC_CTOR block.

2.4 Verifying the Functionality

Now that you have written a model in SystemC, how do you test the functionality of the module? Well, SystemC provides a framework and a set of functions to accomplish this task. This includes clock generation and waveform tracing.

The testing aspects described in this section are not synthesizable, that is, not part of SystemC RTL. Most of the non-SystemC RTL features presented in this section are described in further detail in Chapters 8 and 9.

Let us look at the module `full_adder` again. Let's say we want to test this module by exercising all possible values of input patterns. Each pattern is applied every 5ns, and the outputs of the module are recorded every time there is a change in the `full_adder` module's inputs or outputs. Here is a testbench that accomplishes this task.

```
// File: driver.h
#include "systemc.h"

SC_MODULE (driver) {
  sc_out<bool> d_a, d_b, d_cin;

  void prc_driver ();

  SC_CTOR (driver) {
    SC_THREAD (prc_driver);
  }
};
```

```
// File: driver.cpp
#include "driver.h"

void driver::prc_driver () {
  sc_uint<3> pattern;
  pattern = 0;

  while (1) {
    d_a = pattern[0];
    d_b = pattern[1];
    d_cin = pattern[2];
    wait (5, SC_NS);
```

```
    pattern++;
  }
}

// File: monitor.h
#include "systemc.h"

SC_MODULE (monitor) {
  sc_in<bool> m_a, m_b, m_cin, m_sum, m_cout;

  void prc_monitor ();

  SC_CTOR (monitor) {
    SC_METHOD (prc_monitor);
    sensitive << m_a << m_b << m_cin << m_sum << m_cout;
  }
};

// File: monitor.cpp
#include "monitor.h"

void monitor::prc_monitor () {
  cout << "At time " << sc_time_stamp() << "::";
  cout << "(a, b, carry_in): ";
  cout << m_a << m_b << m_cin;
  cout << "  (sum, carry_out): " << m_sum
       << m_cout << endl;
}

// File: full_adder_main.cpp
#include "driver.h"
#include "monitor.h"
#include "full_adder.h"

int sc_main(int argc, char* argv[]) {
  sc_signal<bool> t_a, t_b, t_cin, t_sum, t_cout;

  full_adder f1 ("FullAdderWithHalfAdder");
  // Connect using positional association:
  f1 << t_a << t_b << t_cin << t_sum << t_cout;

  driver d1 ("GenerateWaveforms");
  // Connect using named association:
```

```
    d1.d_a(t_a);
    d1.d_b(t_b);
    d1.d_cin(t_cin);

    monitor mo1 ("MonitorWaveforms");
    mo1 << t_a << t_b << t_cin << t_sum << t_cout;

    sc_start(100, SC_NS);

    return(0);
}
```

argv and argc have the same meaning and functionality as in a standard C++ main() function.

To simulate any SystemC model, you first have to write a testbench as a function called sc_main(). The function takes two arguments: argc, the count of the number of command line arguments, and argv, an array containing the arguments.

The module full_adder is tested by writing a driver and a monitor module. The driver module generates the input patterns, one every 5ns. The monitor module displays the value of all the full_adder ports every time any of them changes value.

Let us look at the driver module first. The driver module has three output ports and no input ports. The SC_CTOR block for this module declares a process of kind SC_THREAD. An SC_THREAD process has the capability to suspend itself due to wait statements. A wait statement can wait for some time or wait for certain events to occur or could be a combination of these. The SC_THREAD process prc_driver defines a local variable pattern which is a three-bit unsigned integer. The while loop iterates and assigns each pattern to the output ports during each iteration the pattern is incremented. pattern is an example of a *variable*, as opposed to a signal or a port, and it does not exhibit the delta delay behavior. In other words, assignment to a variable occurs instantaneously.

A variable behaves different from a signal or a port.

SystemC allows bit selection of an sc_uint type via the [] operator. For example, pattern[0] refers to the 0th bit of the unsigned integer. The three assignment statements cause the 0th bit of the pattern to be assigned to port d_a, 1st bit of the pattern to port d_b and the 2nd bit of the pattern to port d_cin. The one before last statement in the while loop causes the thread process to suspend for 5ns. SC_NS is the time unit for 5.

The monitor module has only input ports. It monitors all the inputs and outputs of the full_adder module instance. This is modeled using an

SC_METHOD process such that any time there is a change in value on its input ports, the process `prc_monitor` is called to print the values of all the inputs of that module. The predefined SystemC function `sc_time_stamp()` returns the current simulation time.

The function `sc_main()` is where all the testbench components are tied together. Also included in this function are all the relevant header files for the modules that are being tested. In our case, these are `full_adder.h`, `monitor.h` and `driver.h`. There are some local signals such as `t_a` and `t_b` that are declared within the `sc_main()` function to be of type `bool`. These signals are used to interconnect the driver, the monitor, the design under test (the module `full_adder`), and the testbench.

To make debugging easier, keep the instance name the same as the string name.

The line:

```
full_adder f1 ("FullAdderWithHalfAdder");
```

instantiates the module `full_adder` in the testbench. Note that we have used a different instantiation mechanism in `sc_main()` than in SC_MODULE. The instance name is `f1`. Further, this instance is associated with signals using positional association (named association could also have been used). The line:

```
f1 << t_a << t_b << t_cin << t_sum << t_count;
```

associates the ports of the `full_adder` with the signals using positional association. The first port `a` of the module `full_adder` is connected to `t_a`, the second port `b` to `t_b`, and so on. Once again, notice that the way in which interconnections are specified in the function `sc_main()` is different from the way interconnections are specified when describing hierarchy within a module. These differences in syntax of specifying hierarchy in `sc_main()` and within a module hierarchy is caused by the fact that within `sc_main()`, a module is declared as an object itself (`f1` is an object of type `full_adder`), whereas in a module hierarchy, a pointer is declared for each instance of the module and therefore has to be dereferenced when used.

The driver and monitor instantiations appear after the `full_adder` instantiation. The ports of the driver instance are associated using named association.

```
d1.d_a(t_a);
d1.d_b(t_b);
d1.d_cin(t_cin);
```

Port d_a of driver is connected to signal t_a, port d_b of driver is connected to the signal t_b and so on. The monitor instance is interconnected using positional association.

The statement:

```
sc_start (100, SC_NS);
```

starts the simulation and runs for 100ns.

To simulate the testbench, a simulator executable has to be created. See Appendix A for details on how to accomplish this. Create a Makefile and specify the following source files: half_adder.cpp, full_adder.cpp, driver.cpp, monitor.cpp, full_adder_main.cpp. After *making* the executable, run the testbench by invoking the executable.

The output produced on executing the testbench is:

```
At time 0 s::(a, b, carry_in): 000 (sum, carry_out): 00
At time 5 ns::(a, b, carry_in): 100 (sum, carry_out): 00
At time 5 ns::(a, b, carry_in): 100 (sum, carry_out): 10
At time 10 ns::(a, b, carry_in): 010 (sum, carry_out): 10
At time 15 ns::(a, b, carry_in): 110 (sum, carry_out): 10
At time 15 ns::(a, b, carry_in): 110 (sum, carry_out): 01
At time 20 ns::(a, b, carry_in): 001 (sum, carry_out): 01
At time 20 ns::(a, b, carry_in): 001 (sum, carry_out): 11
At time 20 ns::(a, b, carry_in): 001 (sum, carry_out): 10
At time 25 ns::(a, b, carry_in): 101 (sum, carry_out): 10
At time 25 ns::(a, b, carry_in): 101 (sum, carry_out): 00
At time 25 ns::(a, b, carry_in): 101 (sum, carry_out): 01
At time 30 ns::(a, b, carry_in): 011 (sum, carry_out): 01
At time 35 ns::(a, b, carry_in): 111 (sum, carry_out): 01
At time 35 ns::(a, b, carry_in): 111 (sum, carry_out): 11
. . .
```

Notice that the output trace lines are printed more than once at a certain time. This is because we are printing values every time there is a change of value on any input or output ports. Such value changes can occur after one or more delta delays at a particular simulation time.

If you want the values printed only when any output port changes value, then change the sensitivity list in the monitor process to:

```
sensitive << m_sum << m_cout;
```

VCD: Value Change Dump format; part of the IEEE 1364 Verilog standard.

We shall look at writing out VCD files, reading and writing patterns from and to text files, and clock generation in Chapter 8.

2.5 Exercises

1. Write a testbench to test the 2-by-4 decoder module.
2. Construct a 4-bit ripple adder using the `full_adder` module and write a testbench to verify its functionality.
3. Modify the testbench for the `full_adder` module described in the previous section to read patterns from an input file. Simulate and verify. Write the results observed to a file.
4. It is typical when testing combinational logic to apply a pattern, wait for a combinational logic delay and then sample the output to look at the stable value. How would you do this for the full-adder testbench? Assume that you want to sample the output 2ns after applying the input pattern.
5. How do you debug your designs? By printing messages to output or to a file? Use a debugger (Appendix A shows one such usage) to single step through your design developed in Exercise 2.

❑

CHAPTER

3

Data Types

In the previous chapter, we saw only one SystemC type, the type `sc_uint`. In this chapter, we describe this type and other SystemC types in more detail including the kind of operations that are allowed on these types. The various kinds of value holders are described in this section. A value holder is of a specific type. A section provides recommendations on what types to use for modeling in SystemC RTL. Of all the types, the most predominant are the two types `bool` and `sc_uint`.

3.1 Value Holders

A value holder is one of:

i. variable,

ii. signal, or

iii. port.

A value holder is declared to be of a specific type.

A *variable* is declared by specifying its type and its name. The declaration is of the form:

```
type variable_name1, variable_name2, . . . ;
```

For example,

```
int mpy;
```

declares a variable called mpy of type int. Variables can be declared and used local to functions including methods. Variables can also be used as member variables provided they are not used for interprocess communication (other uses of variables are described in Chapter 9).

A *signal* is declared using the sc_signal declaration. The declaration is of the form:

```
sc_signal<type> signal_name1, signal_name2, . . .;
```

Signals are used for interprocess communication and for connecting module instances.

sc_signal<>, sc_in<>, sc_out<>, sc_inout<> are parameterized types (a class template) and the declarations are its instantiations.

A *port* is declared using one of the sc_in, sc_out, or sc_inout declaration. The declarations are of the form:

```
sc_in<type> input_name1, input_name2, . . . ;
sc_out<type> output_name1, output_name2, . . .;
sc_inout<type> inout_name1, inout_name2, . . . ;
```

Ports are used to specify the interface to a module.

A multi-dimensional array is declared using standard C++ conventions. Here are some examples.

```
int watch_in [4] [8];
sc_out<sc_uint<4> > addi [6];
sc_signal<bool> mask [256] [16];
```

watch_in is a variable that holds a two-dimensional array of integers. The first dimension is 4 and the second dimension is 8. addi is a one-dimensional array of output ports. The array consists of six ports, where each port is of a 4-bit unsigned integer type. mask is a two-dimensional array of signals with each element of type bool, with the first dimension of size 256 and the second dimension of size 16.

Multi-dimensional arrays cannot be assigned using a single assignment statement. Each element of the array has to be assigned individually (a for loop can be used to accomplish this). Here is an example.

```
for (word = 0; word < 256; word++)
  for (bit = 0; bit < 16; bit++)
    mask[word][bit] = false;
```

An expression is formed using operands and operators. The various operators allowed on the supported types are described in the following sections. An operand may be, amongst others, a variable, signal or a port. In an assignment statement, the target of the assignment can be a:

- variable
- signal
- port
- bit select (wherever allowed)
- range select (wherever allowed).

3.2 Summary of Types

Table 3-1 shows the list of SystemC data types that are synthesizable. Additional data types (those that are not part of SystemC RTL) are described in Chapter 9.

Name	*Description*
sc_bit	Single bit with two values, '0' and '1'
sc_bv<n>	Arbitrary width bit vector

Table 3-1 SystemC data types that are supported in SystemC RTL.

Name	*Description*
sc_logic	Single bit with four values, '0', '1', 'X' and 'Z'
sc_lv<n>	Arbitrary width logic vector
sc_int<n>	Signed integer type, up to 64 bits
sc_uint<n>	Unsigned integer type, up to 64 bits
sc_bigint<n>	Arbitrary width signed integer type
sc_biguint<n>	Arbitrary width unsigned integer type

Table 3-1 SystemC data types that are supported in SystemC RTL.

There are standard C++ data types that can be used in a SystemC RTL model; these are listed in Table 3-2. Many of these types are platform-specific which means that the size of such a type is dependent on how it is implemented on the host machine. These data types can be used in declaring variables, signals and ports.

Name	*Description*
bool	Single bit, two values: true and false
int	Signed integer (32 bits, platform-specific)
unsigned int	Unsigned integer (32 bits, platform-specific)
long	Signed integer (32 bits, platform-specific)
unsigned long	Unsigned integer (32 bits, platform-specific)
signed char	Signed character (8 bits, platform-specific)
unsigned char	Unsigned character (8 bits, platform-specific)
short	Signed integer (16 bits, platform-specific)
unsigned short	Unsigned integer (16 bits, platform-specific)
enum	User-defined enumeration type
struct	All members of synthesizable types

Table 3-2 C++ data types that are supported in SystemC RTL.

The following sections describe the SystemC data types in more detail.

3.3 Bit Type

sc_bit

The bit type is the type sc_bit[1]. It has two values '0' and '1', where '0' represents false and '1' represents true.

Table 3-3 shows the operators that are supported on operands of this type.

These operators have been overloaded to operate on type sc_bit.

A value holder is a variable, signal or a port.

Operator	*Function*	*Usage*
&	Bitwise AND	expr1 & expr2
|	Bitwise OR	expr1 | expr2
^	Bitwise XOR	expr1 ^ expr2
~	Bitwise NOT	~ expr
=	Assignment	value_holder = expr
&=	Compound AND assignment	value_holder &= expr
|=	Compound OR assignment	value_holder |= expr
^=	Compound XOR assignment	value_holder ^= expr
==	Equality	expr1 == expr2
!=	Inequality	expr1 != expr2

Table 3-3 Operators supported for type sc_bit.

Operands of type sc_bit can be freely mixed with operands of type bool in any boolean operation or assignment.

```
// Declares a signal of type sc_bit:
sc_signal<sc_bit> flag;
```

1. Type sc_bit has been deprecated from SystemC 2.0.1 onwards. Use type bool instead.

```
// Declares a variable ready of type bool:
bool ready;

flag = sc_bit('0');  // Assigns the value '0'.

ready = ready & flag; // ok to do this: '0' is interpreted
  // as false, '1' is interpreted as true.

if (ready == flag)    // ok to compare bool with sc_bit.
```

3.4 Arbitrary Width Bit Type

sc_bv<WIDTH>

The type `sc_bv` defines a arbitrary width bit vector (where a bit is `'0'` or `'1'`). It is a vector of type `sc_bit`. The width of the vector is specified in the type. The rightmost index of the vector is 0 and is also the least significant bit. A width of `W` sets the vector size and direction to be `W-1` down to 0 with the `W-1th` bit being the most significant bit.

Here are some examples.

```
sc_bv<8> ctrl_bus;
sc_out<sc_bv<4> > mult_out;
sc_bv<4> mult;
```

The extra space between the two '>' characters is required when declaring signals and ports of arbitrary width. This is to keep the syntax legal with C++.

The first statement declares a variable `ctrl_bus` as a 8-bit bit vector with indices ranging from 7 down to 0. `ctrl_bus[0]` is the least significant bit. The second statement declares an output port `mult_out` as a 4-bit bit vector, with indices ranging from 3 down to 0. When declaring ports and signals with arbitrary width types, remember to provide an extra space character between the bit vector width <WIDTH> and the trailing `'>'` character.

A value (or literal) of type bit vector is specified as a string, which is a sequence of bit values `'0'` and `'1'` enclosed in double quotes. Here are some examples.

```
ctrl_bus = "00110000";
mult_out = "1011";
```

In an assignment of a value to a bit vector, if the size of the value does not match the size of the left hand side, then the value is zero-extended or truncated.

```
ctrl_bus = "10011";
  // Zero-extended to yield "00010011".
```

Table 3-4 shows the operators and methods that are supported on bit vector operands.

The target of an assignment can also be a bit select or a range select.

<table>
<tr><th>Operator</th><th>Function</th><th>Usage</th></tr>
<tr><td>&</td><td>Bitwise AND</td><td>expr1 & expr2</td></tr>
<tr><td>|</td><td>Bitwise OR</td><td>expr1 | expr2</td></tr>
<tr><td>^</td><td>Bitwise XOR</td><td>expr1 ^ expr2</td></tr>
<tr><td>~</td><td>Bitwise NOT</td><td>~ expr</td></tr>
<tr><td><<</td><td>Bitwise shift left</td><td>expr << constant</td></tr>
<tr><td>>></td><td>Bitwise shift right</td><td>expr >> constant</td></tr>
<tr><td>=</td><td>Assignment</td><td>value_holder = expr</td></tr>
<tr><td>&=</td><td>Compound AND assignment</td><td>value_holder &= expr</td></tr>
<tr><td>|=</td><td>Compound OR assignment</td><td>value_holder |= expr</td></tr>
<tr><td>^=</td><td>Compound XOR assignment</td><td>value_holder ^= expr</td></tr>
<tr><td>==</td><td>Equality</td><td>expr1 == expr2</td></tr>
<tr><td>!=</td><td>Inequality</td><td>expr1 != expr2</td></tr>
<tr><td>[]</td><td>Bit selection</td><td>variable [index]</td></tr>
<tr><td>(,)</td><td>Concatenation</td><td>(expr1, expr2, expr3)</td></tr>
<tr><th>Method</th><th>Function</th><th>Usage</th></tr>
<tr><td>range()</td><td>Range selection</td><td>variable.range(index1, index2)</td></tr>
<tr><td>and_reduce()</td><td>Reduction AND</td><td>variable.and_reduce()</td></tr>
<tr><td>nand_reduce()</td><td>Reduction NAND</td><td>variable.nand_reduce()</td></tr>
</table>

Table 3-4 Operators and methods supported on the type `sc_bv`.

Operator	*Function*	*Usage*
or_reduce()	Reduction OR	variable.or_reduce()
nor_reduce()	Reduction NOR	variable.nor_reduce()
xor_reduce()	Reduction XOR	variable.xor_reduce()
xnor_reduce()	Reduction XNOR	variable.xnor_reduce()

Table 3-4 Operators and methods supported on the type `sc_bv`.

In addition to the concatenation operator, the two-argument `concat()` function can also be used to perform concatenation.

Operations worth special mentioning are the bit selection operator `[]`, the concatenation operator `(,)`, the range `range()` method, and the six reduction methods. The `range()` method is used to obtain a bit range of a vector. The `and` reduction method `and_reduce()` works on a vector, performs the logical `and` operation on all the bits, and returns a 1-bit result. The `or` reduction and the `xor` reduction methods perform a similar function except that they perform the logical `or` and the logical `xor` operation on all the bits respectively.

Here are some examples.

```
ctrl_bus[5] = '0';
ctrl_bus.range(0,3) = ctrl_bus.range(7, 4);
mult = (ctrl_bus[0], ctrl_bus[0],
        ctrl_bus[0], ctrl_bus[1]);
ctrl_bus[0] = ctrl_bus.and_reduce();
ctrl_bus[1] = mult.or_reduce();
```

The first statement assigns a bit value `'0'` to the fifth element of `ctrl_bus` using the bit selection operator. In the second statement, the range 7 down to 4 of `ctrl_bus` is assigned to the range 0 to 3 of `ctrl_bus`; in effect, the value of the 7th element is assigned to the 0th element, value of the 6th element is assigned to the 1st element, and so on. The range in the `range()` method can either be increasing or decreasing. The `range()` method can be thought of as a value composed by the concatenation of the specified range of bits. So,

```
ctrl_bus.range(0, 3)
```

implies a value which is a concatenation of values `ctrl_bus[0]`, `ctrl_bus[1]`, `ctrl_bus[2]` and `ctrl_bus[3]`. Similarly,

```
ctrl_bus.range(7, 4)
```

implies a value which is a concatenation of values of `ctrl_bus[7]`, `ctrl_bus[6]`, `ctrl_bus[5]` and `ctrl_bus[4]`.

The specified bits of the variable `ctrl_bus` are concatenated and assigned to the output `mult` in the third statement. The result of the `and_reduce()` method on `ctrl_bus` is assigned to the 0th bit of `ctrl_bus`. In the last statement, an `or` reduction is performed on all the bits of `mult` and the result is assigned to the 1st bit of `ctrl_bus`.

Use a temporary variable to perform a bit selection or a range selection of a port or a signal.

The bit selection operator and the `range()` method can only be applied to variables, not to ports or signals. If a bit selection or a range selection needs to be performed on a port or a signal, a temporary variable has to be used. Here are some examples.

```
sc_signal<sc_bv<4> > dval;
sc_in<sc_bv<8> > addr;
sc_bv<4> var_dval;
sc_bv<8> var_addr;
sc_bit ready;

// To read the 2nd bit of input addr:
var_addr = addr.read();
ready = var_addr[2];

// To assign "011" to a range of signal dval:
var_dval = dval;
var_dval.range(0, 2) = "011";
dval = var_dval;
```

No arithmetic operations are allowed on the bit vector types. To support such an operation, an operand of the bit vector type can be first assigned to a signed or unsigned integer, the required arithmetic operation performed, and then the result can be converted back to a bit vector. Assignments are overloaded to allow translation to and from a bit vector and an integer type. Here is an example. Assume that we want to compute `pha2 - pha1`, where `pha1` and `pha2` are bit vector quantities and they are to be interpreted as unsigned values.

```
sc_in<sc_bv<4> > pha1;
sc_signal<sc_bv<6> > pha2;
sc_uint<4> uint_pha1;
sc_uint<6> uint_pha2;

uint_pha1 = pha1;
uint_pha2 = pha2;
uint_pha2 = uint_pha2 - uint_pha1;
pha2 = uint_pha2;
```

A local variable can be initialized to all '1' values during its declaration.

```
// Initialize to all 1's:
sc_bv<8> all_ones ('1');
sc_bv<4> dtack (true);          // Sets all bits to '1'.
```

A local variable can be initialized to an arbitrary value in its declaration. For example,

```
sc_bv<8> test_pattern = "01010101";
sc_bv<4> wbus = "0110";
```

To print the value of a bit vector, use the variable in an output statement.

```
cout << "The value of var_addr is " << var_addr << endl;
```

Assuming var_addr has a value "0011", the statement will print:

```
The value of var_addr is 0011
```

3.5 Logic Type

sc_logic

The logic type is the type sc_logic. This type has four values:

- '0', SC_LOGIC_0[1]: false
- '1', SC_LOGIC_1: true

- `'X'`, `'x'`, `SC_LOGIC_X`: unknown
- `'Z'`, `'z'`, `SC_LOGIC_Z`: high-impedance

Table 3-5 shows the operators that are supported on operands of this type.

The overloaded operator functions of this type are defined as part of the SystemC class library.

Operator	*Function*	*Usage*
&	Bitwise AND	expr1 & expr2
|	Bitwise OR	expr1 | expr2
^	Bitwise XOR	expr1 ^ expr2
~	Bitwise NOT	~ expr
=	Assignment	value_holder = expr
&=	Compound AND assignment	value_holder &= expr
|=	Compound OR assignment	value_holder |= expr
^=	Compound XOR assignment	value_holder ^= expr
==	Equality	expr1 == expr2
!=	Inequality	expr1 != expr2

Table 3-5 Operators supported for type `sc_logic`.

Operands of type `sc_logic` can be freely mixed with operands of type `sc_bit` when using the assignment, equality and the inequality operators.

```
sc_logic pulse, trig;
sc_bit select;
sc_signal<sc_logic> stack_end;
sc_inout<sc logic> load_stack;

stack_end = SC_LOGIC_Z;  // Assign high impedance value.
pulse != select;         // Compare sc_bit to sc_logic: ok.
```

1. Prior to SystemC 2.0.1, the values `sc_logic_0`, `sc_logic_1`, `sc_logic_X`, `sc_logic_Z` were also supported. These are now deprecated.

```
select = trig;          // sc_logic to sc_bit: ok; warnings
                        // issued if trig is 'X' or 'Z'.
load_stack = SC_LOGIX_X; // Assign 'X' to inout port.
```

The behavior of the bitwise operations on the logic type is defined in the following tables.

& (and)	'0'	'1'	'X'	'Z'
'0'	'0'	'0'	'0'	'0'
'1'	'0'	'1'	'X'	'X'
'X'	'0'	'X'	'X'	'X'
'Z'	'0'	'X'	'X'	'X'

| (or)	'0'	'1'	'X'	'Z'
'0'	'0'	'1'	'X'	'X'
'1'	'1'	'1'	'1'	'1'
'X'	'X'	'1'	'X'	'X'
'Z'	'X'	'1'	'X'	'X'

^ (xor)	'0'	'1'	'X'	'Z'
'0'	'0'	'1'	'X'	'X'
'1'	'1'	'0'	'X'	'X'
'X'	'X'	'X'	'X'	'X'
'Z'	'X'	'X'	'X'	'X'

~ (not)	'0'	'1'	'X'	'Z'
	'1'	'0'	'X'	'X'

In certain situations, it may be required to cast a value of this type explicitly to its type `sc_logic`. This can be done, for example, by casting the value `'Z'` to a `sc_logic` type using one of:

```
sc_logic ('Z')
static_cast <sc_logic> ('Z')
```

An alternate way to write these cast values is by using the predefined cast values:

```
SC_LOGIC_0        // '0' value
SC_LOGIC_1        // '1' value
SC_LOGIC_X        // 'X' value
SC_LOGIC_Z        // 'Z' value
```

An example of such a usage is:

```
trig = SC_LOGIC_Z; // This is identical to:
trig = sc_logic ('Z');
```

To convert an `sc_logic` value to a `bool` value, use the `to_bool()` method.

```
bool wrn;
sc_logic pena (SC_LOGIC_1); // Initialize to '1'.

wrn = pena.to_bool();

if (pena.to_bool())
  cout << "pena is "<< pena << endl;
```

3.6 Arbitrary Width Logic Type

`sc_lv<WIDTH>` The type `sc_lv` defines a arbitrary width logic vector (where a logic bit is `'0'`, `'1'`, `'X'`, or `'Z'`). It is a vector of logic type `sc_logic`. The width of the vector is specified in the type. The rightmost index is 0 and is the least significant bit. A size of `W` sets the vector size and direction to be `W-1` down to 0 with the `W-1th` bit to be the most significant bit.

Here are some examples.

```
sc_lv<4> data_bus;
sc_signal<sc_lv<8> > counter_state;
sc_out<sc_lv<16> > sensor;
```

The first statement declares a variable `data_bus` as a 4-bit logic vector with indices ranging from 3 down to 0. `data_bus[0]` is the least significant bit. The second statement declares a signal `counter_state` as a 8-bit logic vector ranging from 7 down to 0. The last statement declares an output port `sensor` as a 16-bit logic vector ranging from 15 down to 0. When declaring ports and signals of arbitrary width types, remember to provide an extra space character between the width `<WIDTH>` and the trailing `'>'` character.

A value of type `sc_lv` is specified as a string containing a sequence of logic values `'0'`, `'1'`, `'X'` and `'Z'`. For example:

```
data_bus = "0011";
sensor = "10110XX011000ZZZ";

// To specify as a decimal value:
data_bus = "0d14";

// To specify as a hexadecimal value:
sc_lv<8> dtack_read = "0XFE"; // Loads "11111110".
sc_lv<4> coh_rd = "0XA";      // Loads "1001".
```

Watch out when logic vectors start with "0X".

Be careful when logic vector strings start with a `"0x"` or `"0X"` as these are values represented in the hexadecimal form. If you want to use the logic value `'X'` as the second bit, then add an additional `'0'` prefix to the string. For example:

```
sc_lv<4> mbfr;
mbfr = "00X11";     // mbfr has the logic vector "0X11".
```

In an assignment of a value to a logic vector, if the size of the value does not match the size of the left hand side, then the value is zero-extended or truncated as the case may be.

```
data_bus = "00XX11"; // Since data_bus is only 4 bits,
                     // truncation occurs yielding "XX11".
```

A local variable can be initialized to all 'Z' values or all 'X' values during its declaration.

```
// Initialize to all Z's:
sc_lv<8> allzs (SC_LOGIC_Z);
// Initialize to all X's:
sc_lv<4> allxs (SC_LOGIC_X);
```

Just like a bit vector, a variable can be initialized to all 0's or all 1's.

```
sc_lv<4> mbpc ('0');                  // All bits to '0'.
sc_lv<8> prog_ctr (SC_LOGIC_1);  // All bits to '1'.
sc_lv<4> as_byte (true);             // All bits to '1'.
```

The set of operators supported for logic vector operands is identical to that supported for bit vectors and are shown in Table 3-4. Here are some examples.

```
data_bus[2] = 'X';
data_bus[0] = data_bus[3];

counter_state = (data_bus[3], data_bus[3], data_bus[3],
    data_bus[3], data_bus[3], data_bus[2],
    data_bus[1], data_bus[0]);

sc_lv<4> reverse_bits;
sc_logic parity;
sc_lv<8> c_state;

// Compute parity of all bits of c_state:
parity = c_state.xor_reduce();
// Copy three bits over:
c_state.range(7, 5) = reverse_bits.range (2, 0);
// Store bits of data_bus in reverse order:
reverse_bits = data_bus.range (0, 3);
```

As with bit vectors, bit selection and range selection cannot be performed on ports and signals of logic vector type directly. A temporary variable can be used to perform the intended assignment as shown in the following example.

```
// Want to assign rx_ok and tx_ok to bit 4 and bit 7
// of bmask:
sc_out<sc_lv<8> > bmask;
sc_lv<8> temp;
sc_logic rx_ok, tx_ok;

temp = bmask;
temp[4] = rx_ok;
temp[7] = tx_ok;
bmask = temp;
```

To read one bit of a signal vector, read the vector into a temporary variable and then perform the bit selection.

```
sc_signal<sc_lv<4> > sabm;
sc_logic sel_bit;
sc_lv<4> q_temp;

q_temp = sabm;
// Now perform the bit select from the variable:
sel_bit = q_temp[3];
```

No arithmetic operations are allowed on the logic vector types. To support such an operation, an operand of logic vector type can be first assigned to a signed or unsigned integer, the arithmetic operation performed and then the result converted back to a logic vector. Here is an example. The intent is to add two logic vectors `index1` and `index2`, and store the result in `index2`. It is assumed that the vectors are signed quantities.

```
sc_lv<4> index1;
sc_lv<8> index2;
sc_int<4> int_index1;
sc_int<8> int_index2;

int_index1 = index1;
int_index2 = index2;
int_index2 += int_index1;
index2 = int_index2;
```

Two temporary variables `int_index1` and `int_index2` of type `sc_int` (signed integer type) are introduced which save the logic vectors in signed form. The arithmetic operation is performed and the result is saved back in index2.

Assignments are overloaded to allow translation to and from a logic vector and an integer type. The bit vector type and the logic vector type can be assigned to each other. If during assignment, the value assigned to an integer or a bit vector contains an 'X' or 'Z', the result is undefined and a runtime warning is issued. Here are some examples.

```
sc_uint<4> driver;
sc_int<8> q_array;

// Assignment of logic vector to an unsigned integer:
driver = data_bus; // Presence of 'X' or 'Z' causes a
  // runtime warning and the result is undefined.

// Assignment of logic vector to signed integer:
q_array = data_bus; // Since the right hand side is an
  // unsigned value, zeros are filled into
  // the remaining bits of q_array.

// Assignment of an integer to a logic vector:
sensor = q_array; // The leftmost bit q_array[7] is the
  // sign bit and is extended to all the remaining
  // bits of sensor.

// Assignment of an unsigned integer to a logic vector:
data_bus = driver;

// Use the to_int() method to convert logic vector
// to an integer:
int srw;
sc_lv<8> crd_value;

srw = data_bus.to_int();
driver.range (2, 0) = crd_value.range (7, 5).to_int();
q_array.range (7, 2) = crd_value.range (1, 6).to_int();
```

To print the value of a logic vector, simply use the variable in an output statement.

```
cout << "Data bus has value = " << data_bus << endl;
```

Assuming data_bus has a value "OX1Z", this will cause the following to appear on standard output.

```
Data bus has value = OX1Z
```

3.7 Signed Integer Type

sc_int
<WIDTH>

The signed integer type is the type sc_int. It is a fixed precision integer type because the maximum precision is limited to 64 bits. The width of the integer type can be explicitly specified. This type is interpreted as a signed integer type in which a value is represented in 2's complement form. An sc_int type specified with a width of W has the sign bit at index W-1 and the least significant bit is the 0th bit.

The underlying implementation for this type is 64 bits. All operations are performed using 64 bits and the result is truncated based on the target size.

Table 3-6 shows the operators and methods that are supported on operands of this type.

A value holder is a variable, signal or a port. The target of an assignment can also be a bit select or a range select.

<table>
<tr><th>Operator</th><th>Function</th><th>Usage</th></tr>
<tr><td>&</td><td>Bitwise AND</td><td>exprl & expr2</td></tr>
<tr><td>|</td><td>Bitwise OR</td><td>exprl | expr2</td></tr>
<tr><td>^</td><td>Bitwise XOR</td><td>exprl ^ expr2</td></tr>
<tr><td>~</td><td>Bitwise NOT</td><td>~ expr</td></tr>
<tr><td>>></td><td>Arithmetic right shift</td><td>expr >> constant</td></tr>
<tr><td><<</td><td>Arithmetic left shift</td><td>expr << constant</td></tr>
<tr><td>+</td><td>Addition</td><td>exprl + expr2</td></tr>
<tr><td>-</td><td>Minus</td><td>exprl - expr2</td></tr>
<tr><td>*</td><td>Multiply</td><td>exprl * expr2</td></tr>
<tr><td>/</td><td>Divide</td><td>exprl / expr2</td></tr>
<tr><td>%</td><td>Modulus</td><td>exprl % expr2</td></tr>
<tr><td>=</td><td>Assignment</td><td>value_holder = expr</td></tr>
<tr><td>+=</td><td>Compound + assignment</td><td>value_holder += expr</td></tr>
<tr><td>-=</td><td>Compound - assignment</td><td>value_holder -= expr</td></tr>
<tr><td>*=</td><td>Compound * assignment</td><td>value_holder *= expr</td></tr>
<tr><td>/=</td><td>Compound / assignment</td><td>value_holder /= expr</td></tr>
<tr><td>%=</td><td>Compound % assignment</td><td>value_holder %= expr</td></tr>
<tr><td>&=</td><td>Compound AND assignment</td><td>value_holder &= expr</td></tr>
<tr><td>|=</td><td>Compound OR assignment</td><td>value_holder |= expr</td></tr>
<tr><td>^=</td><td>Compound XOR assignment</td><td>value_holder ^= expr</td></tr>
<tr><td>==</td><td>Equality</td><td>exprl == expr2</td></tr>
<tr><td>!=</td><td>Inequality</td><td>exprl != expr2</td></tr>
<tr><td><</td><td>Less than</td><td>exprl < expr2</td></tr>
</table>

Table 3-6 Operators and methods supported for type `sc_int`.

Operator	*Function*	*Usage*
<=	Less than or equal to	expr1 <= expr2
>	Greater than	expr1 > expr2
>=	Greater than or equal to	expr1 >= expr2
++	Increment	value_holder ++
--	Decrement	value_holder --
[]	Bit selection	variable [index]
(,)	Concatenation	(expr1, expr2, . . .)
Method	*Function*	*Usage*
range()	Range selection	variable.range (index1, index 2)
and_reduce()	Reduction AND	variable.and_reduce()
nand_reduce()	Reduction NAND	variable.nand_reduce()
or_reduce()	Reduction OR	variable.or_reduce()
nor_reduce()	Reduction NOR	variable.nor_reduce()
xor_reduce()	Reduction XOR	variable.xor_reduce()
xnor_reduce()	Reduction XNOR	variable.xnor_reduce()

Table 3-6 Operators and methods supported for type `sc_int`.

All the bitwise operators work on the integer quantity using its equivalent bit vector representation. A bit of an integer quantity can be accessed using the bit selection operator `[]`. A range of an integer can be accessed by using the `range()` method. The reduction operators operate on the vector representation of an integer to yield a single bit result. The `concat()` function can also be used for performing concatenation.

Here are some examples.

```
sc_int<4> sel_addr, inc_pc;
sc_int<8> opcode;
sc_int<12> sel_data;
#define N 7
```

```
sc_in<sc_int<N+1> > cpu_control[4]; // Array port.
sc_int<16> hr_reg_file [32];        // A variable array.

opcode = sel_addr + inc_pc;

sel_data = -12;
opcode = sel_data << 2;

sel_addr = 6;
inc_pc = -5;
sel_addr = sel_addr ^ inc_pc;

sel_data = 100;
inc_pc = sel_data.range (3, 0);
opcode.range(1, 0) = (sel_data[6], sel_data[7]);
hr_reg_file[2] = concat (sel_data, sel_addr);

bool stop_clk;
bool start_clk;

stop_clk = inc_pc.and_reduce();
start_clk = hr_reg_file[15].xor_reduce();
```

In the first assignment statement with the addition operator, sel_addr and inc_pc are expanded to 64 bits by preserving the sign bit (since these are signed quantities), the addition operation performed, and the result is truncated to the size of opcode and then assigned to opcode. In the next assignment, sel_data gets the bit value 0xFF4 (the 2's complement of -12). opcode gets the bit value 0xD0; this is obtained by filling zeros from the right after shifting and truncating to 8 bits, the size of opcode. In the xor operation, the sel_addr gets 0xC, which is the result of 0x06 ^ 0xFB. The range select 3 down to 0 of sel_data yields the value 0x4. The concatenation in the following statement yields the result "11" that is then placed in the range 1 down to 0 of opcode. An example of using the concat() function is also shown. The last two statements show examples of using the reduction methods.

The type sc_int is compatible with other C++ integer types and can be used interchangeably.

To convert a bit vector or a logic vector to a signed integer value, the `to_int()` method[1] can be used.

```
sc_bv<8> tic;
sc_lv<4> itf;
sc_int<8> int_tic;
sc_int<4> int_itf;

int_tic = tic.to_int();
int_itf = itf.to_int();
```

To print values of this type in a bit form, cast the variable to a bit vector.

```
cout << "Select address bus has " <<
  (sc_bv<4>) sel_addr << endl;
```

Assuming `sel_addr` has a 4-bit integer value of `1`, this will print the following to standard output.

```
Select address bus has 0001
```

The `to_string()` method can be used to print integer values in different formats. It can optionally be provided a value that specifies the kind of format in which the value is to be printed. The format kind is one of:

i. `SC_BIN` for binary in 2's complement,
ii. `SC_BIN_US` for binary unsigned,
iii. `SC_BIN_SM` for binary in sign magnitude,
iv. `SC_CSD` for canonical signed digit,
v. `SC_OCT` for octal,
vi. `SC_HEX` for hexadecimal, and
vii. `SC_DEC` for decimal (default).

1. The two methods `to_unsigned()` and `to_signed()` that were present in SystemC 2.0 have been deprecated and replaced by `to_uint()` and `to_int()` methods respectively.

```
sc_int<8> rx_data = 106;
sc_int<4> tx_buf = -11;

cout << "Default: rx_data=" << rx_data.to_string()
     << endl;
cout << "Binary: rx_data=" << rx_data.to_string(SC_BIN)
     << endl;
cout << "Binary unsigned: rx_data="
     << rx_data.to_string (SC_BIN_US) << endl;
cout << "Binary sign magnitude: rx_data="
     << rx_data.to_string (SC_BIN_SM) << endl;
cout << "Canonical signed: tx_buf="
     << tx_buf.to_string (SC_CSD) << endl;
cout << "Octal: tx_buf=" << tx_buf.to_string (SC_OCT)
     << endl;
cout << "Hexadecimal: tx_buf="
     << tx_buf.to_string (SC_HEX) << endl;
cout << "Decimal: tx_buf=" << tx_buf.to_string(SC_DEC)
     << endl;
```

Here is the output produced.

```
Default: rx_data=106
Binary: rx_data=0b01101010
Binary unsigned: rx_data=0bus1101010
Binary sign magnitude: rx_data=0bsm01101010
Canonical signed: tx_buf=0csd0-0-
Octal: tx_buf=0o73
Hexadecimal: tx_buf=0xb
Decimal: tx_buf=-5
```

By default, the string value of the signed type is printed with the base information. An optional second parameter with value `false` causes no base information to be printed.

```
cout << "Binary without base: rx_data="
     << rx_data.to_string(SC_BIN, false) << endl;
cout << "Hexadecimal without base: tx_buf="
     << tx_buf.to_string(SC_HEX, false) << endl;
cout << "Decimal without base: tx_buf="
     << tx_buf.to_string(SC_DEC, false) << endl;
```

prints:

```
Binary without base: rx_data=01101010
Hexadecimal without base: tx_buf=b
Decimal without base: tx_buf=-5
```

3.8 Unsigned Integer Type

sc_uint <WIDTH>

The unsigned integer type is the type sc_uint. It is a fixed precision integer type with a maximum width of 64 bits. The width of the integer type can be explicitly specified. This type is interpreted as an unsigned integer type. An sc_uint type with a width W has the least significant bit in the 0th index.

The same set of operators as those shown in Table 3-6 are supported for this type. Here is an example of a concatenation operator.

```
const sc_uint<4> mif_adr = 0xD;
sc_uint<4> sac_mode = (mif_adr[3], mif_adr[1],
                       mif_adr[0], mif_adr[2]);
```

Operands of type sc_uint can be converted to type sc_int and vice versa by using assignment statements. When assigning an integer to an unsigned operand, the integer value in 2's complement form is interpreted as an unsigned number. When assigning an unsigned to a signed operand, the unsigned is expanded to a 64 bit unsigned number and then truncated to get the signed value. Here are some examples.

```
sc_uint<4> accumulator;
sc_int<8> data_out;
#define M 4
sc_signal<sc_uint<2*M+4> > dtack_data[64];
// dtack_data is a signal array.
sc_lv<8> intr_bus;

accumulator = data_out; // data_out in 2's complement
  // form is assigned to accumulator.
accumulator = -1;        // Assigns 15 to accumulator.
```

```
data_out = accumulator; // accumulator expanded to
  // 64 bits and then truncated to get data_out.

// Convert logic vector to unsigned integer:
dtack_data[3] = intr_bus.to_uint();
```

Unsigned integer values can be printed in different formats, similar to signed integers, using the `to_string()` method. Here are some examples.

```
sc_uint<8> hdlc_dbus = 72;

cout << hdlc_dbus.to_string (SC_HEX) << endl;
cout << hdlc_dbus.to_string (SC_BIN) << endl;
```

These statements print the following values.

```
0x048
0b001001000
```

3.9 Arbitrary Precision Signed Integer Type

sc_bigint <WIDTH>

The type `sc_bigint` is an arbitrary precision integer type with any width specification. This type should be used if a precision of more than 64 bits is required; for a precision of 64 bits or less, the fixed precision integer type `sc_int` can be used (leads to faster simulations).

The arbitrary width signed integer type stores signed numbers. Its values are represented using 2's complement form.

The same operators as those for fixed precision signed type listed in Table 3-6 are supported for operands of this type.

```
sc_bigint<100> comp, big_reg; // Declares two integer
  // variables with a precision size of 100 bits.
sc_bigint<70> con_sig;        // A 70-bit integer.
```

For all its underlying operations, arbitrary precision is used. For example, a multiplication of 16 and 64 bits yields a result of 80 bits but if the target precision is 70 bits, the 10 (most significant) bits are truncated.

The sc_bigint type is compatible with other C++ integer types and can be assigned using the assignment operator to targets of other integer types.

To print a value of this type, the to_string() method can be used.

```
big_reg = 1000248;
con_sig = 606193;
cout << "The value of big_reg is " <<
       big_reg.to_string() << endl;
// Prints in decimal form, by default.

// To print in hexadecimal form:
cout << "The value of big_reg is " <<
       big_reg.to_string(SC_HEX) << endl;

// To print in octal form without base:
cout << con_sig.to_string (SC_OCT, false) << endl;
```

These statements print the following values.

```
The value of big_reg is 1000248
The value of big_reg is 0x000000000000000000000f4338
00000000000000002237761
```

3.10 Arbitrary Precision Unsigned Integer Type

sc_biguint <WIDTH>

The type sc_biguint is an arbitrary precision integer type with any width specification. This type should be used if a precision of more than 64 bits is required. For a precision of 64 bits or less, the fixed precision unsigned type sc_uint can be used (to obtain faster simulations).

The same set of operators as those defined for fixed precision signed type listed in Table 3-6 are supported for operands of this type.

```
sc_biguint<256> ram, rom; // Declares two unsigned
  // integer variables with a width of 256 bits.
sc_biguint<70> fef_rw;     // A 70-bit unsigned integer.
```

The sc_biguint type is compatible with other C++ integer types and can be assigned using the assignment operator to targets of other integer types.

The to_string() method can be used to print a value of this type in different forms.

```
fef_rw = 560000;
// Print in octal form with base:
cout << "Octal form=" << fef_rw.to_string(SC_OCT, true)
      << endl;

// Print in binary form with base (second
// parameter to to_string() is optional):
cout << "Hex form:" << fef_rw.to_string (SC_HEX)
      << endl;
```

The following output occurs.

```
Octal form=0o000000000000000002105600
Hex form=0x000000000000088b80
```

3.11 Resolved Types

Resolved types are useful for modeling multiple drivers where resolution between two or more drivers is necessary. SystemC provides resolved logic scalar and vector types for ports and signals.

```
// Resolved logic scalar port type:
sc_out_resolved
sc_inout_resolved

// Resolved logic vector port type:
sc_out_rv<WIDTH>
sc_inout_rv<WIDTH>

// Resolved logic scalar signal type:
sc_signal_resolved
```

```
// Resolved logic vector signal type:
sc_signal_rv<WIDTH>
```

Each process that contains an assignment to a signal or a port contributes a driver for the signal or port. So if the same signal or port is driven from multiple processes, resolution of the signal or port is required. The resolution occurs based on the following table.

Resolved value	'0'	'1'	'X'	'Z'
'0'	'0'	'X'	'X'	'0'
'1'	'X'	'1'	'X'	'1'
'X'	'X'	'X'	'X'	'X'
'Z'	'0'	'1'	'X'	'Z'

A resolved type such as `sc_out_rv<WIDTH>` is similar to `sc_out<sc_lv<WIDTH> >`, except that it has the additional semantic that the final value is resolved using the above table when there are more than one driver driving the port. It is an error to have multiple drivers for a port or a signal that is of type `sc_lv`.

```
sc_signal<sc_lv<4> > mem_word; // Cannot have multiple
  // drivers (assignments in multiple processes).
sc_signal_rv<4> cycle_counter; // Can be assigned in
  // multiple processes (have multiple drivers).
```

3.12 User-defined Data Types

New data types can be created by using the enum types and the struct types. A signal can be declared to be of such a type. However in such a case, the following four additional overloaded functions that operate on the new data type have to be provided before the functions can be used on a signal of the new data type.

You only need to provide those functions that you plan to use. For example, if you do not plan on using `sc_trace()` on such a data type, then there is no need to provide the function.

i. Operator = (assignment)

ii. Operator == (equality)

iii. Operator << (stream output)

iv. `sc_trace()`

Consider the following user-defined type `micro_bus` and the four functions defined for this type.

```
// File: micro_bus.h
#include "systemc.h"
const int ADDR_WIDTH = 16;
const int DATA_WIDTH = 8;

struct micro_bus {
  sc_uint<ADDR_WIDTH> address;
  sc_uint<DATA_WIDTH> data;
  bool read, write;

  micro_bus& operator= (const micro_bus&);
  bool operator== (const micro_bus&) const;
};

inline micro_bus&
micro_bus::operator= (const micro_bus& arg) {
  address = arg.address;
  data = arg.data;
  read = arg.read;
  write = arg.write;
  return (*this);
}

inline bool
micro_bus::operator== (const micro_bus& arg) const {
  return (
    (address == arg.address) &&
    (data == arg.data) &&
    (read == arg.read) &&
    (write == arg.write));
}
```

```
inline ostream&
operator<< ( ostream& os, const micro_bus& arg) {
  os << "address=" << arg.address <<
      " data=" << arg.data << " read=" << arg.read <<
      " write=" << arg.write << endl;
  return os;
}

inline void sc_trace (sc_trace_file *tf,
    const micro_bus& arg, const sc_string& name) {
  sc_trace (tf, arg.address, name+".address");
  sc_trace (tf, arg.data, name+".data");
  sc_trace (tf, arg.read, name+".read");
  sc_trace (tf, arg.write, name+".write");
}
```

Here are two signals declared to be of type `micro_bus`. The defined operations can now be performed on these signals.

```
sc_signal<micro_bus> bus_a, bus_b;
```

3.13 Recommended Data Types

Here are the recommended guidelines on what types to use in a SystemC RTL model. By far, the `bool` and the `sc_uint` types should suffice for most of the designs.

i. For one bit, use the `bool` data type.

ii. For vectors and unsigned arithmetic, use the `sc_uint<n>` data type.

iii. For signed arithmetic, use `sc_int<n>` data type.

iv. If vector size is more than 64 bits, use the `sc_bigint` or `sc_biguint` accordingly.

v. For loop indices etc., use the `int` type or any other C++ integer type. However do not depend on the size of this integer type to model your design.

vi. Use `sc_logic` and `sc_lv<n>` types for only those signals that will carry the four logic values.

vii. Use the resolved types only when resolution is required such as when a port or a signal has multiple drivers.

3.14 Exercises

1. Declare a 4 bit signal `counter` of a logic vector type.
2. Declare two output ports `pdata` and `paddr` which are signed integer types with a width of 8 and 12 respectively.
3. Declare a two-dimensional array variable `ctrl_ram` of unsigned integer type with a width of 8. Initialize all its values with `0xFF`.
4. Declare a resolved logic type signal `result` of size 4. Determine the resolved value of `result` when the following waveforms appear on its two drivers.

```
Driver 1 of result:
  0 at 0ns,
  5 at 5ns,
  10 at 10ns,
  12 at 15ns.
Driver 2 of result:
  6 at 0ns,
  4 at 3ns,
  8 at 8ns,
  0 at 12ns.
```

5. Declare an enumeration type called `color_type` that has values `red`, `green`, `yellow`, `blue` and `orange`. Declare a signal `next_state` of this type. In addition, define the `=`, `==`, `<<` and the `sc_trace()` functions for this type.

❑

CHAPTER

4

Modeling Combinational Logic

This chapter describes how to model combinational logic. Examples using various SystemC constructs and how these can be synthesized are also shown. Flip-flop and latch modeling are described in the next chapter.

4.1 SC_MODULE

Before explaining how to model combinational logic, let us look at the syntax of SC_MODULE in a bit more detail.

SC_MODULE, SC_THREAD, SC_METHOD and SC_CTOR are macros in SystemC.

```
SC_MODULE ( module_name ) {
  // Declarations of ports: input, output and inout.
  // Declarations of signals used in interprocess
  // communication.
  // Process method declarations.
  // Other (non-process) methods.
  // Child module instantiation pointer declarations.
  // Data variable declarations.

  SC_CTOR ( module_name ) {
    // Child module instantiations and interconnections.
    SC_METHOD ( process_method_name );
    // Sensitivity list for process.
    SC_THREAD ( process_method_name );
    // Sensitivity list for process.
    // ... <any number of SC_METHODs and SC_THREADs>
  }
};
```

SC_CTOR is the constructor for the class specified by SC_MODULE.

The basic building block in SystemC is the module. It is a container class in which processes and other modules can be instantiated. A module can have one or more processes, each describing either a synchronous or a combinational logic process. A module can have multiple child modules to specify hierarchy and can have one or more member function declarations that are called by the process methods.

A method is a function defined within a class.

The processes within a module are concurrent and they execute only when a signal in their sensitivity list changes. The processes describe the parallel behavior of the system. The code within a process is sequential though; that is, a process executes sequentially.

A process is a method.

A process is registered in the module constructor implying that it is recognized as a SystemC process rather than as an ordinary member function.

SC_THREAD processes are not allowed in a SystemC RTL description and are explained in more detail in Chapter 9. Data variables within an SC_MODULE are allowed provided they are not used to communicate between processes. Data variables are also allowed inside processes and functions.

Each module requires a constructor block (SC_CTOR). It is used to register processes and to declare their sensitivity lists. Any hierarchy in the module, that is, child module instantiations and interconnections are also described in the constructor block. No other statements are allowed in a module constructor as part of a SystemC RTL description (this rule is relaxed in Chapter 9 where modeling beyond RTL is considered).

All processes are executed once during the initialization phase of simulation.

A process method declaration must have a return type of `void` and have no arguments. The SC_METHOD declaration takes one argument, which is the name of the process method.

The "other methods" are other member functions that a process may call. This class of member functions is not registered in the constructor block. Additionally, these functions can return any data type that is synthesizable. A function can also be defined external to a module and used within a process.

Signals declared within a module are used to communicate between multiple processes. A port connects a module with its environment. An important property here is that a signal or a port update occurs one delta cycle after the assignment occurs and that multiple drivers can exist for a port or a signal.

4.1.1 File Structure

So far, we have shown that the process definitions reside in a separate file from the module declaration. While this is the recommended style in C++ programming, it is also possible to:

i. place the process definitions and the module declarations in the same file.

ii. place the process definitions directly within the module.

We show these approaches here for completeness.

```
// File: half_adder1.cpp
#include "systemc.h"

SC_MODULE (half_adder) {
  sc_in<bool> a, b;
  sc_out<bool> sum, carry;

  void prc_half_adder ();
```

```
  SC_CTOR (half_adder) {
    SC_METHOD (prc_half_adder);
    sensitive << a << b;
  }
};

inline void half_adder::prc_half_adder () {
  sum = a ^ b;
  carry = a & b;
};
```

It is recommended not to name files starting with an sc_ prefix as these may potentially clash with names used in the SystemC library.

In this case, the process definition and the module declaration appear in one file. Here is the same example written with the process definition inside the module declaration.

```
// File: half_adder2.cpp
#include "systemc.h"

SC_MODULE (half_adder) {
  sc_in<bool> a, b;
  sc_out<bool> sum, carry;

  void prc_half_adder () {
    sum = a ^ b;
    carry = a & b;
  };

  SC_CTOR (half_adder) {
    SC_METHOD (prc_half_adder);
    sensitive << a << b;
  }
};
```

In this book, we shall follow the standard C++ programming style and stick with writing the declaration (interface) and its definition (functionality) in separate files.

4.2 An Example

So how do you model combinational logic? Simply by using an SC_METHOD process with an event sensitivity list (using an edge triggered sensitivity list models storage devices; this is the topic of the next chapter). Here is a model for a built-in self test (BIST) cell.

```
// File: bist_cell.h
#include "systemc.h"

SC_MODULE (bist_cell) {
  sc_in<bool> b0, b1, d0, d1;
  sc_out<bool> z;

  void prc_bist_cell();

  SC_CTOR (bist_cell) {
    SC_METHOD (prc_bist_cell);
    sensitive << b0 << b1 << d0 << d1;
  }
};

// File: bist_cell.cpp
#include "bist_cell.h"
```

The :: is the scope resolution operator.

```
void bist_cell::prc_bist_cell () {
  bool s1, s2, s3;

  s1 = ! (b0 & d1);
  s2 = ! (d0 & b1);
  s3 = ! (s2 | s1);
  s2 = s2 & s1;
  z = !(s2 | s3);
}
```

The name of the module is `bist_cell`. It has four input ports and one output port, all of type `bool`. The module also has one SC_METHOD process declaration `prc_bist_cell` which is sensitive to any event on the input ports of the module. The `bist_cell.cpp` describes the behavior of the SC_METHOD process. `s1`, `s2`, `s3` are variables local to the process. Assignment to the port `z` occurs after a delta delay. So if, say, `d1` changes at

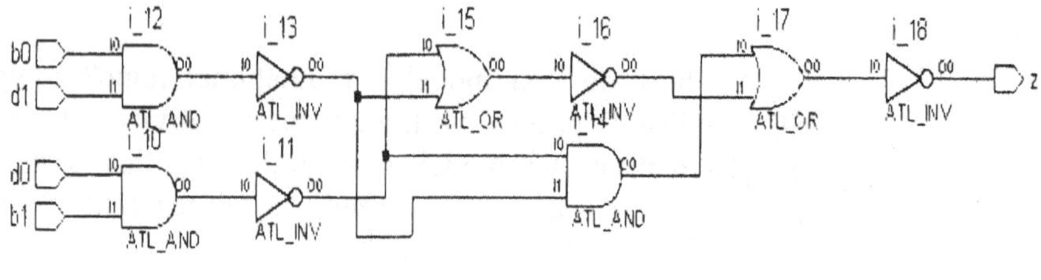

Figure 4-1 A BIST cell.

time 10ns, the process `prc_bist_cell` would execute at `10ns` and the value of `z` computed gets scheduled for assignment at `10+1Δns`. Figure 4-1 shows the synthesized logic.

When describing combinational logic, all the signals and ports that are read within a process should appear as part of the sensitivity list for that process. What happens if, say, port `b0` is missing from the sensitivity list? In such a case, it is not really modeling combinational logic. If an event occurs on `b0`, it does not affect the behavior of the module, but in the synthesized logic, an event on `b0` will propagate to the output. To avoid this mismatch in semantics, ensure that all signals and ports whose values are read within a process appear in its sensitivity list.

The local variables used in the process, `s1`, `s2` and `s3`, do not directly synthesize to wires. In fact, a variable can represent many wires. For example `s2` is the output of gate `i_11` and also the output of gate `i_14`. The complete behavior of this process could be rewritten using no local variables. Here is such a process.

```
void bist_cell:: prc_bist_cell () {
  z = ! ((!(d0 & b1) & !(b0 & d1)) |
        !(!(d0 & b1) | !(b0 & d1)));
  // Though it is harder to read and understand.
}
```

The purpose of using local variables is threefold.

i. Local variables can be used within a process to hold temporary values and to improve readability.

ii. Local variables are assigned values instantaneously (as opposed to a signal or a port that gets a value after a delta delay).

iii. Simulation is likely to be faster when local variables are used.

4.3 Reading and Writing Ports and Signals

In the examples so far, we have read and written values to ports and signals by directly referencing their names. In certain cases, however, this may not be possible. For example, when the port type that you are reading is different from the type you are assigning to, implicit type conversion as defined by C++ may not be sufficient. Here is an example of what a compiler error message may look like for the following module.

```
// File: xor_gates.h
#include "systemc.h"
SC_MODULE (xor_gates) {
  sc_in<sc_uint<4> > bre, sty;
  sc_out<sc_uint<4> > tap;

  void prc_xor_gates();

  SC_CTOR (xor_gates) {
    SC_METHOD (prc_xor_gates);
    sensitive << bre << sty;
  }
};

// File: xor_gates.cpp
#include "xor_gates.h"
void xor_gates::prc_xor_gates() {
  tap = bre ^ sty;
}
```

The compiler (gcc) error message is:

Other compilers may give different-looking error messages.

```
xor_gates.cpp: In method 'void
xor_gates::prc_xor_gates()':
xor_gates.cpp:19: no match for 'sc_in<sc_uint<4> > & ^
sc_in<sc_uint<4> > &'
. . .
```

It is often strongly recommended to always use `read()` and `write()` methods for signals and ports.

For such cases, SystemC provides the `read()` and `write()` methods for reading and writing values from and to a port or signal respectively. Here is how the line with the error in the above example can be modified to behave correctly.

```
tap = bre.read() ^ stdy.read();
```

If a signal or port is read more than once using the `read()` method, one suggestion that can help speed up simulation is to read the signal or port only once and use a temporary variable.

If `count_done` were an output port, then it can be assigned the value 0 by using the `write()` method such as:

```
sc_out<bool> count_done;
. . .
count_done.write (0);
```

It is safe and often strongly recommended to always use the `read()` and `write()` methods to ensure that no compiler errors related to reading and writing values from and to a port or a signal occur.

The value of an output port can be read using the `read()` method.

4.4 Logical Operators

Logical operators can be synthesized directly by expressing the operators in the behavior. Here is an example that uses the `^ (xor)`, `& (and)` and the `| (or)` operators.

```
// File: full_adder.h
#include "systemc.h"

SC_MODULE (full_adder) {
  sc_in<bool> a, b, cin;
  sc_out<bool> sum, cout;

  void prc_full_adder();

  SC_CTOR (full_adder) {
    SC_METHOD (prc_full_adder);
    sensitive << a << b << cin;
```

```
  }
};

// File: full_adder.cpp
#include "full_adder.h"

void full_adder::prc_full_adder () {
  sum = (a ^ b) ^ cin;
  cout = (a & b) | (a & cin) | (b & cin);
}
```

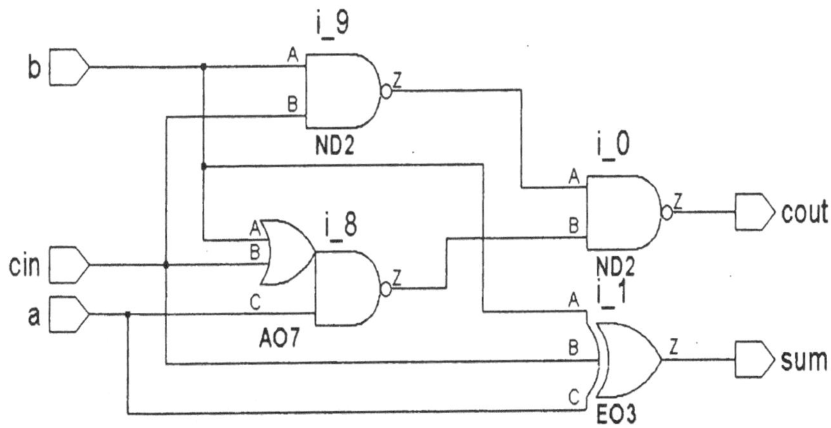

Figure 4-2 A full-adder.

Figure 4-2 shows the synthesized logic for the full-adder. Logical operations can also be performed between vectors. Here is an example. The output is the exclusive-or of the module inputs. Figure 4-3 shows the synthesized logic.

```
// File: xor_gates.h
#include "systemc.h"
const int SIZE = 4;

SC_MODULE (xor_gates) {
  sc_in<sc_uint<SIZE> > bre, sty;
  sc_out<sc_uint<SIZE> > tap;

  void prc_xor_gates();
```

```
  SC_CTOR (xor_gates) {
    SC_METHOD (prc_xor_gates);
    sensitive << bre << sty;
  }
};

// File: xor_gates.cpp
#include "xor_gates.h"

void xor_gates::prc_xor_gates() {
  tap = bre.read() ^ sty.read();
}
```

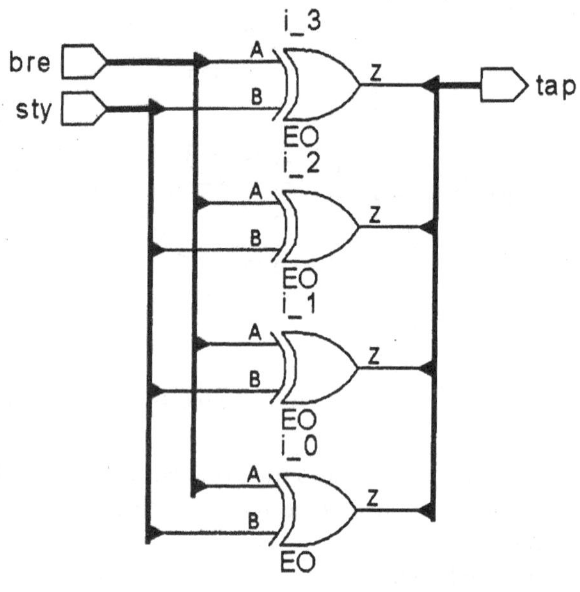

Figure 4-3 A bank of logic gates.

4.5 Arithmetic Operators

When using arithmetic operators, the type of the operands dictates the kind of implied logic, whether signed or unsigned. Examples of signed types are the C++ integer types and sc_int. An example of an unsigned type is sc_uint. Note that in all fixed precision integer type calculations, all computations occur based on a 64-bit representation and appropriate truncation occurs depending on the target result size. So in the example:

```
sc_uint<4> write_addr;
sc_int<5> read_addr;

read_addr = write_addr + read_addr;
```

read_addr and write_addr are first expanded to 64 bits, zero-extended for write_addr since it is an unsigned type, sign-extended (read_addr[4] is the sign bit) for read_addr since it is a signed type, the + operation is performed and the result is assigned back to read_addr by truncating it to a 5-bit result.

4.5.1 Unsigned Arithmetic

Unsigned arithmetic can be modeled using the types sc_uint and sc_biguint. Here is an example of an unsigned adder.

```
//File: unsigned_adder.h
#include "systemc.h"

SC_MODULE (unsigned_adder) {
  sc_in<sc_uint<4> > arb, tbe;
  sc_out<sc_uint<5> > sum;

  void prc_unsigned_adder();

  SC_CTOR (unsigned_adder) {
    SC_METHOD (prc_unsigned_adder);
    sensitive << arb << tbe;
  }
};

// File: unsigned_adder.cpp
#include "unsigned_adder.h"

void unsigned_adder::prc_unsigned_adder() {
  sum = arb.read() + tbe.read();
}
```

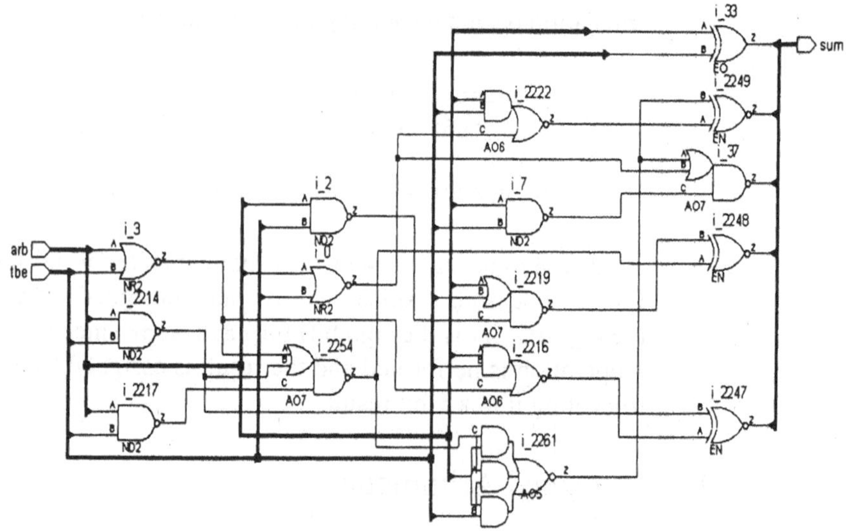

Figure 4-4 A 4-bit adder.

Figure 4-4 shows the synthesized logic. Note that the result is five bits long. The range of values on any input can be from 0 to 15.

4.5.2 Signed Arithmetic

Here is the same example as in the previous section but using signed numbers. Signed numbers are identified by using the types `sc_int` and `sc_bigint`. C++ integer types can also be used to perform signed arithmetic operations.

```
// File: signed_adder.h
#include "systemc.h"

SC_MODULE (signed_adder) {
  sc_in<sc_int<4> > arb, tbe;
  sc_out<sc_int<5> > sum;

  void prc_signed_adder();
```

```
  SC_CTOR (signed_adder) {
    SC_METHOD (prc_signed_adder);
    sensitive << arb << tbe;
  }
};

// File: signed_adder.cpp
#include "signed_adder.h"

void signed_adder::prc_signed_adder() {
  sum = arb.read() + tbe.read();
}
```

The synthesized logic is the same as the unsigned adder case since a signed adder in 2's complement behaves exactly the same as an unsigned adder. The difference is that the signed adder can add input values in the range -8 to 7, while the unsigned adder can add input values in the range 0 to 15.

The result size of an arithmetic operation can be set to any size of 64 bits or less when using the fixed precision integer types; all arithmetic operations are performed internally using 64 bits and then truncated to the target size.

Modeling a carry is easily done by keeping track of the last bit. The signed adder example is rewritten here with an explicit carry out port (`sum[4]` is the carry out bit in the module `signed_adder`).

```
// File: adder_with_carry.h
#include "systemc.h"

SC_MODULE (adder_with_carry) {
  sc_in<sc_int<4> > arb, tbe;
  sc_out<sc_int<4> > sum;
  sc_out<bool> carry_out;

  void prc_adder_with_carry();

  SC_CTOR (adder_with_carry) {
    SC_METHOD (prc_adder_with_carry);
    sensitive << arb << tbe;
  }
};
```

```
// File: adder_with_carry.cpp
#include "adder_with_carry.h"

void adder_with_carry::prc_adder_with_carry() {
  sc_int<5> temp;

  temp = arb.read() + tbe.read();
  sum = temp.range (3, 0);
  carry_out = temp[4];
}
```

4.6 Relational Operators

Relational operators can be modeled similar to arithmetic operators. The logic inferred for relational operators for the unsigned and the signed cases is different. Here is an example of a relational operator used with unsigned numbers. The model checks whether the lower four bits of input a is greater than the upper four bits of input b. If so, the output z is true, else it is false. The synthesized logic is shown in Figure 4-5.

```
// File: gt.h
#include "systemc.h"
const int WIDTH = 8;

SC_MODULE (gt) {
  sc_in<sc_uint<WIDTH> > a, b;
  sc_out<bool> z;

  void prc_gt();

  SC_CTOR (gt) {
    SC_METHOD (prc_gt);
    sensitive << a << b;
  }
};
```

```
// File: gt.cpp
#include "gt.h"

void gt::prc_gt() {
  sc_uint<WIDTH> atemp, btemp;

  atemp = a.read();
  btemp = b.read();
  z = sc_uint<WIDTH>(atemp.range(WIDTH/2-1, 0)) >
      sc_uint<WIDTH>(btemp.range(WIDTH-1, WIDTH/2));
}
```

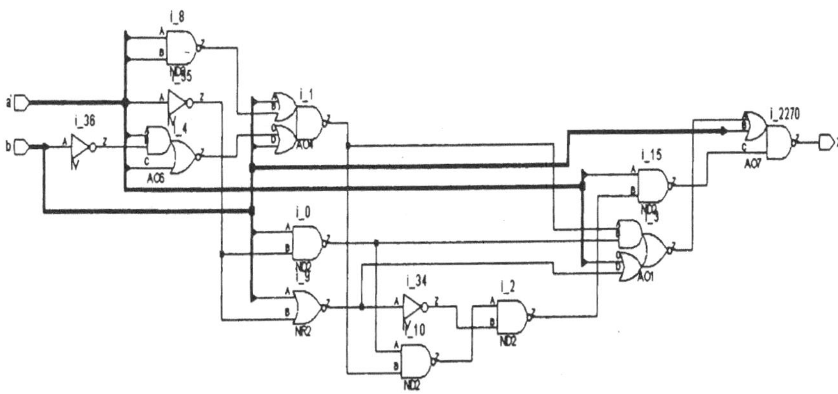

Figure 4-5 Unsigned ">" relational operator.

The assignments to the temporaries are necessary so that the `range()` operation can be performed (the `range()` method is not allowed on a port). The casting of the `range()` operation's result to `sc_uint` is required to ensure that the value of the range stays as an unsigned integer quantity.

Here is an example that uses signed numbers with an inequality operation. In this model, output `z` is true if input `a` is not equal to input `b`. The inputs are signed numbers. The type `sc_int` is used. Figure 4-6 shows the synthesized logic.

```
// File: not_equals.h
#include "systemc.h"
const int WIDTH = 4;

SC_MODULE (not_equals) {
  sc_in<sc_int<WIDTH> > a, b;
  sc_out<bool> z;

  void prc_not_equals();

  SC_CTOR (not_equals) {
    SC_METHOD (prc_not_equals);
    sensitive << a << b;
  }
};

// File: not_equals.cpp
#include "not_equals.h"

void not_equals::prc_not_equals() {
  z = a != b;
}
```

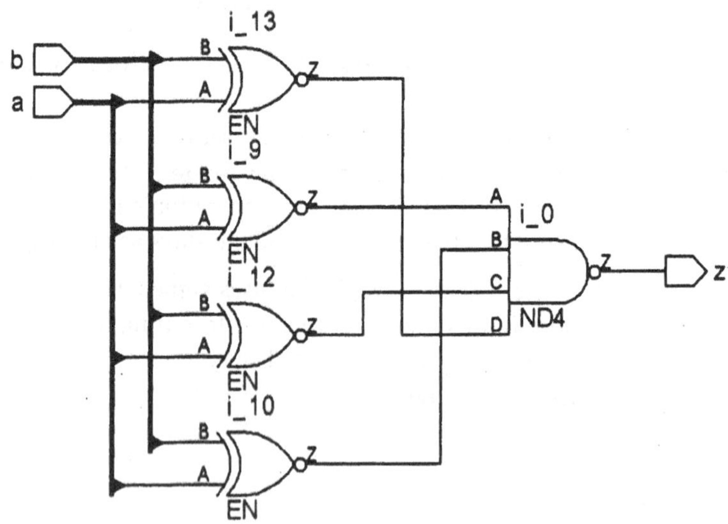

Figure 4-6 Signed "!=" inequality operator.

4.7 Vectors and Ranges

Operations using vectors, bit selects, range selects and concatenations can be used in a SystemC RTL model to infer logic.

As described in the previous chapter, a bit select or a range select of a port or a signal is not allowed. Instead, a temporary variable can be used to achieve the desired functionality. Here is an example.

```
sc_in<sc_uint<4> > data;
sc_signal<sc_bv<6> > counter;
sc_uint<4> temp;
sc_uint<6> cnt_temp;
bool mode, preset;

mode = data[2]; // Not allowed.
// Instead, the following two statements can be used:
temp = data.read();
mode = temp[2];

counter[4] = preset; // Not allowed.
// Instead, the following three statements can be used:
cnt_temp = counter;
cnt_temp[4] = preset;
counter = cnt_temp;
```

4.7.1 Constant Index

Here is an example that uses the `range()` method, concatenation, and array indices with constant values.

```
// File: vectors.h
#include "systemc.h"
const int SIZE = 4;
const int TWOD = 2;

SC_MODULE (vectors) {
  sc_in<sc_uint<SIZE> > a, b, c, d;
  sc_out<sc_uint<SIZE> > zcat;
  sc_out<bool> membit_x;
```

```
    void prc_vectors();

    SC_CTOR (vectors) {
      SC_METHOD (prc_vectors);
      sensitive << a << b << c << d;
    }
  };

  // File: vectors.cpp
  #include "vectors.h"

  void vectors::prc_vectors () {
    sc_uint<SIZE> atemp, btemp, ctemp, dtemp,
      r1, r0, ztemp;
    sc_uint<SIZE> reg_bank[TWOD];

    atemp = a.read();
    btemp = b.read();
    ctemp = c.read();
    dtemp = d.read();

    // First set:
    ztemp.range(3, 1) = (atemp[2], ctemp.range(3, 2));
    ztemp[0] = btemp[0];
    zcat = ztemp;

    // Second set:
    reg_bank[1] = ctemp & dtemp;
    reg_bank[0] = atemp | btemp;

    // Third set:
    r1 = reg_bank[1];
    r0 = reg_bank[0];
    membit_x = (r1[3] & r0[3]) | (r1[2] & r0[2]);
  }
```

The first set of statements in the process show the reading of an element of a vector, a range selection and the concatenation of a bit and a range. It also shows an assignment to a bit of an output port. The second set of statements show a vector operation and its result being assigned to one dimension of a two-dimensional array. The last set of statements show how an element of a two-dimensional array can be read and used to

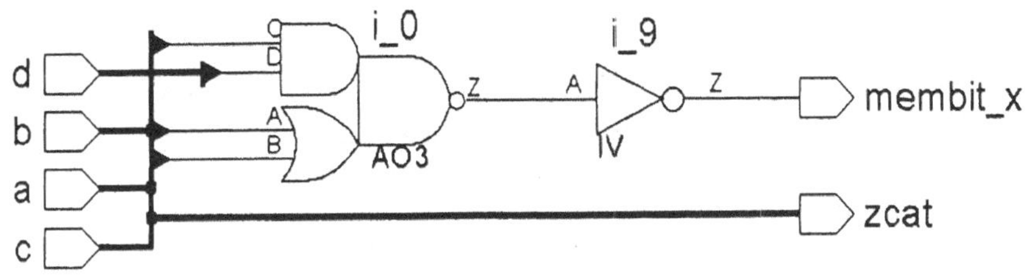

Figure 4-7 Vectors and slices.

form the expression for `membit_x`. The synthesized logic is shown in Figure 4-7.

4.7.2 Non-constant Index

It is possible to use a non-constant as an index in an array element selection as shown in the following module.

```
// File: non_compute_right.h
#include "systemc.h"
const int DSIZE = 4;
const int ISIZE = 2;

SC_MODULE (non_compute_right) {
  sc_in<sc_uint<DSIZE> > data;
  sc_in<sc_uint<ISIZE> > index;
  sc_out<bool> dout;

  void prc_non_compute_right();

  SC_CTOR (non_compute_right) {
    SC_METHOD (prc_non_compute_right);
    sensitive << data << index;
  }
};
```

```
// File: non_compute_right.cpp
#include "non_compute_right.h"

void non_compute_right::prc_non_compute_right () {
  sc_uint<DSIZE> dtemp;
  sc_uint<ISIZE> itemp;

  dtemp = data.read();
  itemp = index.read();
  dout = dtemp[itemp];
}
```

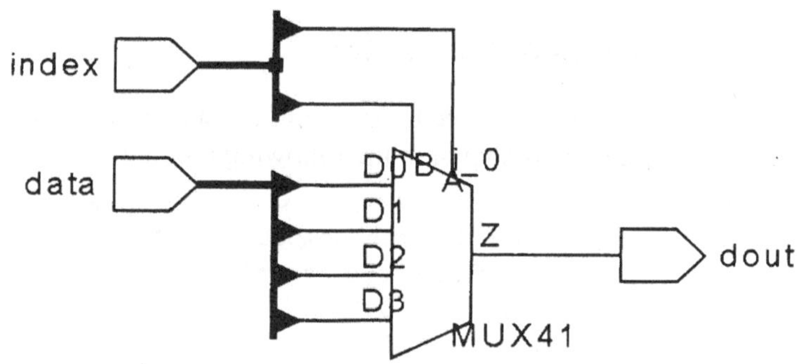

Figure 4-8 Non-constant index generates a multiplexer.

In this case, a multiplexer is generated as shown in the synthesized logic of Figure 4-8.

Here is another example of a non-constant index; this time it is used on the left hand side of an assignment. A decoder is synthesized for this behavior as shown in Figure 4-9.

```
// File: non_compute_left.h
#include "systemc.h"
const int DSIZE = 4;
const int ISIZE = 2;

SC_MODULE (non_compute_left) {
  sc_in<bool> store;
  sc_in<sc_uint<ISIZE> > addr;
  sc_out<sc_uint<DSIZE> > mem;
```

```
  void prc_non_compute_left();

  SC_CTOR (non_compute_left) {
    SC_METHOD (prc_non_compute_left);
    sensitive << store << addr;
  }
};

// File: non_compute_left.cpp
#include "non_compute_left.h"

void non_compute_left::prc_non_compute_left () {
  sc_uint<DSIZE> mem_temp;
  sc_uint<ISIZE> addr_temp;

  addr_temp = addr.read();
  mem_temp [addr_temp] = store;
  mem = mem_temp;
}
```

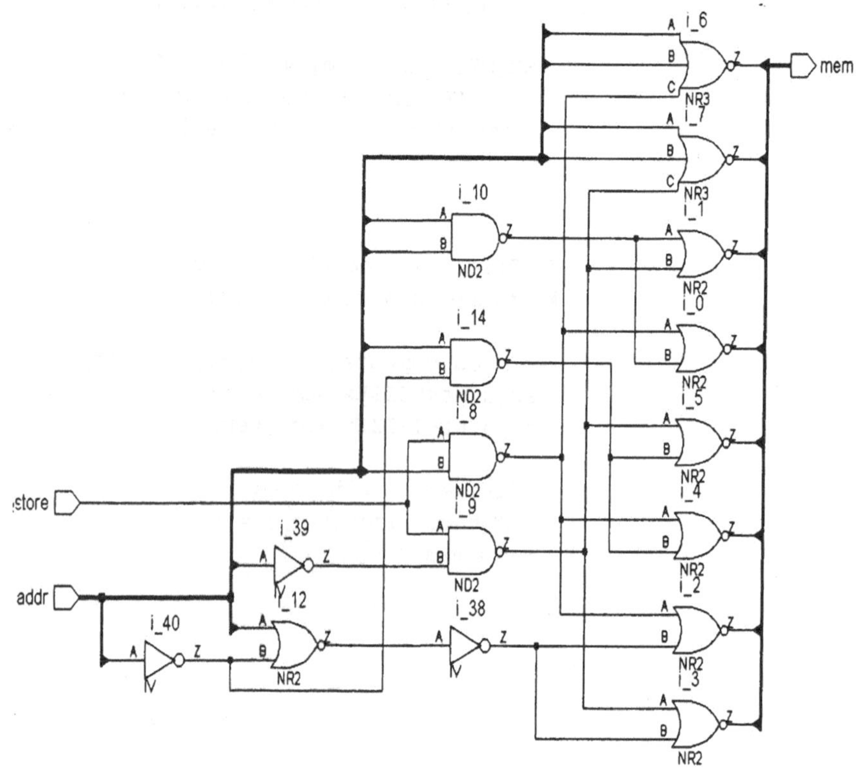

Figure 4-9 A decoder generated from a non-constant index.

4.8 If Statement

An `if` statement represents logic that is conditionally executed. Here is an example.

```
// sync, mode and cond are all of type bool.
if (sync > mode)
  cond = mode;
else
  cond = sync;
```

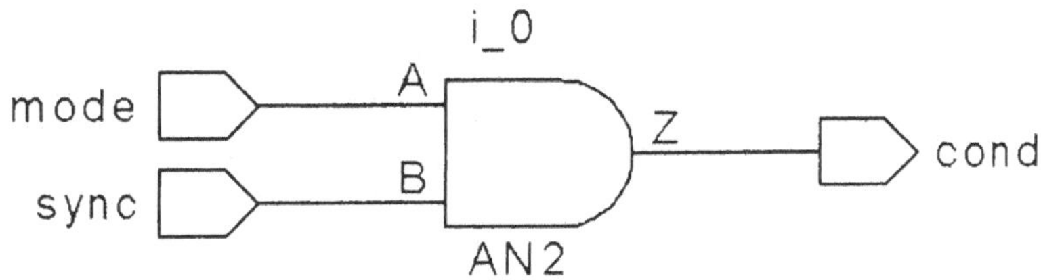

Figure 4-10 Logic derived from an `if` statement.

Figure 4-10 shows the logic corresponding to this `if` statement. Here is another example of an `if` statement. Figure 4-11 shows the synthesized logic.

```
// File: simple_alu.h
#include "systemc.h"
const int WORD_SIZE = 4;

SC_MODULE (simple_alu) {
  sc_in<sc_uint<WORD_SIZE> > a, b;
  sc_in<bool> ctrl;
  sc_out<sc_uint<WORD_SIZE> > z;

  void prc_simple_alu();

  SC_CTOR (simple_alu) {
    SC_METHOD (prc_simple_alu);
    sensitive << a << b << ctrl;
  }
};

// File: simple_alu.cpp
#include "simple_alu.h"

void simple_alu::prc_simple_alu() {
  if (ctrl)
    z = a.read() & b.read();
  else
    z = a.read() | b.read();
}
```

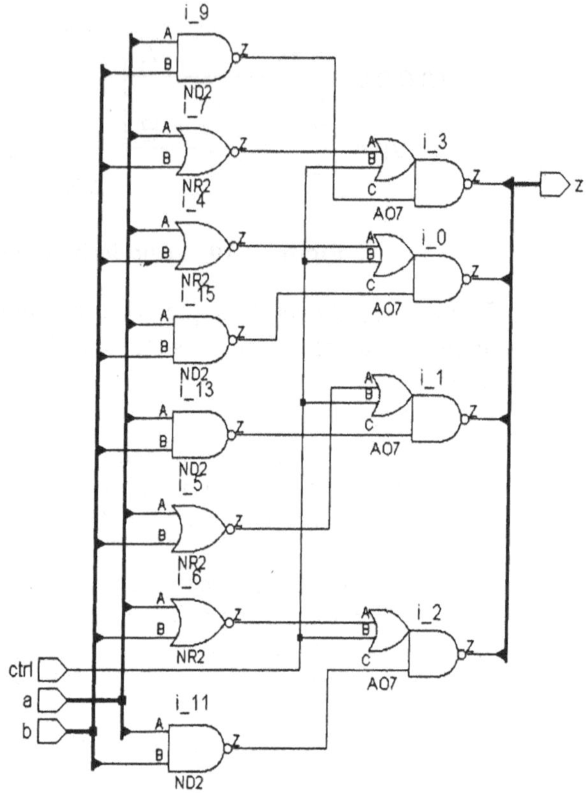

Figure 4-11 Conditional selection of operations.

The if statement provides a natural way of modeling a priority encoder, a model of which is shown next. Figure 4-12 shows the synthesized logic.

```
// File: priority.h
#include "systemc.h"
const int INPUT_SIZE = 4;
const int OUTPUT_SIZE = 3;

SC_MODULE (priority) {
  sc_in<sc_uint<INPUT_SIZE> > sel;
  sc_out<sc_uint<OUTPUT_SIZE> > z;

  void prc_priority();
```

```
  SC_CTOR (priority) {
    SC_METHOD (prc_priority);
    sensitive << sel;
  }
};

// File: priority.cpp
#include "priority.h"

void priority::prc_priority() {
  sc_uint<INPUT_SIZE> tsel;

  tsel = sel.read();

  if (tsel[0])
    z = 0;
  else if (tsel[1])
    z = 1;
  else if (tsel[2])
    z = 2;
  else if (tsel[3])
    z = 3;
  else
    z = 7;
}
```

The target `z` is assigned in all the branches of the `if` statement. This rule must be followed to model or synthesize combinational logic. We shall see in the next chapter what the consequence is if this rule is not followed.

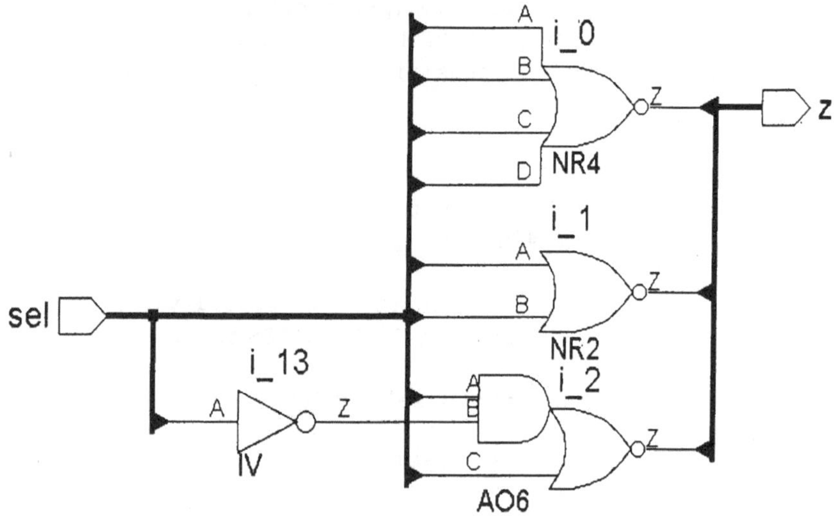

Figure 4-12 A priority encoder.

4.9 Switch Statement

Here is an example of a switch statement.

```
// File: alu.h
#include "systemc.h"
const int WORD = 2;
enum op_type {add, subtract, multiply, divide};

SC_MODULE (alu) {
  sc_in<sc_uint<WORD> > a, b;
  sc_in<op_type> op;
  sc_out<sc_uint<WORD> > z;

  void prc_alu();

  SC_CTOR (alu) {
    SC_METHOD(prc_alu);
    sensitive << a << b << op;
```

```
  }
};

// File: alu.cpp
#include "alu.h"

void alu::prc_alu() {
  sc_uint<WORD> ta, tb;

  ta = a.read();
  tb = b.read();

  switch (op) {
    case add        : z = ta + tb; break;
    case subtract   : z = ta - tb; break;
    case multiply   : z = ta * tb; break;
    case divide     : z = ta / tb; break;
  }
}
```

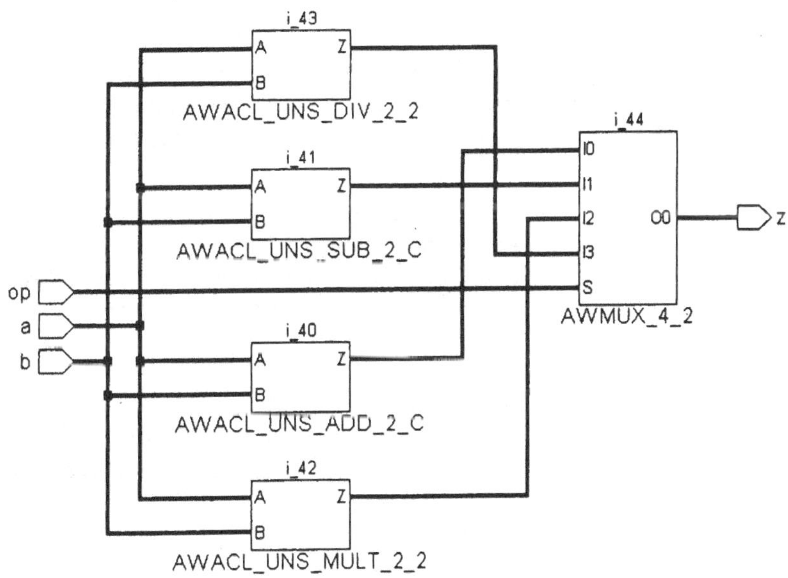

Figure 4-13 A 2-bit ALU.

A switch statement behaves like a nested `if` statement, that is, the value of the switch expression `op` is checked with the first case label, if it does not match, the second case label is checked and so on. If a case label matches, then the set of statements associated with that case label is executed. A break statement causes the switch statement to exit, that is, execution continues with the statement following the switch statement, if any. SystemC RTL supports both the presence or the absence of a break statement (the absence of a break statement is a fall through). The equivalent `if` statement for the above switch statement follows.

```
if (op == add)
  z = ta + tb;
else if (op == subtract)
  z = ta - tb;
else if (op == multiply)
  z = ta * tb;
else if (op == divide)
  z = ta / tb;
```

The synthesized logic in shown in Figure 4-13. An alternate way to generate logic for a switch statement is as a decoder.

Here is another example of a switch statement. Figure 4-14 shows the synthesized logic. This example shows the use of an user-defined enumeration type and its use as an input port type.

```
// File: case_ex.h
#include "systemc.h"
enum weekday {sunday, monday, tuesday, wednesday,
    thursday, friday, saturday};
const int OUT_SIZE = 4;

SC_MODULE (case_ex) {
  sc_in<weekday> day_of_week;
  sc_out<sc_uint<OUT_SIZE> > sleep_time;

  void prc_case_ex();

  SC_CTOR (case_ex) {
    SC_METHOD (prc_case_ex);
    sensitive << day_of_week;
```

```
  }
};

// File: case_ex.cpp
#include "case_ex.h"

void case_ex::prc_case_ex() {
  switch (day_of_week) {
    case monday     :
    case tuesday    :
    case wednesday  : sleep_time = 6; break;
    case friday     : sleep_time = 8; break;
    case saturday   : sleep_time = 9; break;
    case sunday     : sleep_time = 7; break;
    default         : sleep_time = 6; break;
  }
}
```

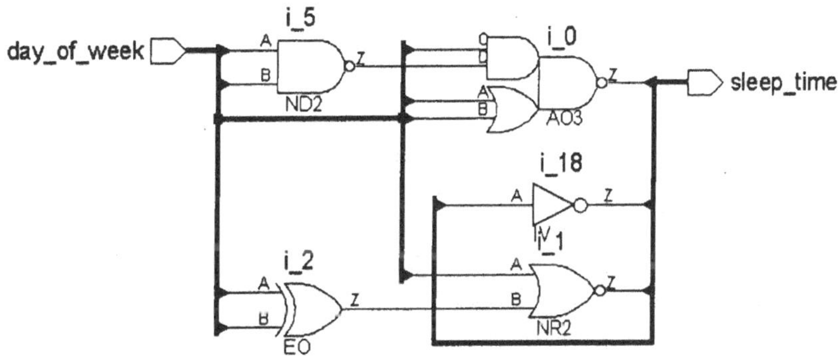

Figure 4-14 A switch statement example.

As in the `if` statement case, it is important to assign a value to a target for all possible values of the switch expression. This rule is necessary to infer combinational logic. In the next chapter, we see what happens if this rule is not followed. To cover the assignment of `sleep_time` in all possible branches of the switch statement, the default case branch in the above example is required.

4.10 Loops

There are three kinds of loop statements in C++.

i. For loop statement

ii. While statement

iii. Do while statement

The for loop statement is the only one supported in SystemC RTL. In addition, the for loop iteration must be a compile time constant, that is, you should be able to unroll the for loop at compile time. This implies that the only kind of expression allowed in a for loop is one that can be computed at compile time. Here is an example of a for loop statement.

```
// File: demux.h
#include "systemc.h"
const int IN_WIDTH = 2;
const int OUT_WIDTH = 4;

SC_MODULE (demux) {
  sc_in<sc_uint<IN_WIDTH> > a;
  sc_out<sc_uint<OUT_WIDTH> > z;

  void prc_demux();

  SC_CTOR (demux) {
    SC_METHOD (prc_demux);
    sensitive << a;
  }
};

// File: demux.cpp
#include "demux.h"

void demux::prc_demux() {
  sc_uint<3> j;
  sc_uint<OUT_WIDTH> temp;

  for (j=0; j<OUT_WIDTH; j++)
    if (a == j)
      temp[j] = 1;
    else
```

```
        temp[j] = 0;

    z = temp;
}
```

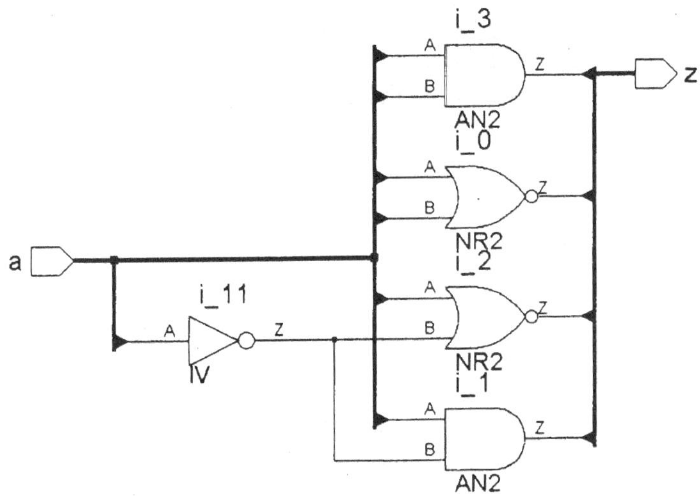

Figure 4-15 A for-loop example.

Note that a temporary variable is required for the output port since bit selection is not allowed directly on an output port. When the for loop is expanded (unrolled), as is typically done by a synthesis tool, the following four `if` statements are obtained.

```
j = 0;
if (a == j) temp[j] = 1; else temp[j] = 0;
j = 1;
if (a == j) temp[j] = 1; else temp[j] = 0;
j = 2;
if (a == j) temp[j] = 1; else temp[j] = 0;
j = 3;
if (a == j) temp[j] = 1; else temp[j] = 0;
```

The synthesized logic is shown in Figure 4-15.

4.11 Methods

A method is a member function of a class.

Methods other than the SC_METHOD processes can be used in a SystemC RTL model. Such methods can be called from within an SC_METHOD process or from another method. A method is synthesized typically by expanding the method call into inline code. Any local variables declared within a method are temporary variables and may map to wires in the synthesized logic. Here is an example.

```
// File: odd_ones.h
#include "systemc.h"
const int SIZE = 6;

SC_MODULE (odd_ones) {
  sc_in<sc_uint<SIZE> > data_in;
  sc_out<bool> is_odd;

  bool compute_if_odd (sc_uint<SIZE> abus);
  void prc_odd_ones ();

  SC_CTOR (odd_ones) {
    SC_METHOD (prc_odd_ones);
    sensitive << data_in;
  }
};

// File: odd_ones.cpp
#include "odd_ones.h"

void odd_ones::prc_odd_ones () {
  is_odd = compute_if_odd(data_in);
}

bool odd_ones::compute_if_odd (sc_uint<SIZE> abus) {
  bool result;
  int i;

  result = false;

  for (i=0; i<SIZE; i++)
    result = result ^ abus[i];
```

```
  return (result);
}
```

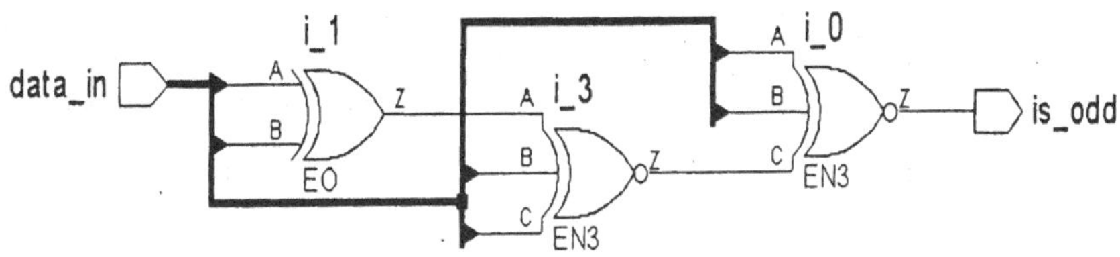

Figure 4-16 Odd numbers of ones logic.

The method compute_if_odd() is called from the SC_METHOD process prc_odd_ones. Notice the additional declaration for the compute_if_odd() method in the module declaration. The size of the input data has been parameterized by using a constant SIZE. This example is used to illustrate the support of a method call in SystemC RTL. The predefined xor_reduce() reduction method could have been used to perform the intended function in this case instead of using the compute_if_odd() method. However, the reduction method is supported only on bit vector and logic vector types. So the sc_uint type has to be first converted to a bit-vector type and then the reduction method can be used, as shown below.

```
#include "odd_ones.h"

void odd_ones::prc_odd_ones() {
  sc_bv<SIZE> temp;

  temp = data_in.read();
  is_odd = temp.xor_reduce();
}
```

Figure 4-16 shows the synthesized netlist.

A function need not be a method (a member function).

Here is an example of a function, which is not a method, that is called from an SC_METHOD process. A 4-bit full-adder logic is implemented by calling a function that computes a full single bit add four times. Figure 4-17 shows the synthesized logic.

```
// File: one_bit_adder.h
void one_bit_adder
  (bool a, bool b, bool cin, bool &sum, bool &cout);

// File: one_bit_adder.cpp
void one_bit_adder
  (bool a, bool b, bool cin, bool &sum, bool &cout) {
  sum = a ^ b ^ cin;
  cout = (a & b) | (a & cin) | (b & cin);
}

// File: four_bit_adder.h
#include "systemc.h"
const int SIZE = 4;

SC_MODULE (four_bit_adder) {
  sc_in<sc_uint<SIZE> > sha, shb;
  sc_in<bool> shcarry_in;
  sc_out<sc_uint<SIZE> > shsum;
  sc_out<bool> shcarry_out;

  void prc_four_bit_adder();

  SC_CTOR (four_bit_adder) {
    SC_METHOD (prc_four_bit_adder);
    sensitive << sha << shb << shcarry_in;
  }
};

// File: four_bit_adder.cpp
#include "four_bit_adder.h"
#include "one_bit_adder.h"

void four_bit_adder::prc_four_bit_adder () {
  sc_uint<SIZE+1> tcarry;
  sc_uint<SIZE> tsum, tsha, tshb;
  int j;
  bool sum_bit, carry_bit;

  tsha = sha.read();
  tshb = shb.read();
  tcarry[0] = shcarry_in.read();
```

```
    for (j=0; j<SIZE; j++) {
      one_bit_adder ((bool)tsha[j], (bool)tshb[j],
        (bool)tcarry[j], sum_bit, carry_bit);
      tsum[j] = sum_bit;
      tcarry[j+1] = carry_bit;
    }

    shcarry_out = tcarry[SIZE];
    shsum = tsum;
}
```

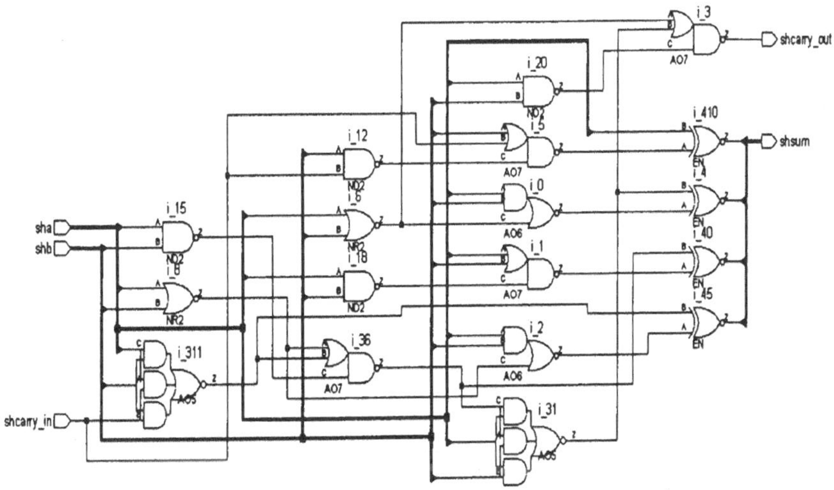

Figure 4-17 A four-bit adder.

In this model, the function `one_bit_adder` updates the variables associated with its `sum` and `cout` parameters. The for loop in the process `prc_four_bit_adder` mimics the generation of four one-bit adders.

4.12 Structures

A structure that has members only of synthesizable types can be used in a SystemC RTL model. Here is such an example. The structure `packet` contains two members `packet_id` and `packet_state`. Figure 4-18 shows the synthesized logic.

```
// File: init_packet.h
#include "systemc.h"
const int XMIT_ID = 3;
const int DONE_ID = 1;
enum states {xmit, rcv, init, done};

struct packet {
  sc_uint<2> packet_id;
  states packet_state;
};

SC_MODULE (init_packet) {
  sc_in<bool> send;
  sc_out<packet> tsq;

  void prc_init_packet();

  SC_CTOR (init_packet) {
    SC_METHOD (prc_init_packet);
    sensitive << send;
  }
};

// File: init_packet.cpp
#include "init_packet.h"

void init_packet::prc_init_packet() {
  packet temp;            // Temporary structure variable.

  if (send) {
    temp.packet_id = XMIT_ID;
    temp.packet_state = xmit;
  }
```

```
    else {
      temp.packet_id = DONE_ID;
      temp.packet_state = done;
    }

    tsq = temp;
  }
```

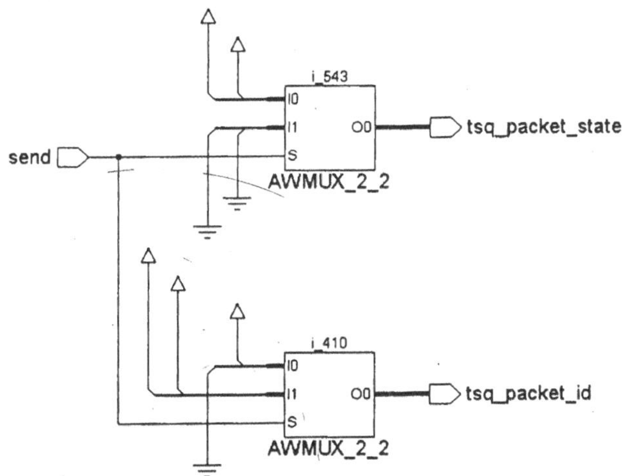

Figure 4-18 An example using a structure type.

The port tsq is of a structure type and it has elements packet_id and packet_state. During synthesis, a structure is typically expanded (split up) into its individual elements. For packet tsq, two output ports tsq.packet_id and tsq.packet_state are identified. A local temporary variable temp is also declared to be of the user-defined structure type. The local variable is necessary in this case since writing to individual elements of an aggregate output port is not allowed. So the temporary structure is first filled in and then assigned to the output port using a single assignment.

4.13 Multiple Processes and Delta Delay

Communication between processes must be done by means of signals to avoid non-determinism.

Combinational logic can be modeled using more than one process within a module. Each such process uses an event sensitivity list. Communication between the processes occurs using signals. Additionally, an assignment to a signal (or a port) always takes effect after a delta delay. These concepts are illustrated using a simple model that contains a chain of three inverters, with each inverter modeled as a separate process.

```
// File: mult_procs.h
#include "systemc.h"

SC_MODULE (mult_procs) {
  sc_in<bool> source;
  sc_out<bool> drain;

  sc_signal<bool> connect1, connect2;
  void mult_procs_1();
  void mult_procs_2();
  void mult_procs_3();

  SC_CTOR (mult_procs) {
    SC_METHOD (mult_procs_1);
    sensitive << source;
    SC_METHOD (mult_procs_2);
    sensitive << connect1;
    SC_METHOD (mult_procs_3);
    sensitive << connect2;
  }
};

// File: mult_procs.cpp
#include "mult_procs.h"

void mult_procs:: mult_procs_1 () {
  connect1 = ! source;
}

void mult_procs::mult_procs_2() {
  connect2 = ! connect1;
}
```

```
void mult_procs::mult_procs_3() {
  drain = ! connect2;
}
```

The module mult_procs has three processes. Each process models combinational logic, in this case an inverter. The output of one process becomes the input to the next process and so on. Two signals are used to communicate between the three processes. So if the input port source changes value say at 5ns, signal connect1 will get a new value at 5+1Δns (after execution of process mult_procs_1), signal connect2 will get a new value at 5+2Δns (after execution of process mult_procs_2), and drain will get its new value at time 5+3Δns (after execution of process mult_procs_3). Figure 4-19 shows the synthesized logic.

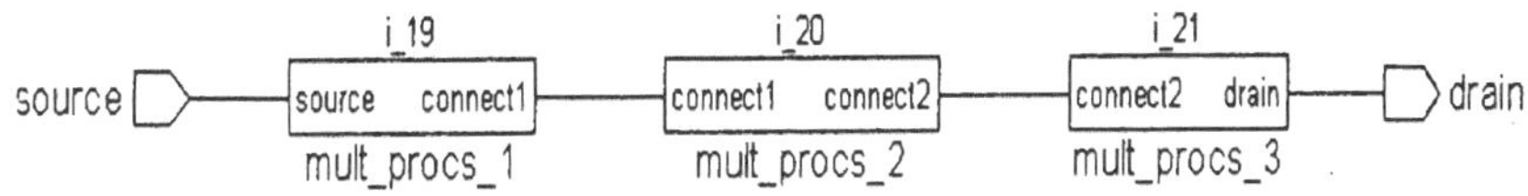

Figure 4-19 A chain of three inverters.

4.14 Summary

To summarize, combinational logic is modeled using:

- One or more SC_METHOD processes.
- Each process has an event sensitivity list.
- All signals and ports read within a process appear in its sensitivity list.
- A signal or port is assigned in all branches of a conditional statement (if or switch).

In this chapter, we saw a number of SystemC features and C++ constructs that were used to model combinational logic. The same exact features can be used for modeling synchronous logic as well. For example, a for loop can be used to model combinational logic as well as synchronous logic. We will say more on this in the next chapter.

4.15 Exercises

1. Write a Gray code to binary code converter.
2. Write a model for an arithmetic logic unit that performs four functions: add, nand, greater than, and xor of the two signed operands. The arithmetic logic unit has two outputs, the data output and the comparator output. Assume an encoded 2-bit select input.
3. Write a model for a 4-by-1 word multiplexer with two select lines. Each word has a width of 8.
4. Write a combinational barrel shifter which has inputs `data_in` and `num_bits`, the number of bits to be shifted. The output is `data_out`.
5. Consider a 4-byte word. Write a method that converts a word containing data in little-endian form to a word in the big-endian form.

❑

CHAPTER

5

Modeling Synchronous Logic

This chapter provides guidelines for modeling synchronous logic and provides examples of such. All the SystemC statements that we looked at in the previous chapter can also be used to model synchronous logic by using the appropriate synchronous logic style. For example, loop statements and switch statements can all be used in a synchronous logic model. More specifically, this chapter discusses:

- modeling of flip-flops,
- with asynchronous set / reset,
- with synchronous set / reset, and
- modeling of latches.

5.1 Modeling Flip-flops

The key to flip-flop modeling is the specification of the sensitivity list. For flip-flop modeling, the basic SC_MODULE construct stays exactly the same except that edge sensitivity is used instead of event sensitivity. The following kind of (edge) sensitivity list specification is employed:

```
// To specify rising edge:
sensitive_pos

// To specify falling edge:
sensitive_neg
```

Such an edge can be specified for a signal or a port of type `bool` or of type `sc_logic`. For a `sc_logic` type, a non-zero to zero transition is treated as a falling edge, while a non-one to one transition is treated as a rising edge.

Here is a model of a basic D-type flip-flop.

```
// File: basic_ff.h
#include "systemc.h"

SC_MODULE (basic_ff) {
  sc_in<bool> d, clk;
  sc_out<bool> q;

  void prc_basic_ff();

  SC_CTOR (basic_ff) {
    SC_METHOD (prc_basic_ff);
    sensitive_pos << clk;        // Edge sensitivity.
  }
};

// File: basic_ff.cpp
#include "basic_ff.h"

void basic_ff::prc_basic_ff () {
  q = d;
}
```

The sensitivity list contains the edge sensitivity `sensitive_pos` specified on the port `clk`, which indicates that only on a rising edge of port `clk` does the data input `d` gets transferred to the output `q`.

So what kind of value holders infer flip-flops? Ports and signals that get assigned values under the control of a clock edge (edge sensitivity) get inferred as flip-flops. In the above example, `q` is a port assigned under the control of a rising edge of a clock and therefore infers a flip-flop.

Here is another example of flip-flop inference, this one on a multi-bit (vector) port.

```
// File: gang_ffs.h
#include "systemc.h"
const int WIDTH = 4;

SC_MODULE (gang_ffs) {
  sc_in<sc_uint<WIDTH> > current_state;
  sc_in<bool> clock;
  sc_out<sc_uint<WIDTH> > next_state;

  void prc_gang_ffs();

  SC_CTOR (gang_ffs) {
    SC_METHOD (prc_gang_ffs);
    sensitive_neg << clock;
  }
};

// File: gang_ffs.cpp
#include "gang_ffs.h"

void gang_ffs::prc_gang_ffs() {
  next_state = current_state;
}
```

Figure 5-1 shows the synthesized logic. In this case, negative edge triggered flip-flops are inferred by virtue of the fact that negative edge sensitivity is specified for the process `prc_gang_ffs`.

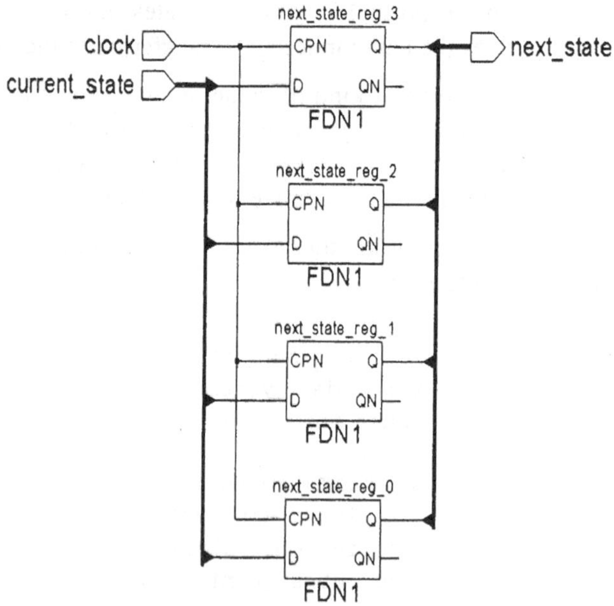

Figure 5-1 A group of flip-flops.

5.2 Multiple Processes

A module can have multiple SC_METHOD processes. Each process can either model combinational logic (when event sensitivity is used) or can model synchronous logic (when edge sensitivity is used). Communication between the processes occur using signals.

In a non SystemC RTL model, a process can have a mix of edge sensitivity and event sensitivity.

A process cannot have both an edge sensitivity and an event sensitivity. Furthermore, only signals and ports of `bool` type can be used in an edge sensitive specification.

Here is an example of a pipelined sequence detector. In this example, flip-flops are inferred for signals. The output of the detector is a 1 if a sequence "101" is detected on the input data stream. The synthesized logic is shown in Figure 5-2.

```
// File: seq_det.h
#include "systemc.h"

SC_MODULE (seq_det) {
  sc_in<bool> clk, data;
  sc_out<bool> seq_found;

  // Synchronous logic process:
  void prc_seq_det();
  // Combinational logic process:
  void prc_output();

  // Interprocess communication signals:
  sc_signal<bool> first, second, third;

  SC_CTOR (seq_det) {
    SC_METHOD (prc_seq_det);
    // Edge sensitivity:
    sensitive_pos << clk;
    SC_METHOD (prc_output);
    // Event sensitivity:
    sensitive << first << second << third;
  }
};

// File: seq_det.cpp
#include "seq_det.h"

void seq_det::prc_seq_det() {
  first = data;
  second = first;
  third = second;
}

void seq_det::prc_output() {
  seq_found = first & (!second) & third;
}
```

There are two SC_METHOD processes in this example. The first process `prc_seq_det` models synchronous logic because of the edge sensitivity. The second process `prc_output` models combinational logic that

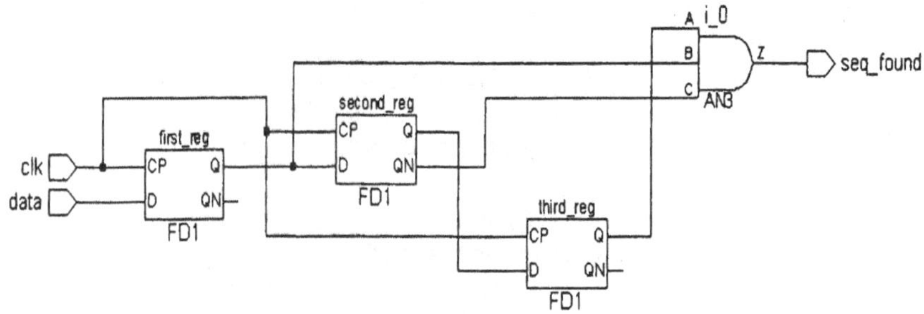

Figure 5-2 A pipelined sequence detector.

computes the output as a combinational value of the signals `first`, `second` and `third`.

If only one process were used to model the sequence detector, done by placing the assignment to `seq_found` in process `prc_seq_det`, then the synthesized logic would consist of an additional flip-flop for `seq_found`.

This example highlights the delta delay assignment of signals and ports. An assignment to a signal or a port does not occur immediately but always occurs one delta delay later. So when the rising edge of the clock occurs, the process `prc_seq_det` is called. The assignment to signal `first` occurs, but the value of `first` does not get updated immediately. Next the second statement executes. Since the value of signal `first` has not yet been updated, signal `second` gets assigned the old value of `first`. Similarly, the previous value of signal `second` gets assigned to signal `third`. This can be seen from the synthesized logic that shows the input of the flip-flop `second` comes from the output of the flip-flop `first`, and the input of the flip-flop `third` comes from the output of flip-flop `second`.

5.3 Flip-flop with Asynchronous Preset and Clear

First we show an example of inferring a flip-flop with asynchronous clear. In this modeling style, the appropriate edge of the clear input is additionally specified as part of the edge sensitivity list. So if the asynchronous clear is an active low clear, the falling edge is used (`sensitive_neg`), if it is an active high clear, the rising edge is used (`sensitive_pos`).

Here is an example of an up-down counter with asynchronous clear. Figure 5-3 shows the synthesized logic.

```
// File: count4.h
#include "systemc.h"
const int COUNT_SIZE = 4;

SC_MODULE (count4) {
  sc_in<bool> mclk, clear, updown;
  sc_out<sc_uint<COUNT_SIZE> > data_out;

  void sync_block();

  SC_CTOR (count4) {
    SC_METHOD(sync_block);
    sensitive_pos << mclk;     // Positive clock edge.
    sensitive_neg << clear;    // Negative active clear.
  }
};

// File: count4.cpp
#include "count4.h"

void count4::sync_block() {
  if (! clear)                 // Asynchronous condition.
    data_out = 0;
  else                         // Else rising clock edge.
    if (updown)
      data_out = data_out.read() + 1;
    else
      data_out = data_out.read() - 1;
}
```

An output port can be read and written to.

The module `count4` has one process `sync_block` which models the synchronous logic. The first `if` condition identifies the asynchronous condition under which `data_out` gets initialized to 0. Its `else` part implicitly refers to the second sensitivity edge, the rising edge of the clock `mclk` in this case. Notice that the output port can be read as well as written to.

In a similar manner, to model both asynchronous preset and clear, the appropriate edges of the preset and clear inputs have to be specified as

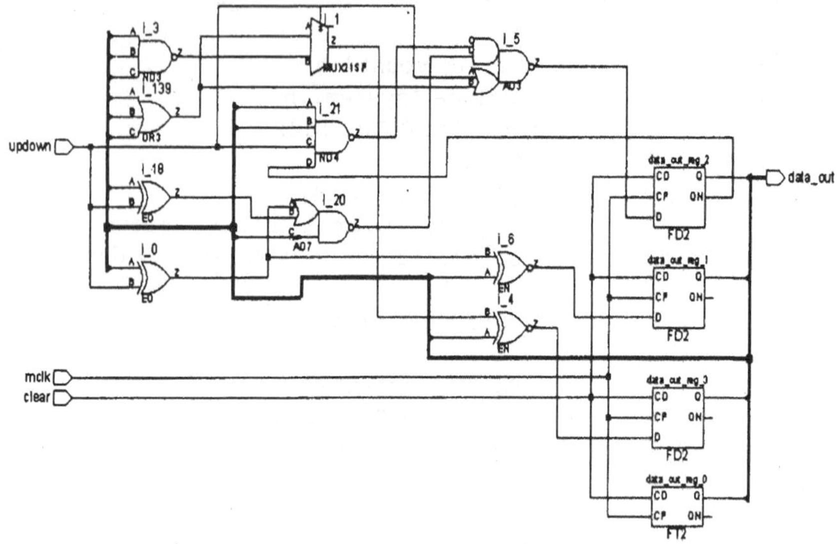

Figure 5-3 Counter with asynchronous clear.

part of the sensitivity list. Here is such an example, the synthesized logic of which is shown in Figure 5-4.

```
// File: async_states.h
#include "systemc.h"
const int STATE_BITS = 4;

SC_MODULE (async_states) {
  sc_in<bool> clk, reset, set;
  sc_in<sc_uint<STATE_BITS> > current_state;
  sc_out<sc_uint<STATE_BITS> > next_state;

  void prc_async_states ();

  SC_CTOR (async_states) {
    SC_METHOD (prc_async_states);
    // Negative edge clock and active low reset:
    sensitive_neg << clk << reset;
    sensitive_pos << set;       // Active high set.
  }
};
```

```
// File: async_states.cpp
#include "async_states.h"

void async_states::prc_async_states() {
  if (!reset)          // First asynchronous condition.
    next_state = 0;
  else if (set)        // Second asynchronous condition.
    next_state = 5;
  else                 // Negative clock edge (implicit).
    next_state = current_state;
}
```

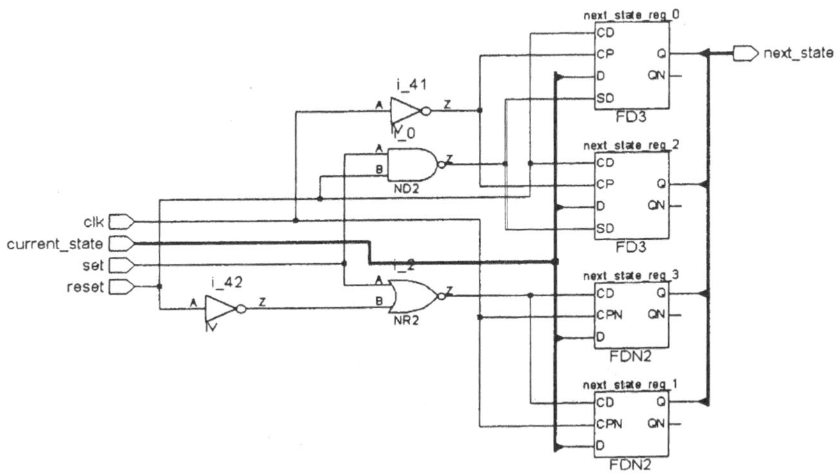

Figure 5-4 Flip-flops with asynchronous preset and clear.

In general, a process may have multiple edges specified as part of its sensitivity along with a clock edge specification.

```
SC_METHOD (my_process);
sensitive_pos << a << b << clk;
sensitive_neg << d << e << f;
```

`sensitive_pos` is used to model rising edge sensitivity (active high logic), while `sensitive_neg` is used to model falling edge sensitivity (active low logic). Furthermore, the process behavior is written using a single `if` statement of the form in which all the non-clock condition checks appear first and the last `else` branch is implicitly the clock condition. Also the logical not of the non-clock condition is used if a negative edge sensitivity is specified, else the positive value of the non-clock condition is used. Here is the template for such a process.

```
void my_module::my_process () {
  if (a)            // Positive value used, since positive
                    // edge specified.
    <asynchronous behavior>
  else if (b)
    <asynchronous behavior>
  else if (! d)     // Logical-not used, since negative
                    // edge specified.
    <asynchronous behavior>
  else if (! e)
    <asynchronous behavior>
  else if (! f)
    <asynchronous behavior>
  else              // Rising clock edge.
    <clocked behavior>
}
```

The various combinations of set and reset conditions that are desired can be achieved by using the above template. For example, to get a negative set and a negative reset flip-flop, the following would be the process declaration and the process behavior.

```
SC_METHOD (ff_neg_set_reset);
sensitive_pos << clk;
sensitive_neg << set << reset;
. . .

if (!set)
  <asynchronous set behavior here>
else if (! reset)
  <asynchronous reset behavior here>
else
  <clocked behavior here>
```

5.4 Flip-flop with Synchronous Preset and Clear

For modeling a flip-flop with synchronous preset and clear, only the clock edge needs to be specified in the sensitivity list. The preset and clear conditions are explicitly coded in the SC_METHOD process itself.

Here is an example of a counter with a low active synchronous preset. Figure 5-5 shows the synthesized logic.

```
// File: sync_count4.h
#include "systemc.h"
const int COUNT_BITS = 4;

SC_MODULE (sync_count4) {
  sc_in<bool> mclk, preset, updown;
  sc_in<sc_uint<COUNT_BITS> > data_in;
  sc_out<sc_uint<COUNT_BITS> > data_out;

  void prc_counter();

  SC_CTOR (sync_count4) {
    SC_METHOD(prc_counter);
    sensitive_pos << mclk; // Only clock edge specified.
  }
};

// File: sync_count4.cpp
#include "sync_count4.h"

void sync_count4::prc_counter() {
  if (! preset)
    data_out = data_in;
  else
    if (updown)
      data_out = data_out.read() + 1;
    else
      data_out = data_out.read() - 1;
}
```

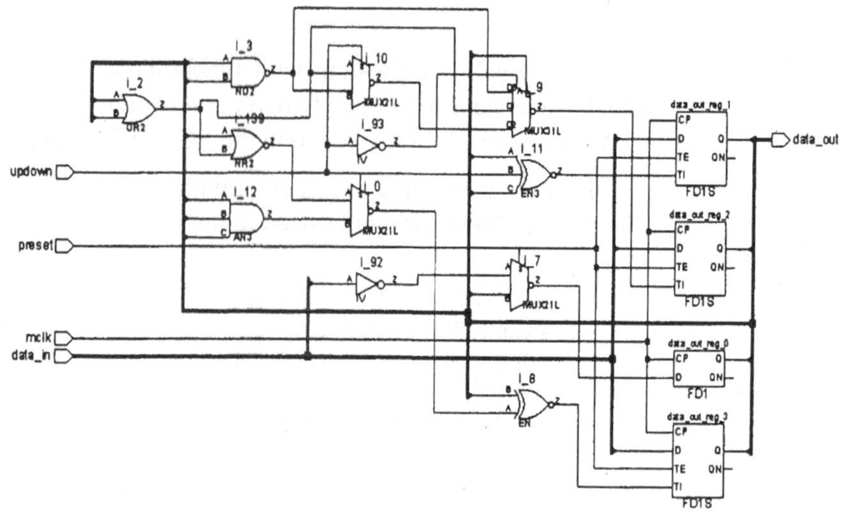

Figure 5-5 Flip-flops with synchronous preset and clear.

If a synchronous preset and clear flip-flip is not available in a target library, quite often the logic for preset and clear is attached to the data input of the flip-flop.

5.5 Multiple and Multi-phase Clocks

In a single module, any number of SC_METHOD processes can be written with each process being either synchronous or a combinational process. When multiple synchronous processes are present, multiple clocks in different processes can be used to model your logic, as shown in the following example. Process `prc_vt15ck` triggers on the negative edge of the clock `vt15ck`, while the process `prc_ds1ck` triggers on the positive edge of the clock `ds1ck`.

```
// File: mult_clks.h
#include "systemc.h"

SC_MODULE (mult_clks) {
  sc_in<bool> vt15ck, addclk, adn, resetn, subclr,
              subn, ds1ck;
```

```
  sc_out<bool> ds1_add, ds1_sub;

  void prc_vt15ck();
  void prc_ds1ck();
  sc_signal<bool> add_state, sub_state;

  SC_CTOR (mult_clks) {
    SC_METHOD (prc_vt15ck);
    sensitive_neg << vt15ck;
    SC_METHOD (prc_ds1ck);
    sensitive_pos << ds1ck;
  }
};

// File: mult_clks.cpp
#include "mult_clks.h"

void mult_clks::prc_vt15ck () {
  add_state = !(addclk | (adn | resetn));
  sub_state = subclr ^ (subn & resetn);
}

void mult_clks::prc_ds1ck() {
  ds1_add = add_state;
  ds1_sub = sub_state;
}
```

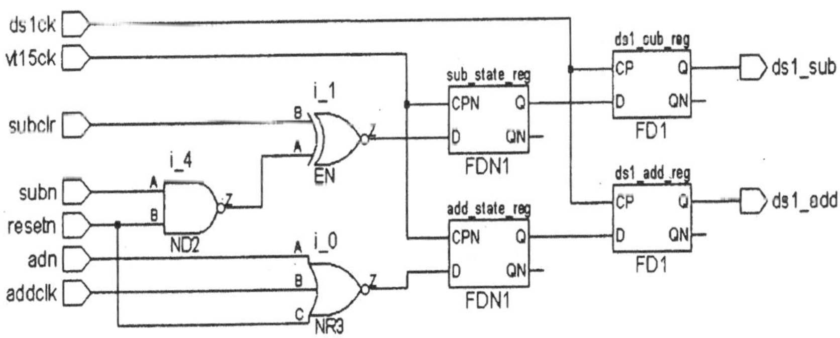

Figure 5-6 Multiple clocks in a module.

Figure 5-6 shows the synthesized logic. The signals add_state and sub_state are assigned on the negative edge of the clock vt15ck and their values gets assigned to ds1_add and ds1_sub on the positive edge of another clock ds1ck. A typical RTL modeling restriction is that the same signal or port cannot be assigned by different clock edges.

Here is an example of a design that uses different phases of the same clock in a module. Once again, a signal or a port is restricted from being assigned under more than one such clock edge. Figure 5-7 shows the synthesized logic for the following example. Process prc_rising triggers on the positive edge of clock zclk, while process prc_falling triggers on the negative edge of clock zclk. The output of the first process is the input to the second process; this is achieved by using the signal d for interprocess communication.

```
// File: multiphase.h
#include "systemc.h"

SC_MODULE (multiphase) {
  sc_in<bool> zclk, a, b, c;
  sc_out<bool> e;

  void prc_rising();
  void prc_falling();

  sc_signal<bool> d;

  SC_CTOR (multiphase) {
    SC_METHOD (prc_rising);
    sensitive_pos << zclk;
    SC_METHOD (prc_falling);
    sensitive_neg << zclk;
  }
};

// File: multiphase.cpp
#include "multiphase.h"

void multiphase::prc_rising() {
  e = d & c;
}
```

```
void multiphase::prc_falling() {
  d = a & b;
}
```

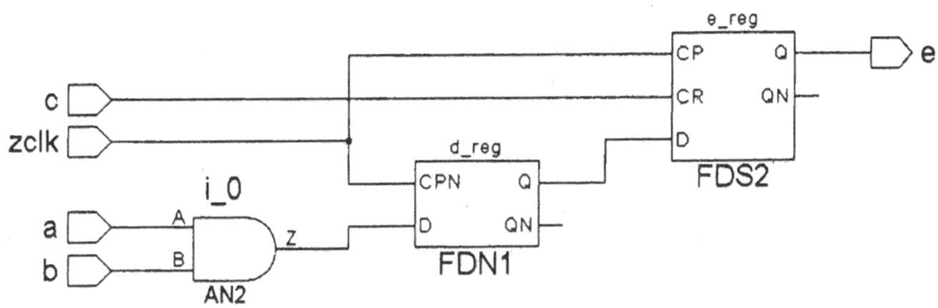

Figure 5-7 Different edges of same clock in a module.

5.6 Modeling Latches

A latch is inferred for a signal or a port when in all possible executions of a process, it is not assigned a value in all the possible paths. The conditional statements, `if` and `switch`, are the two statements that can cause multiple execution paths to occur within a process. Let us consider each one in turn.

5.6.1 If Statement

Consider the `if` statement in the following model.

```
// File: incr.h
#include "systemc.h"
const int COUNTER_SIZE = 2;

SC_MODULE (incr) {
  sc_in<bool> phy;
  sc_in<sc_uint<COUNTER_SIZE> > one_count;
  sc_out<sc_uint<COUNTER_SIZE> > z;

  void prc_incr();
```

```
  SC_CTOR (incr) {
    SC_METHOD (prc_incr);
    sensitive << phy << one_count;
  }
};

// File: incr.cpp
#include "incr.h"

void incr::prc_incr() {
  if (phy)
    z = one_count.read() + 1;
}
```

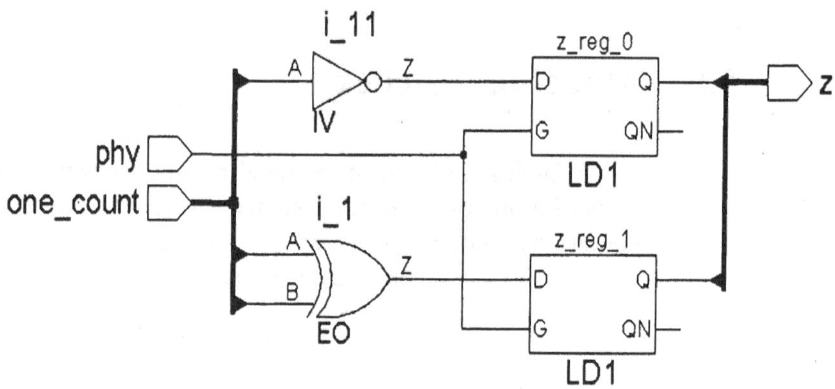

Figure 5-8 Unassigned port becomes a latch.

The semantics for the SC_METHOD process specifies that every time there is an event on the input phy or one_count, the process prc_incr executes and the output z gets an incremented value of input one_count if phy is 1. If phy is 0, the output z retains its old value. This data retention is implemented in hardware using a latch. Figure 5-8 shows the synthesized logic .

A general rule for latch inferencing, when using an if statement, is that if a signal or a port is not assigned a value in all branches of the if statement, then a latch is inferred for that signal or port. This rule does not apply to local variables that are declared and used within a process, a non-process method or in a function.

Here is another example of latch inferencing.

```
// File: compute.h
#include "systemc.h"
const int BITS = 4;
enum grade_type {fail, pass, excellent};

SC_MODULE (compute) {
  sc_in<sc_uint<BITS> > marks;
  sc_out<grade_type> grade;

  void prc_compute();

  SC_CTOR (compute) {
    SC_METHOD (prc_compute);
    sensitive << marks;
  }
};

// File: compute.cpp
#include "compute.h"
void compute::prc_compute() {
  if (marks.read() < 5)
    grade = fail;
  else if (marks.read() < 7)
    grade = pass;
}
```

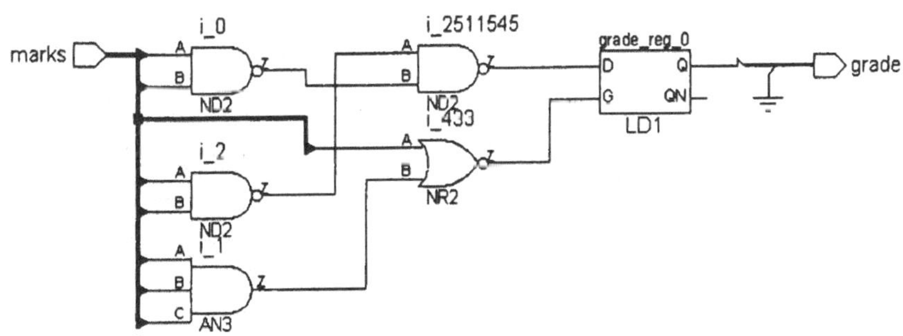

Figure 5-9 The output port is latched.

In this example, what should the value of `grade` be if `marks` has a value of 8? The semantics of the port specifies that `grade` should retain its previous value and therefore infer a latch upon synthesis. Figure 5-9 shows the synthesized logic.

Here is another example on latch inferencing.

```
// File: latched_alu.h
#include "systemc.h"

SC_MODULE (latched_alu) {
  sc_in<bool> clk, a, b;
  sc_out<bool> z;

  void prc_alu();

  SC_CTOR (latched_alu) {
    SC_METHOD (prc_alu);
    sensitive << clk << a << b;
  }
};

// File: latched_alu.cpp
#include "latched_alu.h"

void latched_alu::prc_alu() {
  if (clk)
    z = !(a | b);
}
```

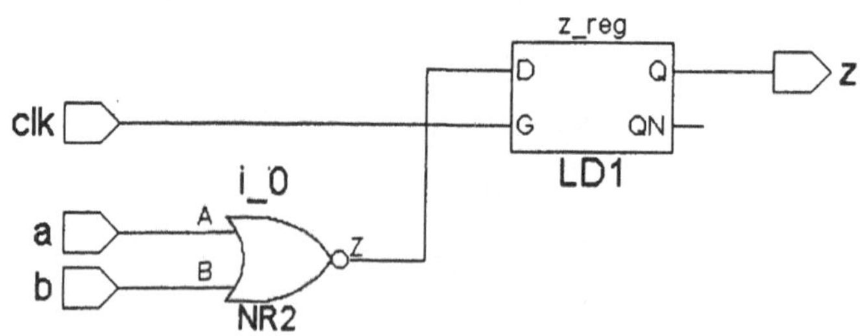

Figure 5-10 A latched ALU.

The output port z is not assigned a value when input clk is 0. Therefore in keeping with the semantics of the model, a latch is inferred for port z. Figure 5-10 shows the synthesized logic.

5.6.2 Switch Statement

A switch statement is another conditional statement that exhibits multiple paths of execution in a process. So if a port or a signal is assigned a value in one of its branches but not assigned in all the branches, a latch is inferred. This indicates that the value of the port or signal needs to be saved between multiple invocations of the process. Here is an example.

```
// File: state_update.h
#include "systemc.h"
enum states {s0, s1, s2, s3};
const int Z_SIZE = 2;

SC_MODULE (state_update) {
  sc_in<states> current_state;
  sc_out<sc_uint<Z_SIZE> > z;

  void prc_state_update();

  SC_CTOR (state_update) {
    SC_METHOD (prc_state_update);
    sensitive << current_state;
  }
};

// File: state_update.cpp
#include "state_update.h"

void state_update::prc_state_update() {
  switch (current_state) {
    case s0:
    case s3: z = 0; break;
    case s1: z = 3; break;
  }
}
```

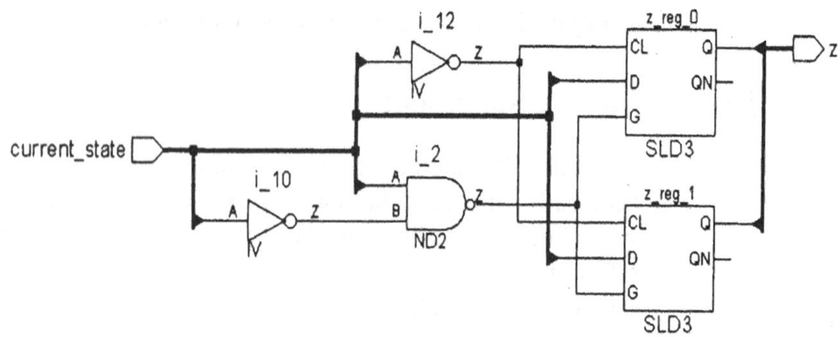

Figure 5-11 Inferring latches from a switch statement.

The port z is not assigned a value for all possible values of the input current_state, more specifically, z is not assigned a value when current_state has the value s2. Therefore in keeping with the behavior of the process, a latch is inferred for port z. Figure 5-11 shows the synthesized logic.

5.6.3 Avoiding Latches

It is important to understand how to avoid latches. In most cases, latches are inferred when they are really not required. The key to avoiding latches is to make sure that a signal or a port, if assigned in a conditional statement, is assigned a value in all possible branches of the conditional statement.

For the switch statement example in the previous section, this can easily be achieved by initializing the output port z to some value prior to the switch statement. This ensures that the port z always has a value assigned to it in all branches of the switch statement.

```
// File: state_update2.cpp
#include "state_update.h"

void state_update::prc_state_update() {
  z = 1;       // Initialize z to a value.

  switch (current_state) {
    case s0:
    case s3: z = 0; break;
    case s1: z = 3; break;
  }
}
```

So when input current_state has the value s2, z has the value 1 (by virtue of the first assignment statement).

Another way for avoiding a latch in a switch statement is to use the default case branch. That is, specify a default value for the signal or port in the default case branch to ensure that a value has been assigned in all possible branches of the switch statement. Here is the previous example written using a default case branch.

```
// File: state_update3.cpp
#include "state_update.h"

void state_update::prc_state_update() {
  switch (current_state) {
    case s0:
    case s3: z = 0; break;
    case s1: z = 3; break;
    default: z = 1; break;
  }
}
```

Similarly, for the module compute in Section 5.6.1, latches can be avoided by ensuring that the output grade is assigned in all branches of the if statement. An example of this is shown below.

```
// File: compute2.cpp
#include "compute.h"

void compute::prc_compute() {
  if (marks.read() < 5)
    grade = fail;
  else if (marks.read() < 7)
    grade = pass;
  else                        // A catchall else branch.
    grade = excellent;
}
```

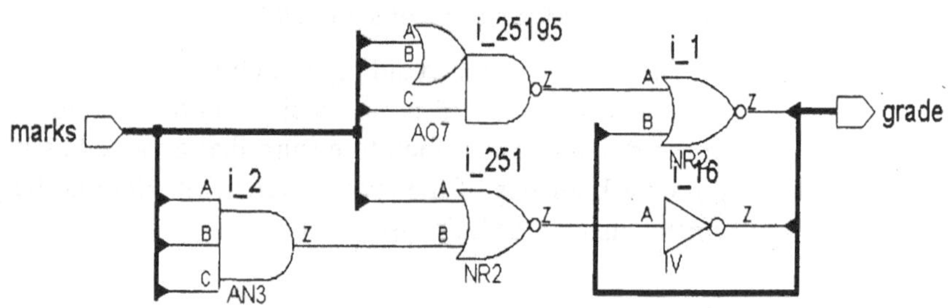

Figure 5-12 No latch inferred for grade.

The port grade does not infer a latch since it is assigned a value in all possible executions of the process. Figure 5-12 shows the synthesized logic.

Another way to avoid a latch in the above case would be to assign a value to port grade before the if statement, as was done with the switch statement example. Either approach provides the same semantics and no latches are inferred. The approach with an initial assignment prior to the if statement is shown next.

```
// File: compute3.cpp
#include "compute.h"

void compute::prc_compute() {
  grade = excellent;                     // Initialize value.

  if (marks.read() < 5)
    grade = fail;
```

```
    else if (marks.read() < 7)
      grade = pass;
}
```

5.7 Summary

- To model synchronous logic, use SC_METHOD process with edge sensitivity.
- A module can contain any number of processes, with each process either being a combinational process or a synchronous process.
- A flip-flop is inferred for a signal or port if it is assigned a value in a process that is sensitive to a clock edge.
- Asynchronous set and reset in synchronous logic can be modeled using a special form of `if` statement.
- A latch is inferred for a signal or a port if it is not assigned a value in all possible branches of an `if` statement or a switch statement.
- A latch can be avoided for a signal or a port by initializing it before an `if` statement or a switch statement, or by ensuring that the signal or port is assigned a value in all possible branches of the conditional statement.

5.8 Exercises

1. Write a model for a shift register state machine that goes through the sequence: 0000 1000 1100 1110 1111 0111 0011 0001 0000. Ensure that redundant flip-flops are not modeled.
2. Write a model for a sequence detector that detects three consecutive 1's on an input stream. The input stream is checked on every rising edge of the clock. Set the output to true when such a sequence is found, else set the output to false.

3. Write a model for a pulse counter. The pulse counter counts the number of clock edges that occur between `start` and `stop`. A rising edge on `start` starts the count, while a falling edge on `stop` stops the counter. If the count exceeds 32, an overflow bit is set. A reset signal resets the pulse counter to 0. The pulse count is an output.
4. Write a synchronous model for a car controller. The controller has the following ports:
   `accel`: to increase the speed,
   `brake`: to decrease the speed (one step per clock cycle),
   `reset`: to reset the speed to 0 (synchronous reset),
   `clk`: controller clock,
   `speed`: is the output port.
   Assume that the speed can go up or down 4 steps.
5. Write a model for a blackjack program. This program is played with a deck of cards. Cards 2 through 10 have values equal to their face value and an ace has a value of either 1 or 11. The object of the game is to accept a number of random cards such that the total score is as close as possible to 21 without exceeding 21. Inputs are card value, a clock, a card inserted flag, and a new game start flag. Outputs are the total points accumulated so far and two flags `won` and `lost`.
6. Write a model for a clock divider. The inputs are the clock `clk`, an asynchronous reset `rst`, and a divide by value `div_by`. The output is the resultant divided clock.
7. Write a model for a serial-in, serial-out, parallel_load, 8-bit shift register. An active low `clear` input clears the shift register. The parallel load occurs when the `data_load` signal is active high and the rising edge of `clock` occurs. Shifting occurs when `data_load` is inactive and `shift_enable` is active. Shifting occurs synchronously on the rising edge of `clock`.
8. Write a model for a M-deep N-bit FIFO. Input `push` causes data to be loaded into the FIFO. Input `pop` causes data to be read from the FIFO. Output `empty` indicates when the FIFO is empty, while output `full` indicates when the FIFO is full. Issue assertion messages when pushing to a full FIFO or reading an empty FIFO. All operations occur synchronously on the falling edge of a clock.

❑

CHAPTER

6

Miscellaneous Logic

In this chapter, we look at the modeling of three-state drivers, don't-cares, parameterized modules, and hierarchy. We saw examples of using user-defined data types as port and signal types in the previous two chapters.

6.1 Three-state Drivers

A three-state driver can be modeled by assigning the value `'Z'` to a signal or a port of the logic type `sc_logic` or `sc_lv`. The assignment of `'Z'` must be done within a conditional statement (`if` or `switch` statement). Here is an example.

```
// File: tri_state.h
#include "systemc.h"

SC_MODULE (tri_state) {
  sc_in<bool> ready, dina, dinb;
  sc_out<sc_logic> selectx;

  void prc_tri_state();

  SC_CTOR (tri_state) {
    SC_METHOD (prc_tri_state);
    sensitive << ready << dina << dinb;
  }
};

// File: tri_state.cpp
#include "tri_state.h"

void tri_state::prc_tri_state() {
  if (ready)
    selectx = sc_logic('Z');
    // or selectx = SC_LOGIC_Z;
  else
    selectx = sc_logic (dina.read() & dinb.read());
}
```

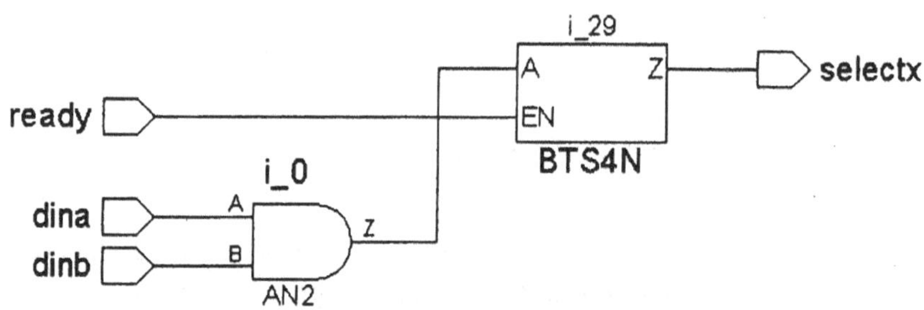

Figure 6-1 Inferring three-state drivers.

Port `selectx` has to be a logic type since only a logic type models the value `'Z'` (high-impedance value). The example states that if input `ready` is true then output `selectx` gets the high-impedance value (three-state driver is off), and if input `ready` is false, then `selectx` gets the value of the expression `dina & dinb`. Notice that the value `'Z'` and the expression `dina & dinb` need to be cast to type `sc_logic` so that the types on both sides of the assignment match. An alternate way of casting the value `'Z'` is to use the predefined value `SC_LOGIC_Z` which is shown in the commented text. Figure 6-1 shows the synthesized logic.

Here is another example of modeling a three-state driver. In this case, the assignments are done under the control of a clock edge. Flip-flops are inferred for output `main_bus` and three-state drivers are inferred at the output of these flip-flops. Figure 6-2 shows the synthesized logic.

```
// File: driver_bank.h
#include "systemc.h"
const int BUS_SIZE = 4;

SC_MODULE (driver_bank) {
  sc_in<bool> myclk, read_state;
  sc_in<sc_lv<BUS_SIZE> > cpu_bus;
  sc_out<sc_lv<BUS_SIZE> > main_bus;

  void prc_driver_bank();

  SC_CTOR (driver_bank) {
    SC_METHOD (prc_driver_bank);
    sensitive_pos << myclk;
  }
};

// File: driver_bank.cpp
#include "driver_bank.h"

void driver_bank::prc_driver_bank() {
  sc_lv<BUS_SIZE> temp;
  int i;

  if (read_state) {
    for (i=0; i<BUS_SIZE; i++)
      temp[i] = 'Z';
  }
  else
    temp = cpu_bus.read();
```

```
        main_bus = temp;
    }
```

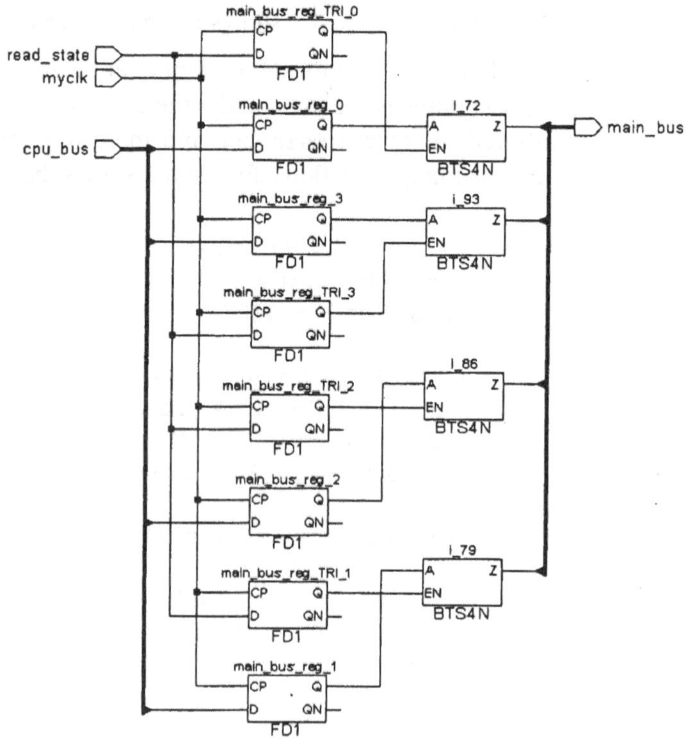

Figure 6-2 Three-state drivers at outputs of flip-flops.

Use a for loop to assign 'Z' to a vector if the vector is parameterizable.

If the size of the input bus cpu_bus were fixed, then the assignment of 'Z' to output main_bus could be written as a single statement. However, since we want to parameterize the 'Z' assignment based on BUS_SIZE, one way to accomplish this is by using a for loop statement that assigns the value 'Z' to each bit of a temporary variable temp, and then the temporary as a whole is assigned to output main_bus. No flip-flops are inferred for the temporary temp as it is a local variable.

A local variable within a process does not get inferred as a flip-flop (i.e. no storage).

Instead of using a for statement to set all bits of temp to 'Z', the local variable temp can be initialized with the value when it is declared. For example, to initialize a variable stbuf with all 'Z' values, you can write the declaration of stbuf as:

```
sc_lv<8> stbuf (SC_LOGIC_Z);
```

To initialize with all 'X' values, use SC_LOGIC_X. Here is the process prc_driver_bank rewritten using this feature.

```
// File: driver_bank2.cpp
#include "driver_bank.h"

void driver_bank::prc_driver_bank() {
  sc_lv<BUS_SIZE> temp (SC_LOGIC_Z);

  if (read_state)
    main_bus = temp;
  else
    main_bus = cpu_bus.read();
}
```

This is a much more compact description.

An interesting point to note is that an extra set of flip-flips is inferred for the control signal read_state that is driving the three-state drivers. This is because the check for the condition also occurs at the rising edge of the clock and any changes on input read_state that occur between clock edges have no effect on the output main_bus. To avoid this extra set of flip-flops, the synchronous logic and the three-state drivers can be modeled in separate processes, as shown in the following module.

```
// File: driver_bank_noff.h
#include "systemc.h"
const int BUS_SIZE = 4;

SC_MODULE (driver_bank_noff) {
  sc_in<bool> clock, read_state;
  sc_in<sc_lv<BUS_SIZE> > cpu_bus;
  sc_out<sc_lv<BUS_SIZE> > main_bus;

  void ff_logic();
  void z_logic();
  sc_signal<sc_lv<BUS_SIZE> > saved_value;
```

Edge sensitivity is used to model a synchronous process, while event sensitivity is used to model a combinational logic process.

```
  SC_CTOR (driver_bank_noff) {
    // This is a synchronous process:
    SC_METHOD (ff_logic);
    sensitive_pos << clock;
    // This is a combinational process:
    SC_METHOD (z_logic);
    sensitive << saved_value << read_state;
  }
};

// File: driver_bank_noff.cpp
#include "driver_bank_noff.h"

void driver_bank_noff::z_logic() {
  sc_lv<BUS_SIZE> temp (SC_LOGIC_Z);

  if (read_state)
    main_bus = temp;
  else
    main_bus = saved_value.read();
}

void driver_bank_noff::ff_logic() {
  saved_value = cpu_bus.read();
}
```

Figure 6-3 shows the synthesized netlist. The synchronous logic is modeled in the process `ff_logic`. The three-state driver logic is modeled as combinational logic in process `z_logic`. The signal `saved_value` is used to pass values from process `ff_logic` to process `z_logic`. The input `read_state` now combinationally controls the three-state drivers (no extra set of flip-flops is required).

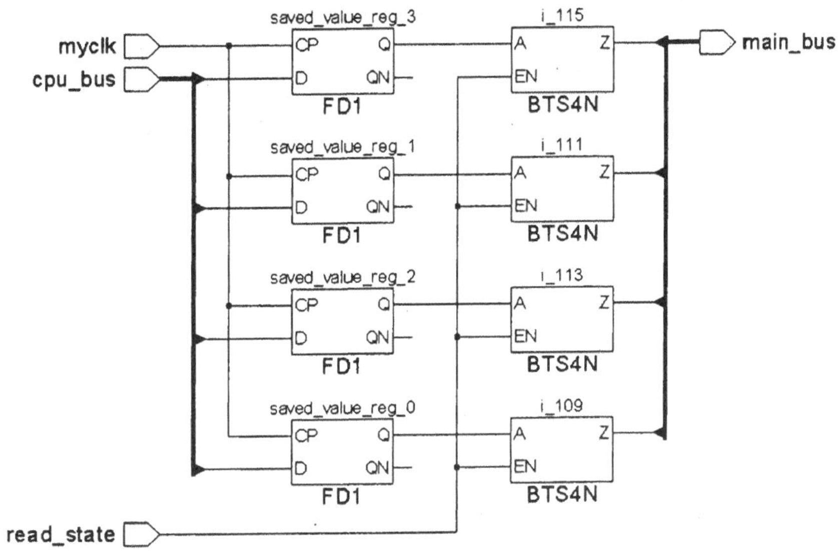

Figure 6-3 With separate flip-flop and three-state processes.

6.2 Multiple Drivers

When multiple drivers drive a signal or a port, a resolution method is required. Here is an example that has multiple drivers and uses a resolved vector port. Figure 6-4 shows the synthesized logic.

```
// File: buses.h
#include "systemc.h"
const int BUS_SIZE = 4;

SC_MODULE (buses) {
  sc_in<bool> a_ready, b_ready;
  sc_in<sc_uint<BUS_SIZE> > a_bus, b_bus;
  sc_out_rv<BUS_SIZE> z_bus;      // Resolved port type.

  void prc_a_bus();
  void prc_b_bus();
```

```
    SC_CTOR (buses) {
      SC_METHOD (prc_a_bus);
      sensitive << a_ready << a_bus;

      SC_METHOD (prc_b_bus);
      sensitive << b_ready << b_bus;
    }
};

// File: buses.cpp
#include "buses.h"

void buses::prc_a_bus() {
  if (a_ready)
    z_bus = a_bus.read();
  else
    z_bus = "ZZZZ";
}
void buses::prc_b_bus() {
  if (b_ready)
    z_bus = b_bus.read();
  else
    z_bus = "ZZZZ";
}
```

Use a for-loop to assign the value 'Z' if you want to parameterize the size of z_bus.

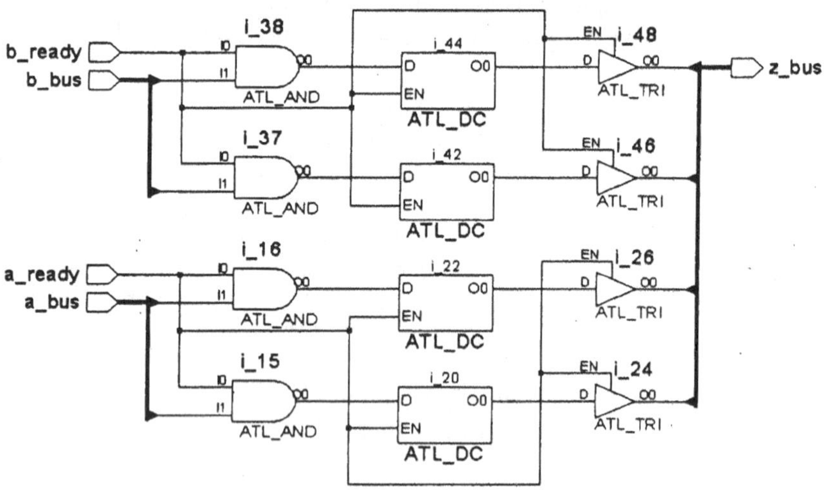

Figure 6-4 A multi-driven bus (shown only for a two bit bus).

The output port z_bus is of a resolved vector type sc_out_rv and it has two drivers, one from process prc_a_bus and another from process prc_b_bus. In process prc_a_bus, the output z_bus is driven with input a_bus if input a_ready is true, else the output gets the high-impedance value. In process prc_b_bus, the same output z_bus is driven with the input b_bus if b_ready is true, else it is driven with a high-impedance value. The effective value of z_bus is obtained by resolving the values on both its drivers using the table shown in Section 3.11.

Here is the same example, but this time modeled using a resolved vector signal. The resolution occurs on the signal driver_bus which is multiply driven.

```
// File: buses2.h
#include "systemc.h"

SC_MODULE (buses2) {
  sc_in<bool> a_ready, b_ready;
  sc_in<sc_uint<4> > a_bus, b_bus;
  sc_out<sc_lv<4> > z_bus;

  sc_signal_rv<4> driver_bus;          // Resolved signal.
  void prc_a_bus();
  void prc_b_bus();
  void prc_ab_bus();

  SC_CTOR (buses2) {
    SC_METHOD (prc_a_bus);
    sensitive << a_ready << a_bus;
    SC_METHOD (prc_b_bus);
    sensitive << b_ready << b_bus;
    SC_METHOD (prc_ab_bus);
    sensitive << driver_bus;
  }
};

// File: buses2.cpp
#include "buses2.h"
void buses2::prc_a_bus() {
  if (a_ready)
    driver_bus = a_bus.read();
  else
```

```
    driver_bus = "ZZZZ";
}

void buses2::prc_b_bus() {
  if (b_ready)
    driver_bus = b_bus.read();
  else
    driver_bus = "ZZZZ";
}

void buses2::prc_ab_bus() {
  z_bus = driver_bus;
}
```

In this case, an internal signal is of a resolved type. The assignment of the multiply driven signal `driver_bus` to the output port `z_bus` is done in the process `prc_ab_bus`. The synthesized logic is the same as that shown in Figure 6-4.

6.3 Handling Don't-cares

Don't-care handling for synthesis is supported by interpreting an assignment of logic value `'X'` as a don't-care assignment. Don't-care assignments are useful in modeling situations in which variables have don't-care values. This provides an opportunity for the synthesis tool to select appropriate values for assignment to the target such that optimized logic may be obtained. Here is an example in which don't-cares are assigned to an output port after all possible values of the input have been considered. The default case branch is required so as to avoid inferencing any latches.

```
// File: encoder.h
#include "systemc.h"
const int IN_SIZE = 8;
const int OUT_SIZE = 3;
```

```
SC_MODULE (encoder) {
  sc_in<sc_uint<IN_SIZE> > data;
  sc_out<sc_lv<OUT_SIZE> > yout;

  void prc_encoder();

  SC_CTOR (encoder) {
    SC_METHOD (prc_encoder);
    sensitive << data;
  }
};

// File: encoder.cpp
#include "encoder.h"

void encoder::prc_encoder() {
  switch (data.read()) {
    case 0x01 : yout = 0;
    case 0x02 : yout = 1;
    case 0x04 : yout = 2;
    case 0x08 : yout = 3;
    // You can assign an integer value or a vector
    // value to output yout.
    case 0x10 : yout = "100";
    case 0x20 : yout = "101";
    case 0x40 : yout = "110";
    case 0x80 : yout = "111";
    default: yout = "XXX";      // Don't-care assignment.
  }
}
```

Simulation mismatches may occur between the model and the synthesized logic when don't-care values are used in the model.

When input data has a value other than any of those explicitly listed in the case branches, a don't-care value is assigned to the output yout. This means that a synthesis tool is free to choose any value for output yout; most synthesis tools will pick a value that leads to a reduction of the synthesized logic. Note that this interpretation of the value 'X' is different from a simulation interpretation where the value 'X' is the value 'X', and not a don't-care. So use caution when using don't-care values as differences may occur in simulation between the synthesis model and the synthesized logic.

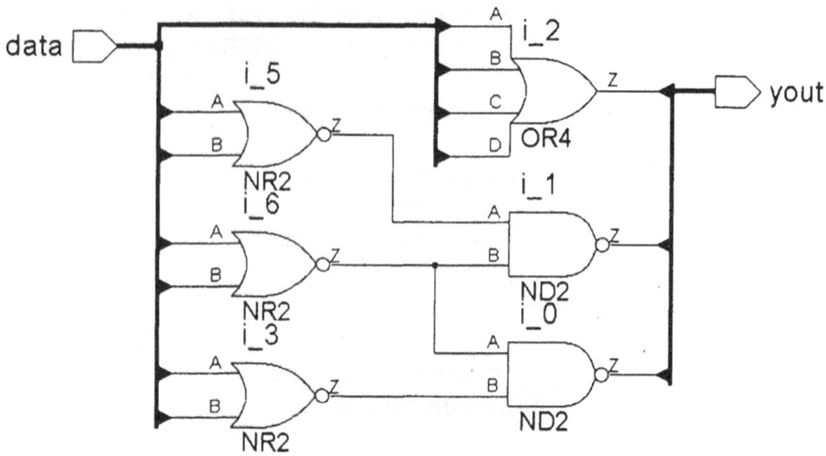

Figure 6-5 Handling don't-cares.

6.4 Hierarchy

A module can contain instances of other modules thus creating hierarchy. Signals are used to connect the various instances. Ports of a parent module may directly connect to the ports of an instance. There are three steps needed to create a hierarchy.

A member variable is a variable declared within a class.

i. Declare the signals used to connect the various instances.

ii. Declare member variables as pointers to the child modules or as instances of the child modules.

iii. Specify the interconnections to the instance ports (could be via named association or positional association).

Here is a skeleton module that shows the various constructs that are used to create a hierarchy. In this case, child modules appear as pointers.

We use the pointer approach when describing hierarchy in this book.

```
#include "systemc.h"

SC_MODULE (top_parent) {
  sc_in<any_type> top_a;
  sc_out<any_type> top_b;
  . . .
```

```
    // Signals for connecting instances:
    sc_signal<any_type> c1, c2, c3;
    . . .
    // Child modules as pointers:
    child_a *a_ptr1, *a_ptr2;
    child_b *b_ptr1;
    . . .
    SC_CTOR (top_parent) {
      // Instantiate the child module:
      a_ptr1 = new child_a ("instancename_a");
      // Specify the interconnections now:
      a_ptr1->x(top_a); // Connect instance port x to
                        // port top_a.
      a_ptr1->y (c1);   // Connect port y to signal c1.
      . . .
      // Above is an example of using named association.
      // Another instantiation:
      b_ptr1 = new child_b ("instancename_b");
      // Using positional association:
      (* b_ptr1) (c2, c1, top_b, . . . );
        // Signal c1 connects instances a_ptr1 and b_ptr1.
        // Port top_b is connected directly to an
        // instance port.
      . . .
    }

    // Destructor:
    ~ top_parent() {
      delete a_ptr1;
      delete a_ptr2;
      delete b_ptr1;
      . . .
    }
  };
```

For debugging, it is often recommended to keep the instance name same as the pointer name.

The destructor is used to deallocate the memory that was allocated via the new operator in the SC_CTOR block. This is required to avoid memory leaks that may occur during simulation.

Here is the same skeleton module shown with child modules appearing as instances.

```
#include "systemc.h"

SC_MODULE (top_parent) {
  sc_in<any_type> top_a;
  sc_out<any_type> top_b;
  . . .
  // Signals for connecting instances:
  sc_signal<any_type> c1, c2, c3;
  . . .
  // Child modules as instances:
  child_a a_inst1, a_inst2;
  child_b b_inst1;
  . . .
  SC_CTOR (top_parent) :
    // Child module initializations:
    a_inst1 ("instancename_a1"),
    a_inst2 ("instancename_a2"),
    b_inst1 ("instancename_b1")
  {
    // Specify the interconnections now:
    a_inst1.x(top_a); // Connect instance port x to
                      // port top_a.
    a_inst1.y (c1);   // Connect port y to signal c1.
    . . .
    // Above is an example of using named association.
    // Using positional association:
     b_inst1 << c2 << c1 << top_b << . . . ;
    // Signal c1 connects instances a_inst1 and b_inst1.
    // Port top_b is connected directly to an
    // instance port.
    . . .
  }
};
```

Here is an example of an up-down counter in which the flip-flop is first described as a basic component, and then later, it is used to build the up-down counter.

```
// File: ff_with_pc.h
#include "systemc.h"

SC_MODULE (ff_with_pc) {
  sc_in<bool> din, clock, preclr;
  sc_out<bool> q, notq;

  void prc_ff_with_pc();

  SC_CTOR (ff_with_pc) {
    SC_METHOD (prc_ff_with_pc);
    sensitive_neg << clock;
    sensitive_pos << preclr;
  }
};
```

```
// File: ff_with_pc.cpp
#include "ff_with_pc.h"

void ff_with_pc::prc_ff_with_pc() {
  if (preclr)
    q = 0;
  else
    q = din;

  notq = ! q;
}
```

```
// File: upc.h
#include "systemc.h"
#include "ff_with_pc.h"

SC_MODULE (upc) {
  sc_in<bool> clk, up_down, pc;
  sc_out<bool> q0, q1, q2;

  void misc_logic();
```

```
  // Member variables as pointers to child module:
  ff_with_pc *lq0, *lq1, *lq2;
  // Signals used to connect instances and process:
  sc_signal<bool> qn0, qn1, qn2, bit11, bit21;

  SC_CTOR (upc) {
    // First instance of module ff_with_pc:
    lq0 = new ff_with_pc ("ff_with_pc_lq0");
    // Using named association:
    lq0->clock(clk);
    lq0->din (qn0);
    lq0->preclr (pc);
    lq0->q(q0);
    lq0->notq(qn0);

    // Second instance of module ff_with_pc:
    lq1 = new ff_with_pc ("ff_with_pc_lq1");
    lq1->clock(clk);
    lq1->din (bit11);
    lq1->preclr (pc);
    lq1->q(q1);
    lq1->notq(qn1);

    // Third instance of module ff_with_pc:
    lq2 = new ff_with_pc ("ff_with_pc_lq2");
    // Using positional association:
    (*lq2) (bit21, clk, pc, q2, qn2);

    SC_METHOD (misc_logic);
    sensitive << qn0 << qn1 << qn2;
    sensitive << q0 << up_down << q1;
  }

  // Destructor:
  ~ upc () {
    delete lq0;
    delete lq1;
    delete lq2;
  }
};
```

```
// File: upc.cpp
#include "upc.h"

void upc::misc_logic() {
  bool t01, t12, t13;

  t01 = up_down ^ q0;
  bit11 = t01 ^ qn1;
  t12 = up_down ^ q1;
  t13 = t01 | t12;
  bit21 = t13 ^ qn2;
}
```

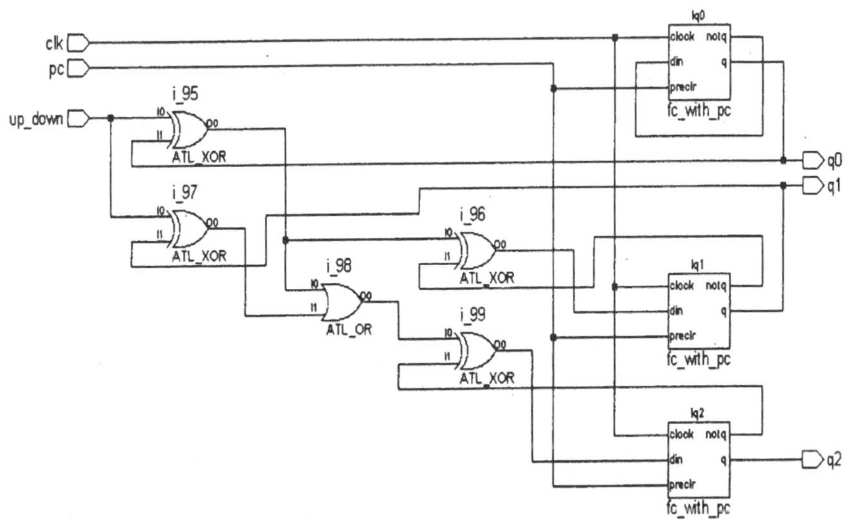

Figure 6-6 An up-down counter.

The new operator is used to create an instance of the flip-flop module. The statements following the new operator perform the association between the instance ports to the signals and ports of the parent module. There are two kinds of associations that can be used: named and positional. Named association is shown in the association of instances `lq0` and `lq1`, while positional association is used in the association of instance `lq2`. Figure 6-6 shows the synthesized logic.

No range selection or bit selection is allowed in an association - use split and merge processes.

The associations in an instantiation can only occur between signals with ports or ports with ports. No range selection or bit selection of a signal or a port is allowed to connect to an instance port. One way to accomplish this is to create a process that acts as a splitter process and returns the split values as separate signals which can then be used for association. This is shown in the following code skeleton. A merge process similarly collects all the values of a bus and assembles them together.

```
// File: parent.h
#include "systemc.h"
#include "child.h"

SC_MODULE (parent) {
  sc_out<sc_uint<4> > arith_bus;
  . . .
  sc_signal<sc_uint<3> > bus_m;
  sc_signal<bool> bus_m0, bus_m1, bus_m2;
  sc_signal<bool> arith0, arith1, arith2, arith3;
  void split_x();
  void merge_z();
  child *ptr1, *ptr2;

  SC_CTOR (parent) {
    // Process splits bus bus_m into its
    // individual elements:
    SC_METHOD (split_x);
    sensitive << bus_m;
    // Process joins individual elements of bus:
    SC_METHOD (merge_z);
    sensitive << arith0 << arith1 << arith2 << arith3;

    ptr1 = new child ("child_instance_name1");
    ptr1->term_a (bus_m1); // bus_m[1] is not allowed.
    ptr1->term_b (arith0);
    . . .
    ptr2 = new child ("child_instance_name2");
    ptr2->term_a (arith1); // arith_bus[1] not allowed.
  }
```

Destructors are ignored in synthesis.

```
  // Destructor:
  ~ parent () {
    delete ptr1;
    delete ptr2;
  }
};

// File: parent.cpp
#include "parent.h"

void parent::split_x () {
  sc_uint<3> tmp_bus;

  tmp_bus = bus_m.read();
  bus_m0 = tmp_bus[0];
  bus_m1 = tmp_bus[1];
  bus_m2 = tmp_bus[2];
}

void parent::merge_z () {
  sc_uint<4> tmp_arith;

  tmp_arith[0] = arith0;
  tmp_arith[1] = arith1;
  tmp_arith[2] = arith2;
  tmp_arith[3] = arith3;
  arith_bus = tmp_arith;
}
```

The module `parent` has an output port `arith_bus` whose elements are assigned to by the child instances `ptr1` and `ptr2`. The process `merge_z` is sensitive to changes on any of the output elements `arith0`, `arith1`, `arith2`, `arith3`, and collects the elements of the output bus into a temporary variable before assigning it to the output bus. Similarly an element of a signal bus `bus_m` is read by instance `ptr1`. This is achieved by using the process `split_x` that splits the signal `bus_m` into its individual elements; the process itself is sensitive to the signal `bus_m`. The appropriate element is then used in the association of instance `ptr1`.

The port type and the signal type in an association must match. For example, if the port type is `sc_uint`, then the port can only be connected to a signal or port of type `sc_uint`. In addition, `read()` and `write()`

methods are not required when connecting ports of a module to its instances.

6.5 Parameterizing Modules

A module can be parameterized in SystemC RTL by using the template mechanism provided by the C++ programming language. Here we consider a simple example of a parameterized N-bit and-gate.

```
// File: generic_and.h
#include "systemc.h"

template <int size>
  SC_MODULE (generic_and) {
    sc_in<sc_uint<size> > a;
    sc_out<bool> z;

    void prc_generic_and();

    SC_CTOR (generic_and) {
      SC_METHOD (prc_generic_and);
      sensitive << a;
    }
  };

template <int size>
  inline void generic_and<size>::prc_generic_and() {
    sc_bv<size> bv_temp;

    bv_temp = a.read();
    z = bv_temp.and_reduce();
  }
```

The template construct is prefixed to the SC_MODULE construct and you can specify any number of parameters between the characters '<' and '>' that follow the keyword `template`, such as:

```
template <int size, bool flag, unsigned int data>
```

After declaring the template parameters, the parameters can then be used within the SC_MODULE declaration. Any methods that are declared within the SC_MODULE need to be independently decorated with the template construct also, as shown for the process prc_generic_and. Note that the template class and all its methods appear in a header file; this is the recommended style. Alternately, the methods could be defined in a program text file (in a .cpp file) for each combination of actual template type parameters that might be required.

Template parameters must be constants, that is, fixed at compile time.

The generic template can then be instantiated in another module that instantiates the parameterized blocks. Here is an example that instantiates a 2-input and a 4-input and-gate from the generic and-gate and exclusive-or's their outputs to produce the final output.

```
// File: generic_instantiate.h
#include "generic_and.h"
// File "systemc.h" included with above include.

const int WIDTH = 6;

SC_MODULE (generic_instantiate) {
  sc_in<sc_uint<WIDTH> > tsq;
  sc_out<bool> rsq;

  void prc_xor();
  void prc_splitter();

  generic_and<2> *and2;
  generic_and<4> *and4;

  sc_signal<bool> and2out, and4out;
  sc_signal<sc_uint<2> > t2;
  sc_signal<sc_uint<4> > t4;

  SC_CTOR (generic_instantiate) {
    SC_METHOD (prc_xor);
    sensitive << and2out << and4out;
    SC_METHOD (prc_splitter);
    sensitive << tsq;
```

```
    and2 = new generic_and<2> ("and2");
    and2->a(t2);
    and2->z(and2out);

    and4 = new generic_and<4> ("and4");
    and4->a(t4);
    and4->z(and4out);
  }

  ~ generic_instantiate() {
    delete and2;
    delete and4;
  }
};

// File: generic_instantiate.cpp
#include "generic_instantiate.h"

void generic_instantiate::prc_xor() {
  rsq = and2out ^ and4out;
}

void generic_instantiate::prc_splitter() {
  sc_uint<WIDTH> temp;

  temp = tsq.read();
  t2 = temp.range(0, 1);
  t4 = temp.range(2, 5);
}
```

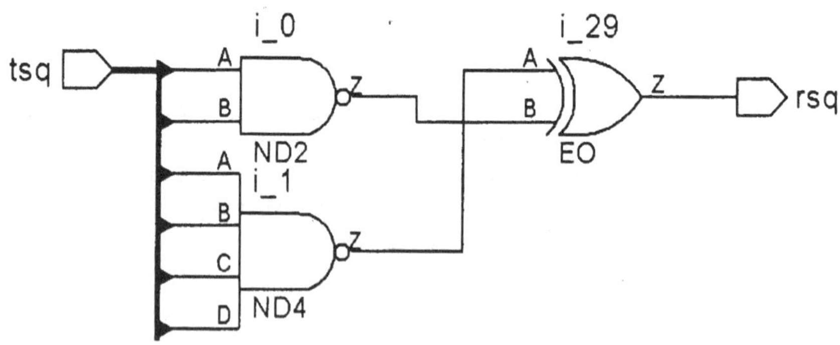

Figure 6-7 Instantiation of a parameterized module.

The parameter values for the generic and-gate are explicitly specified when declaring the pointer to the instance as well as at instantiation time. In the lines:

```
generic_and<2> *and2; // <2> is an instance value.
. . .
and2 = new generic_and<2> ("and2");
    // <2> is instance-specific.
```

the `<2>` is the value of the template parameter `size`. Since range select and bit select of a signal or a port is not allowed to be directly used to connect to a port of an instance, a splitter process `prc_splitter` is used. It copies the range selects to temporary signals which are then used in the association of the instances. Figure 6-7 shows the synthesized logic.

A module can be parameterized not only based on constants but also on types. For example, you can model a generic comparator that can be instantiated with either type `sc_uint` or `sc_int`. An example of such a model is left as an exercise.

6.6 Variable and Signal Assignments

A variable declared within an SC_METHOD process does not have memory, that is, a variable does not retain its value between multiple process invocations. Also a value is assigned to a variable instantaneously. A signal on the other hand has memory and an assignment to a signal always occurs after a delta delay. Consider the following example.

```
// File: var_sig.h
// Example highlights differences between variable
// and signal assignments:
#include "systemc.h"

SC_MODULE (var_sig) {
  sc_in<bool> clk_a, tmq;
  sc_out<bool> bds_1, bds_2, bds_3;

  sc_signal<bool> qst_2;
```

```
    void var_sig_1();
    void var_sig_2();
    void var_sig_3();

    SC_CTOR (var_sig) {
      SC_METHOD (var_sig_1);
      sensitive_pos << clk_a;
      SC_METHOD (var_sig_2);
      sensitive_pos << clk_a;
      SC_METHOD (var_sig_3);
      sensitive << qst_2;
    }
};

// File: var_sig.cpp
#include "var_sig.h"

void var_sig::var_sig_1() {
  bool qst_1;

  qst_1 = tmq;
  bds_1 = qst_1;
}

void var_sig::var_sig_2() {
  qst_2 = ! tmq;
  bds_2 = qst_2;
}

void var_sig::var_sig_3() {
  bds_3 = qst_2;
}
```

Variable qst_1 is declared local to process var_sig_1. There is no delay in the assignment of tmq to qst_1 and from qst_1 to bds_1. On the other hand, in process var_sig_2, since qst_2 is a signal, qst_2 does not get updated immediately but gets updated after a delta delay. Consequently when the second assignment in the process executes, it uses the old value of qst_2 which then gets assigned to bds_2. A flip-flop is therefore inferred for qst_2 and no flip-flop is inferred for qst_1. This is shown in the synthesized logic of Figure 6-8. Signal qst_2 has memory while qst_1 does not. The process var_sig_3 is used only to show that qst_2

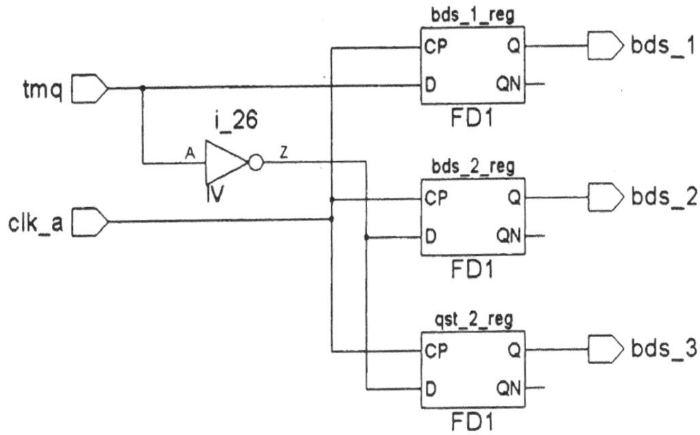

Figure 6-8 A signal vs. a variable assignment.

does infer a memory; if `qst_2` is not used anywhere else, a synthesis tool would remove the unnecessary flip-flop that would have been synthesized for signal `qst_2`. Variables can also be declared as member variables, that is, declared within an SC_MODULE; we see examples of these in Chapter 9.

6.7 Exercises

1. Write a model for a parameterizable arithmetic logic unit that takes in two input data and performs an exclusive-or, less than or an increment by one operation. Make the model generic for any size of input operands.
2. Write a model for a generic adder with N-bit operands and a `carry_in` and with outputs `sum` and `carry_out`. Instantiate this generic adder in another module to model a 4-bit and a 6-bit adder.
3. Use the generic adder in the previous exercise to model an 8-bit arithmetic logic unit that performs an addition or a subtraction. A control signal specifies what operation is to be performed. To perform the subtraction, take the 2's complement of the second operand and add it to the first operand.

4. Write a model for a generic N-bit binary decoder which is parameterized on the size of its input.
5. Write a generic model for an N-bit Gray code up-down counter.
6. Write a model for a rising-edge triggered D-flipflop with an asynchronous reset and a synchronous enable. Use this flip-flop to build a generic N-bit serial-in, serial-out shift register.
7. Using a template, write a model for a splitter (1 to many) that is generic on the type and the number of splits.
8. Write a parameterized function that returns the number of 1's in a logic vector.

❑

CHAPTER

7

Modeling Examples

This chapter shows some common models described using SystemC. Examples include counters, decoders and finite state machines.

7.1 Parameterizable Register with Three-state Output

Here is a model of a parameterizable register file with a three-state output capability. First a parameterized module `tristate` is presented and then a parameterized module `reg` is presented. Both of these are described using templates. Module `tristate_reg` models a 4-bit instantiation of the `reg` and `tristate` modules. Figure 7-1 shows the synthesized logic.

```
// File: tristate_reg.h
// Parameterizable register with three-state output
// built using parameterizable blocks:
#include "systemc.h"

template<int width>
  SC_MODULE (tristate) {
    sc_in<sc_uint<width> > in_bus;
    sc_in<bool> output_enable;
    sc_out<sc_lv<width> > out_bus;

    // The definition can appear inside the template:
    void prc_tristate() {
      sc_lv<width> all_zs (SC_LOGIC_Z);

      if (output_enable)
        out_bus = in_bus.read();
      else
        out_bus = all_zs;
    }

    SC_CTOR (tristate) {
      SC_METHOD (prc_tristate);
      sensitive << in_bus << output_enable;
    }
  };

template<int width>
  SC_MODULE (reg) {
    sc_in<sc_uint<width> > d;
    sc_in<bool> enable, clock, reset;
    sc_out<sc_uint<width> > q;

    void prc_reg () {
      if (reset)
        q = 0;
      else {                    // Clock behavior.
        if (enable)
          q = d;
      }
    }
```

```
    SC_CTOR(reg) {
      SC_METHOD (prc_reg);
      sensitive_pos << reset;
      sensitive_neg << clock;
      // enable is not in list as it is synchronous.
    }
  };

// Even this block can be parameterized if necessary.
const int SIZE = 2;

SC_MODULE (tristate_reg) {
  sc_in<bool> clock, reset, reg_enable, output_enable;
  sc_in<sc_uint<SIZE> > data_in;
  sc_out<sc_lv<SIZE> > data_out;

  reg<SIZE> *inst1;
  tristate<SIZE> *inst2;
  sc_signal<sc_uint<SIZE> > reg_out;

  SC_CTOR (tristate_reg) {
    inst1 = new reg<SIZE> ("regSIZE");
    inst1->d (data_in);
    inst1->enable (reg_enable);
    inst1->clock (clock);
    inst1->reset (reset);
    inst1->q (reg_out);

    inst2 = new tristate<SIZE> ("tristateSIZE");
    inst2->in_bus (reg_out);
    inst2->output_enable (output_enable);
    inst2->out_bus (data_out);
  }

  ~ tristate_reg() {                    // The destructor.
    delete inst1;
    delete inst2;
  }
};
```

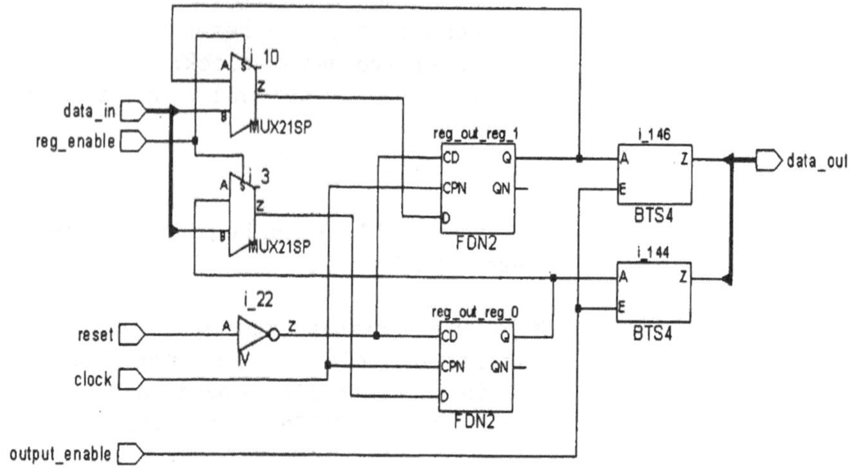

Figure 7-1 A 2-bit register with three-state output.

7.2 A Memory Model

Here is a model of a memory. The memory storage is modeled using a two-dimensional member variable ram. The variable is of a logic vector type to allow the transition of output to the high-impedance value. The output transitions to the high-impedance value when the enable signal en is active low.

It is safe to use a member variable to model storage in this case as there is no inter-process communication.

```
// File: memory.h
#include "systemc.h"
const int WORD_SIZE = 8;
const int ADDR_SIZE = 6;
const int MEM_SIZE = 100;

SC_MODULE (memory) {
  sc_in<bool> en, rw, clk;
  sc_in<sc_uint<ADDR_SIZE> > addr;
  sc_inout<sc_lv<WORD_SIZE> > data;

  void prc_memory();
  sc_lv<WORD_SIZE> ram [MEM_SIZE];
```

```
  SC_CTOR (memory) {
    SC_METHOD (prc_memory);
    sensitive_neg << clk;
  }
};

// File: memory.cpp
#include "memory.h"

void memory::prc_memory() {
  sc_lv<WORD_SIZE> allzs (SC_LOGIC_Z);
  sc_lv<WORD_SIZE> allxs (SC_LOGIC_X);

  if (en) {
    if (rw) {                             // Read.
      if (addr.read() < MEM_SIZE)
        data = ram [addr.read()];
      else {
        data = allxs;                     // 'X's.
#ifndef SYNTHESIS
        cout << "Address " << addr <<
          " is out of range for read operation." << endl;
#endif
      }
    }
    else {                                // Write.
      if (addr.read() < MEM_SIZE)
        ram[addr.read()] = data;
#ifndef SYNTHESIS
      else
        cout << "Address " << addr <<
          " is out of range for write operation." << endl;
#endif
    }
  }
  else
    data = allzs;                         // 'Z's.
}
```

Put non-synthesizable code under #ifndef SYNTHESIS directive.

7.3 Modeling an FSM

A finite state machine (FSM) has two major forms:

i. A Moore machine in which the output of the circuit is dependent only on the state of the machine and not on its inputs.

ii. A Mealy machine in which the output is dependent both on the machine state as well as its inputs.

This is shown pictorially in Figure 7-2. Each of the next state logic, state

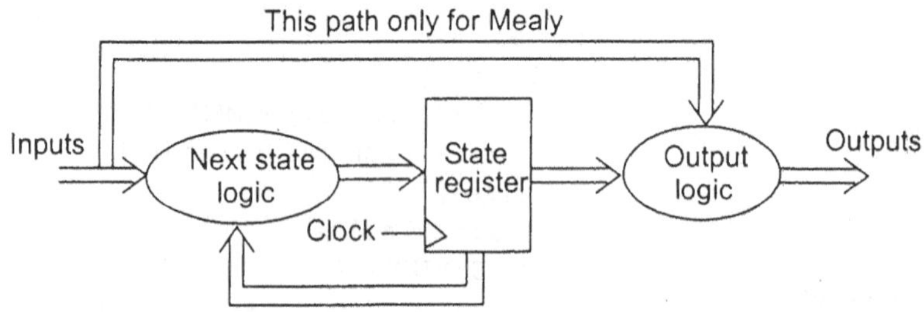

Figure 7-2 A finite state machine.

register and the output logic can be modeled using separate processes or as a single process, or any combination in between. The state register process is inherently a synchronous process. When the state register and the output logic are modeled as a single process, the outputs are synchronously registered into flip-flops. If the outputs do not need to be registered, then it should be modeled as a separate (combinational) process. In some designs, it is quite possible to register some outputs and keep the others combinational; in such cases, a combinational process can be used to model the combinational part of the output logic while a synchronous process can be used to model the synchronous outputs.

7.3.1 Moore FSM

Here is a model of a Moore finite state machine. Figure 7-3 shows the state transition diagram. This FSM is modeled using a single process for the next state logic, state register and the output logic. The process is a single synchronous process with a switch statement that has the outputs assigned in each case branch and the input conditions dictating the value of the next state. The signal moore_state is used to model the machine state which can have one of the four possible states.

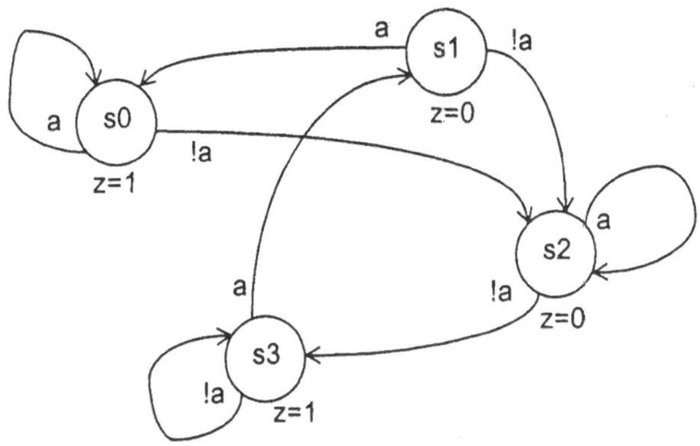

Figure 7-3 State transition diagram for Moore machine example.

A single process is used for modeling next state logic, state register, and output logic.

```
// File: moore.h
#include "systemc.h"

SC_MODULE (moore) {
  sc_in<bool> a, clk, reset;
  sc_out<bool> z;

  enum state_type {s0, s1, s2, s3};
  sc_signal<state_type> moore_state;
  void prc_moore();

  SC_CTOR (moore) {
    SC_METHOD (prc_moore);
    sensitive_pos << clk;
  }
};

// File: moore.cpp
#include "moore.h"

void moore::prc_moore() {
  if (reset)                        // Synchronous reset.
    moore_state = s0;
  else
```

```
        switch (moore_state) {
          case s0: z = 1; moore_state = a ? s0 : s2; break;
          case s1: z = 0; moore_state = a ? s0 : s2; break;
          case s2: z = 0; moore_state = a ? s2 : s3; break;
          case s3: z = 1; moore_state = a ? s1 : s3; break;
        }
    }
```

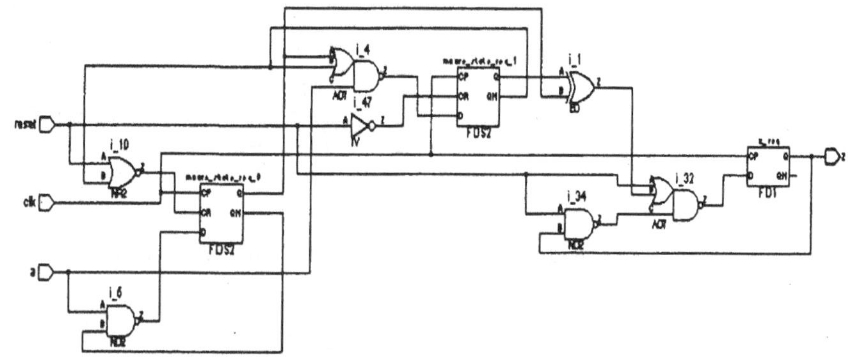

Figure 7-4 A Moore FSM model.

Figure 7-4 shows the synthesized logic. Notice that an extra flip-flop is inferred for the output z, that is, the output z is always synchronized to the clock edge. If this extra flop-flop is not required, then the processing of the output and the processing of the states have to be split up into two separate processes. This is shown in the following module which has the same behavior as the previous one but with the output z strictly being a combinational function of the states. Two processes are used to model this FSM. The first process `prc_states` models the next state logic and the state register while the process `prc_outputs` models the output logic. Figure 7-5 shows the synthesized logic.

One process models the next state logic and the state register, while a second process models the output logic.

```
// File: moore2.h
#include "systemc.h"

SC_MODULE (moore2) {
  sc_in<bool> a, clk, reset;
  sc_out<bool> z;

  enum state_type {s0, s1, s2, s3};
  sc_signal<state_type> moore_state;
  void prc_states();
  void prc_outputs();

  SC_CTOR (moore2) {
    SC_METHOD (prc_states);          // Synchronous.
    sensitive_pos << clk;
    SC_METHOD (prc_outputs);         // Combinational.
    sensitive << moore_state;
  }
};

// File: moore2.cpp
#include "moore2.h"

void moore2::prc_states() {
  if (reset)
    moore_state = s0;
  else
    switch (moore_state) {
      case s0: moore_state = a ? s0 : s2; break;
      case s1: moore_state = a ? s0 : s2; break;
      case s2: moore_state = a ? s2 : s3; break;
      case s3: moore_state = a ? s1 : s3; break;
    }
}

void moore2::prc_outputs() {
  switch (moore_state) {
    case s3:
    case s0: z = 1; break;
    case s1:
    case s2: z = 0; break;
  }
}
```

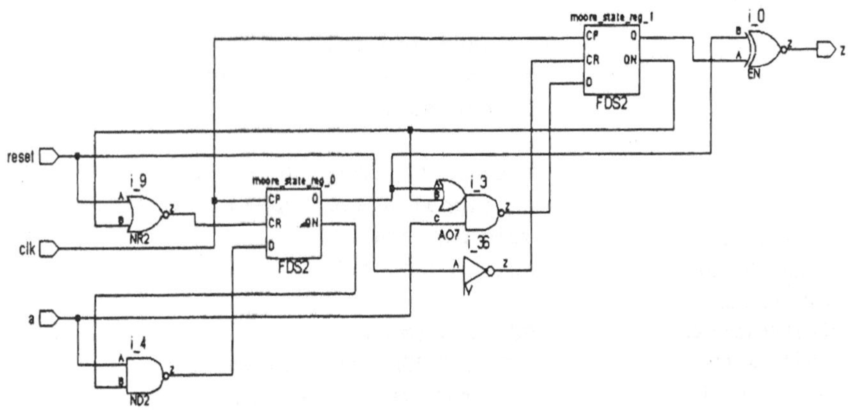

Figure 7-5 Output is combinational.

7.3.2 Mealy FSM

In a Mealy finite state machine, the non-registered outputs can change asynchronously with respect to the clock since such outputs can be directly dependent on the inputs. If the outputs are combinational, two processes can be used to model the Mealy finite state machine, one process that registers the current state on an active clock edge and the second process that determines the outputs of the finite state machine based on the current machine state and input values.

Here is an example of a Mealy finite state machine. Signal `mealy_state` holds the machine state while signal `next_state` is used to pass information from the combinational logic process to the synchronous logic process.

```
// File: mealy.h
#include "systemc.h"

SC_MODULE (mealy) {
  sc_in<bool> clk, reset, a;
  sc_out<bool> z;

  // One-cold encoding:
  enum state_type {S0=0xE, S1=0xD, S2=0xB, S3=0x7};
  sc_signal<state_type> mealy_state, next_state;
  void prc_state();
  void prc_output();

  SC_CTOR (mealy) {
    SC_METHOD (prc_state);
    sensitive_neg << clk;
    sensitive_pos << reset;        // High active reset.
    SC_METHOD (prc_output);
    sensitive << mealy_state << a;
  }
};
```

Two processes are used to model this FSM. One process models the state register and the second process models the next state logic and the output logic.

```
// File: mealy.cpp
#include "mealy.h"

void mealy::prc_state() {
  if (reset)
    mealy_state = S0;
  else
    mealy_state = next_state;
}

void mealy::prc_output() {
  switch (mealy_state) {
    case S0:
      if (a) {
        z = 1;
        next_state = S3;
      }
      else
        z = 0;
      break;
```

```
        case S1:
          if (a) {
            z = 1;
            next_state = S0;
          }
          else
            z = 0;
          break;
        case S2:
          if (!a)
            z = 0;
          else {
            z = 1;
            next_state = S1;
          }
          break;
        case S3:
          z = 0;
          if (! a)
            next_state = S2;
          else
            next_state = S1;
          break;
      }
    }
```

Here is another example of a Mealy finite state machine. In this model, the process `prc_state` models the state register and the process `prc_comb_logic` models the next state logic and the output logic. A user-defined enumeration type `states` is defined and two signals `curr_state` and `nxt_state` of this type are further declared. The encoding for the enumeration literals is explicitly specified in the type declaration.

```
// File: mealy2.h
#include "systemc.h"

SC_MODULE (mealy2) {
  sc_in<bool> clock, resetn, a, b, c, d;
  sc_out<bool> out1, out2;

  enum states {state0=0x0, state1=0x2, state2=0x3,
    state3=0x7, state4=0x5};
```

```
  sc_signal<states> curr_state, nxt_state;
  void prc_comb_logic();
  void prc_state();

  SC_CTOR (mealy2) {
    SC_METHOD (prc_state);
    sensitive_pos << clock;
    sensitive_neg << resetn;      // Asynchronous reset.

    SC_METHOD (prc_comb_logic);
    sensitive << nxt_state << a << b << c << d;
  }
};
```

Two processes are used to model this FSM. One process models the state register and the second process models the next state logic and the output logic.

```
// File: mealy2.cpp
#include "mealy2.h"

void mealy2::prc_state() {
  if (! resetn)
    curr_state = state0;
  else
    curr_state = nxt_state;
}

void mealy2::prc_comb_logic() {
  out1 = 0;
  out2 = 0;
  nxt_state = state0;

  switch (curr_state) {
    case state0:
      if ((a & b) | c)
        nxt_state = state2;
      else
        nxt_state = state1;
      break;
    case state1:
      if (b & d)
        out1 = 1;
      nxt_state = state4;
      break;
```

When writing large switch statements to describe combinational logic, it is a good practice to initialize the outputs of the process so as to avoid latches.

```
            case state2:
              out2 = 1;
              nxt_state = state3;
              break;
            case state3:
              out2 = 1;
              if ((a | b) & (c | d))
                nxt_state = state4;
              else
                nxt_state = state3;
              break;
            case state4:
              nxt_state = state0;
              break;
            default:
              nxt_state = state0;
              break;
          }
        }
```

The initialization of the outputs `out1` and `out2` that appear before the switch statement ensures that no latches are produced for the two outputs.

7.4 Universal Shift Register

Here is a model of an N-bit universal shift register. The universal shift register performs the following functions:

- hold value
- shift left
- shift right
- load value

This universal shift register can be used as a:

- serial-in, serial-out shift register
- parallel-in, serial-out shift register
- serial-in, parallel-out shift register
- parallel-in, parallel-out shift register

Here is the state table for a 3-bit register. Figure 7-6 shows the synthesized logic.

Function	*Next state*		
	q[2]	*q[1]*	*q[0]*
Hold	q[2]	q[1]	q[0]
Shift left	q[1]	q[0]	rin
Shift right	lin	q[2]	q[1]
Load	par_in[2]	par_in[1]	par_in[0]

```
// File: usr_define.h
#ifndef USR_DEFINE_H
#define USR_DEFINE_H
const int WIDTH = 3;
const int SEL_WIDTH = 2;
// Select values:
const int HOLD = 0;
const int SHIFT_LEFT = 1;
const int SHIFT_RIGHT = 2;
const int LOAD = 3;
#endif

// File: usr.h
#include "systemc.h"
#include "usr_define.h"

SC_MODULE (usr) {
  sc_in<bool> clk, clr, lin, rin;
  sc_in<sc_uint<SEL_WIDTH> > select;
  sc_in<sc_uint<WIDTH> > par_in;
  sc_out<sc_uint<WIDTH> > q;

  void prc_usr();

  SC_CTOR (usr) {
    SC_METHOD (prc_usr);
    sensitive_pos << clk;
    sensitive_neg << clr;
```

```
    }
};

// File: usr.cpp
#include "usr.h"
void usr::prc_usr() {
  sc_uint<WIDTH> q_temp;
  sc_uint<SEL_WIDTH> sel_temp;

  if (!clr)
    q = 0;
  else {
    q_temp = q.read();           // Ok to read output port.
    sel_temp = select.read();

    switch (sel_temp) {
      case HOLD: break;          // Hold value.
      case SHIFT_LEFT:
        q = (q_temp.range(WIDTH-2, 0), rin.read());
        break;
      case SHIFT_RIGHT:
        q = (lin.read(), q_temp.range(WIDTH-1, 1));
        break;
      case LOAD:
        q = par_in;
        break;
    }
  }
}
```

7.5 Counters

7.5.1 Modulo-N Counter

Here is a model of a counter that counts modulo-N. Both `q` and `qbar` of the outputs are present. Counting occurs on every rising clock edge and the counter has an active high asynchronous clear. The model has two processes, the first one `prc_counter` models the synchronous counter and the second process `prc_outputs` generates the negated outputs.

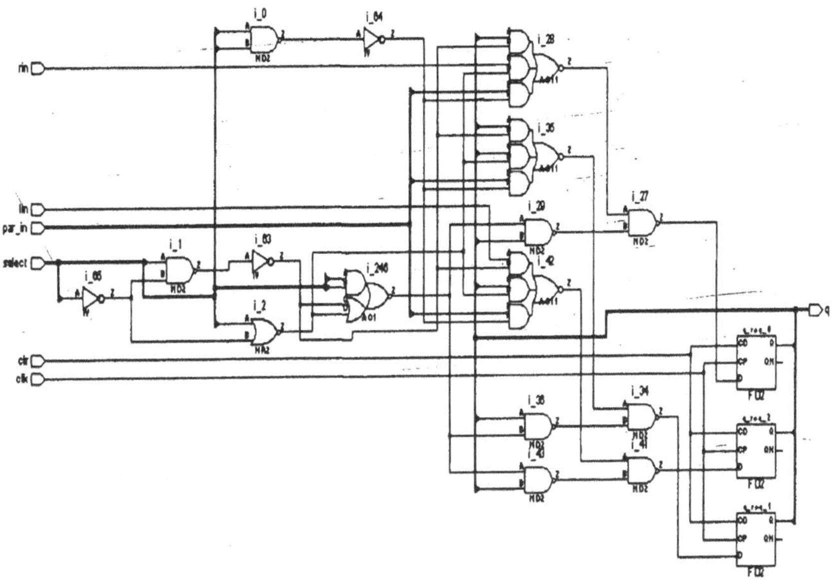

Figure 7-6 A 3-bit universal shift register.

```
// File: mod_counter.h
#include "systemc.h"
const int NBITS = 4;
const int UPTO = 11;

SC_MODULE (mod_counter) {
  sc_in<bool> clk, clear;
  sc_out<sc_uint<NBITS> > q, qbar;

  sc_signal<sc_uint<NBITS> > counter;
  void prc_counter();
  void prc_outputs();

  SC_CTOR (mod_counter) {
    SC_METHOD (prc_counter);          // Synchronous.
    sensitive_pos << clk << clear;

    SC_METHOD (prc_outputs);          // Combinational.
    sensitive << counter;
```

```
  }
};

// File: mod_counter.cpp
#include "mod_counter.h"

void mod_counter::prc_counter() {
  if (clear)
    counter = 0;
  else
    counter = (counter.read() + 1) % UPTO;
}

void mod_counter::prc_outputs() {
  q = counter.read();
  qbar = ~ counter.read();
}
```

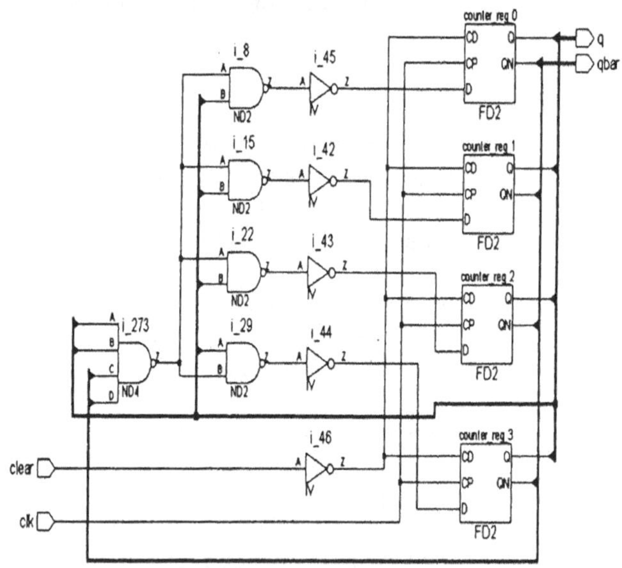

Figure 7-7 A 4-bit modulo-11 binary counter.

Figure 7-7 shows the synthesized logic. Flip-flops are inferred for the signal `counter` since the signal is assigned values synchronously under a clock edge.

7.5.2 Johnson Counter

A Johnson counter is a shift-type counter. Here is an example of a 3-bit Johnson counter stream.

```
000
001
011
111
110
100
000
```

The key to modeling a Johnson counter is to note that if the most significant bit (the leftmost bit) of the counter is a 1, then a 0 has to be shifted in from the right; if the most significant bit is a 0, then a 1 has to be shifted in from the right. Here is a model of a generic N-bit Johnson counter with an asynchronous clear control. Figure 7-8 shows the synthesized logic for a 3-bit counter.

```
// File: johnson_ctr.h
#include "systemc.h"
const int NBITS = 3;

SC_MODULE (johnson_ctr) {
  sc_in<bool> clk, clear;
  sc_out<sc_uint<NBITS> > q;

  void prc_counter();

  SC_CTOR (johnson_ctr) {
    SC_METHOD (prc_counter);          // Synchronous.
    sensitive_pos << clk;
    sensitive_neg << clear;
  }
};
```

```
// File: johnson_ctr.cpp
#include "johnson_ctr.h"

void johnson_ctr::prc_counter() {
  sc_uint<NBITS> t_cnt;

  if (!clear)
    q = 0;
  else {
    t_cnt = q.read();
    q = (t_cnt.range(NBITS-2, 0), !t_cnt[NBITS-1]);
  }
}
```

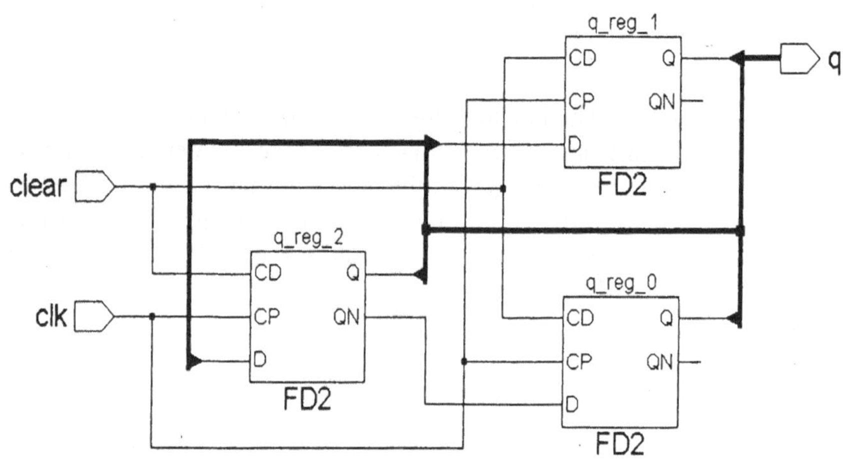

Figure 7-8 A 3-bit Johnson counter.

The temporary variable `t_cnt` is needed since a range select or a bit select cannot be performed directly on the port `q`.

7.5.3 Gray Code Up-down Counter

Here is an example of a 3-bit Gray code up-down counter modeled as a finite state machine. The counter counts up when input `up_down` is a 1, else it counts down. If signal `hold` is active high, the counting is disabled. If input `reset` is high, the counter is reset to 0. Figure 7-9 shows the state diagram.

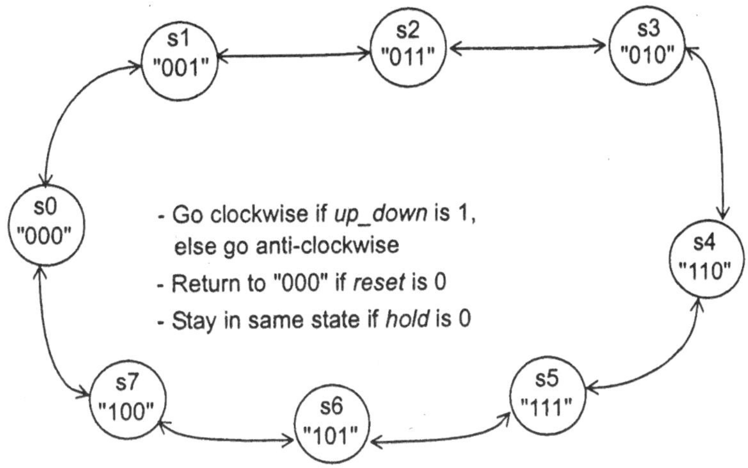

Figure 7-9 State diagram for a 3-bit Gray code up-down counter.

Here is the model for this counter. Figure 7-10 shows the synthesized logic for the counter.

```
// File: gray_ctr.h
#include "systemc.h"
enum gray_states {s0=0x0, s1=0x1, s2=0x3, s3=0x2,
    s4=0x6, s5=0x7, s6=0x5, s7=0x4};

SC_MODULE (gray_ctr) {
  sc_in<bool> clk, reset, up_down, hold;
  sc_out<gray_states> gray_count;

  void prc_counter();

  SC_CTOR (gray_ctr) {
    SC_METHOD (prc_counter);
    sensitive_neg << clk << reset;
  }
};
```

```
// File: gray_ctr.cpp
#include "gray_ctr.h"

void gray_ctr::prc_counter() {
  if (! reset)
    gray_count = s0;
  else
    if (! hold)
      switch (gray_count) {
        case s0 : gray_count = up_down ? s1 : s7; break;
        case s1 : gray_count = up_down ? s2 : s0; break;
        case s2 : gray_count = up_down ? s3 : s1; break;
        case s3 : gray_count = up_down ? s4 : s2; break;
        case s4 : gray_count = up_down ? s5 : s3; break;
        case s5 : gray_count = up_down ? s6 : s4; break;
        case s6 : gray_count = up_down ? s7 : s5; break;
        case s7 : gray_count = up_down ? s0 : s6; break;
        default: gray_count = s0; break;
      }
}
```

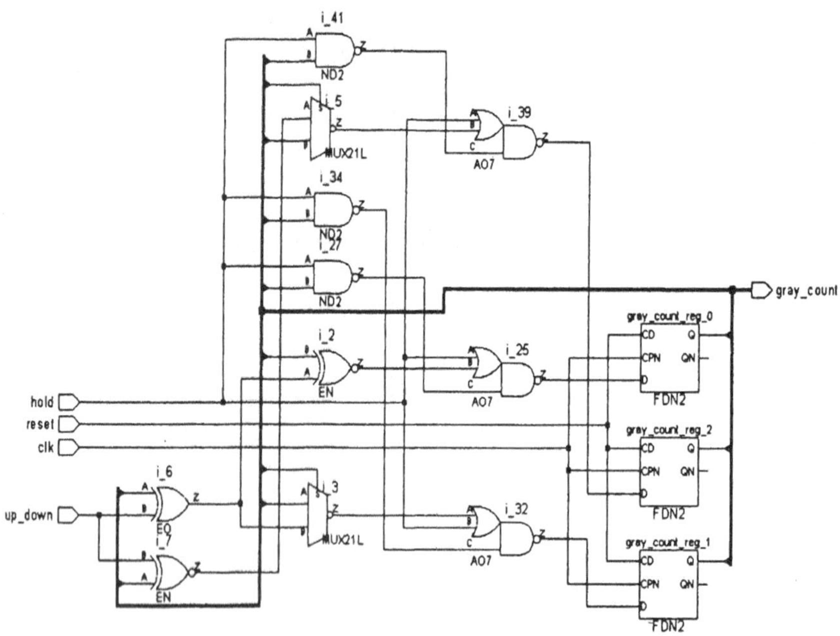

Figure 7-10 A 3-bit Gray code up-down counter.

7.6 Johnson Decoder

Here is a model of a N-bit Johnson decoder with an enable control. Figure 7-11 shows the synthesized logic.

```
// File: johnson_decoder.h
#include "systemc.h"
const int NBITS = 3;
const int TWICENBITS = 2*NBITS;

SC_MODULE (johnson_decoder) {
  sc_in<sc_uint<NBITS> > sel;
  sc_in<bool> enable;
  sc_out<sc_uint<TWICENBITS> > y;

  void prc_decoder();

  SC_CTOR (johnson_decoder) {
    SC_METHOD (prc_decoder);
    sensitive << sel << enable;
  }
};

// File: johnson.decoder.cpp
#include "johnson_decoder.h"

void johnson_decoder::prc_decoder() {
  sc_uint<TWICENBITS> address, y_temp;
  int i;

  if (!enable)
    y = 0;
  else {
    address = 0;
    y_temp = 0;

    for (i=0; i<NBITS; i++)
      if (sel[i])
        address++;
```

```
        if (sel[NBITS-1])
          address = TWICENBITS - address;

        y_temp[address] = 1;
        y = y_temp;
      }
    }
```

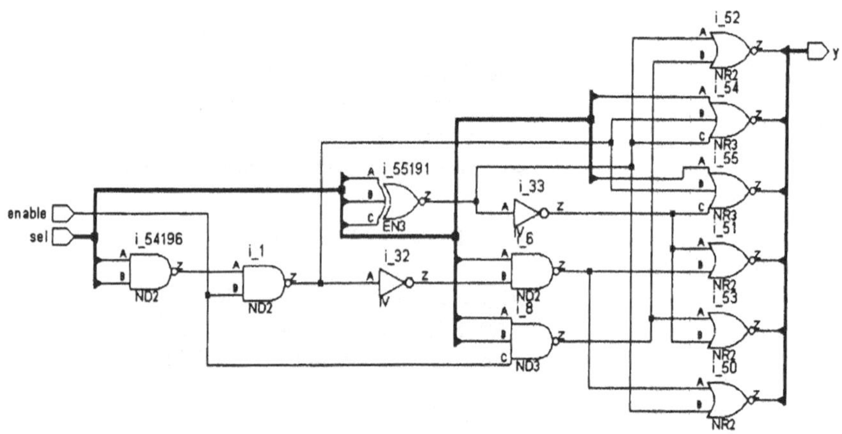

Figure 7-11 A 3-bit Johnson decoder.

7.7 A Factorial Model

Here is a model that generates the factorial of a number specified in `data`. The result is placed in `fac_out` and `exp_out` as mantissa and exponent respectively. The exponent is base 2. The input `reset` causes the model to initialize.

```
// File: fac.h
#include "systemc.h"
const int DATA_SIZE = 5;
const int OUT_SIZE = 8;

SC_MODULE (fac) {
  sc_in<bool> reset, start, clk;
  sc_in<sc_uint<DATA_SIZE> > data;
```

```
  sc_out<bool> done;
  sc_out<sc_uint<OUT_SIZE> > fac_out, exp_out;

  sc_signal<sc_uint<DATA_SIZE> > inlatch;
  void prc_fac();

  SC_CTOR (fac) {
    SC_METHOD (prc_fac);
    sensitive_pos << clk;
  }
};


// File: fac.cpp
#include "fac.h"
const int TEMP_SIZE = 12;

void fac::prc_fac() {
  sc_uint<TEMP_SIZE> next_result, next_inlatch;
  sc_uint<TEMP_SIZE> t_exponent;
  int k;

  if ((start & done) | reset) {
    fac_out = 1;
    exp_out = 0;
    inlatch = data;
    done = 0;
#ifndef SYNTHESIS
    cout << "Being reset ..." << endl;
#endif
  }
  else {
    if ((inlatch.read() > 1) & !done) {
      next_result = fac_out.read() * inlatch.read();
      next_inlatch = inlatch.read() - 1;
    }
    else {
      next_result = fac_out;
      next_inlatch = inlatch;
    }

    if (inlatch.read() <= 1)
      done = 1;
```

```
        t_exponent = exp_out;
        // Normalization:
        for (k = 1; k <= DATA_SIZE; k++) {
          if (next_result > 256) {          // 2 ** OUT_SIZE
            next_result = next_result / 2;
            t_exponent = t_exponent + 1;
          }
        }

        fac_out = next_result;
        exp_out = t_exponent;
        inlatch = next_inlatch;
      }
    }
```

An #ifndef compiler directive is used in the model to print debug statements during simulation. Non-synthesizable statements are typically placed within an #ifndef directive and are turned off for synthesis by setting the define flag.

7.8 Modeling a ROM

Here is a model of a read-only memory (ROM). The ROM data is stored in a constant array.

```
// File: rom.h
#include "systemc.h"
#define DATA_WIDTH 8
#define WORD_DEPTH 1024
#define ADDR_WIDTH 10

SC_MODULE (rom) {
  sc_in<bool> clk;
  sc_in<bool> cen;
  sc_in<sc_uint<ADDR_WIDTH> > addr;

  sc_out<sc_uint<DATA_WIDTH> > que;

  void prc_rom();
```

```
  SC_CTOR (rom) {
    SC_METHOD (prc_rom);
    sensitive_pos << clk;
  }
};

// File: rom.cpp
#include "rom.h"

void rom::prc_rom() {
  static const
    sc_uint<DATA_WIDTH> rom_data [WORD_DEPTH] =
    {0x11, 0x22, 0x33, 0x44, 0x55, 0x66, 0x77,
     0x88, <other values not listed here>};

  if (cen)
    que = rom_data[addr.read()];
  else
    que = 0;
}
```

The ROM table can also be declared within the SC_MODULE class and its values defined externally as shown below.

```
SC_MODULE (rom)
. . .
  static const
    sc_uint<DATA_WIDTH> rom_data [WORD_DEPTH];
. . .
}

const sc_uint<DATA_WIDTH> rom::rom_data [WORD_DEPTH] =
  {0x11, 0x22, 0x33, 0x44, 0x55, 0x66, 0x77,
   0x88, <others not listed here>};
```

It is possible to read the ROM values directly from a text file. This is left as an exercise for the reader.

7.9 Exercises

1. Write a model for an up-down counter with a clear and a preset data load where both of these are asynchronous and active high. The counter counts at the falling edge of the clock.
2. Write a model for a generic comparator whose operands are signed and it performs the following functions: equal to, greater than and less than. Instantiate a 10-bit comparator.
3. Write a model for a generic N-by-M multiplexer. The number of words and the number of bits per word are parameters.
4. Write a model for a parallel to serial converter. The inputs are `par_data`, `clk`, and `data_rdy`. Input `data_rdy` is 1 when data `par_data` is ready. Output appears serially on `serial_out`.
5. Write a model for an N-bit parity generator. The generator produces both an odd parity and an even parity output.
6. Write a model for a 4-by-4 crossbar switch. There are four input ports and four output ports. Each port is 8 bits wide. For each output port, a 2-bit selector selects the appropriate input.
7. Write a model for the transmitter block of an UART. The model accepts data in parallel and shifts the data out serially. It prepends a start bit (with value 1) and shifts the bits out serially starting with the 0th bit and finally sends out a stop bit (with value 1). No new data is allowed to be loaded in while the shift operation is in progress. A ready signal may be provided as an output indicating when the model is ready to accept a new parallel data load.

❑

8

Writing Testbenches

In the chapters so far, we have focused on describing hardware using SystemC, that is, described SystemC RTL. This chapter focuses on verification and on writing testbenches. The next chapter focuses on the more advanced (system-level) capabilities of SystemC.

SystemC is C++. So for testbenches and system level design, every C++ feature can be used.

SystemC is a language not only for describing hardware but also for building a powerful verification test environment. It is C++, so all the power and features of C++ can be used to write any sort of complex verification model. This chapter focuses on some simple aspects of writing test benches such as generating clocks, waveforms, reactive testbenches and dumping results. This chapter also describes the simulation control available in SystemC. Once you have mastered this chapter and understand C++ in more detail, you can write more powerful and advanced verification environments.

8.1 Writing a Testbench

A testbench is a model that is used to exercise and verify the correctness of a design under test. In addition to describing the design in SystemC, a testbench can also be written using the same language, that is, in SystemC. A testbench has three main purposes.

i. To generate stimulus for simulation (waveforms).

ii. To apply the stimulus to the design under test and collect output responses.

iii. To compare output responses with expected results.

There are many different ways of writing a testbench. Figure 8-1 shows one such scenario. The stimulus generation could be written in one module, `stimulus.h` and `stimulus.cpp`, and the output monitoring and comparison could be written in another module, `monitor.h` and `monitor.cpp`. The design under test is in a separate module, `dut.h` and `dut.cpp`. A main program `main.cpp` links in the various modules and interconnects them to form a testbench. Another way would be to embed the stimulus generation in the main program along with the monitoring functionality. Or the stimulus can be generated in one module and the comparison and results logged in the main program. This is really dependent on the user, the style, the tests, and the complexity of the design. In a large design, it is useful to follow the style shown in Figure 8-1, that of separating the stimulus and monitoring into individual modules as these modules themselves tend to be large.

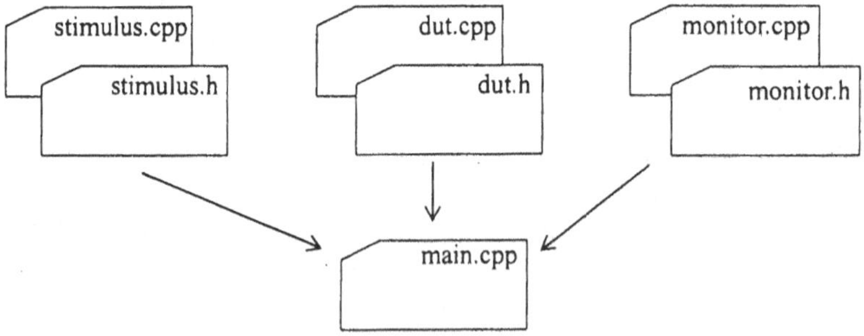

Figure 8-1 A typical testbench structure.

Any C++ code can be used in a testbench.

Here is the structure of a testbench in file main.cpp.

```
// File: main.cpp
// #include files here.

int sc_main (int argc, char *argv[]) {
  // sc_signal declarations here: used to connect the
  // various modules that are instantiated.

  // sc_clock clock declarations.

  // Design under test, stimulus module and
  // monitor module instantiations.

  // Trace file creation and monitoring.
  // Simulation start and control.
}
```

The function sc_main() has to be written for each SystemC design (a module or a module hierarchy) that has to be tested. The function sc_main() is the main program that instantiates the design under test. It is compiled and linked with other used modules to create an executable. This executable when run constitutes the simulation run. The arguments argc and argv have the same meaning as in a C++ main program; argc is the number of arguments that are passed via the command line options into the function sc_main() when executed, and argv is the array containing the option arguments.

A module can be instantiated in the function sc_main() by either declaring it as an object or by using the new operator. Here are examples of two module instantiations in the function sc_main() where the instances are declared as objects.

In this book, we follow the style of instantiating the modules as objects in a testbench.

```
sc_signal<bool> clk, resetn, renable, oenable;
sc_signal<sc_uint<4> > din, qout;
sc_signal<sc_lv<4> > dout;

tristate_reg tr1 ("tristate_reg_tr1");
// Named association:
tr1.clock (clk);
tr1.reset (resetn);
tr1.reg_enable (renable);
```

```
tr1.output_enable (oenable);
tr1.data_in (din);
tr1.data_out (dout);

johnson_ctr jc1 ("johnson_ctr_jc1");
// Positional association:
jc1 << clk << resetn << qout;
// The ports for the Johnson
// counter are: clk, clear and q.
```

Signals declared using `sc_signal` or `sc_clock` declarations are used to connect to the ports of an instance. There are two types of connections, *named* and *positional*. The instance `tr1` is an example where named association is used while the instance `jc1` is an example where positional association is used.

Here is the same example as above but in this case modules are instantiated in the function `sc_main()` using the `new` operator.

```
tristate_reg*
  tr1 = new tristate_reg ("tristate_reg_tr1");
// Named association:
tr1->clock (clk);
tr1->reset (resetn);
tr1->reg_enable (renable);
tr1->output_enable (oenable);
tr1->data_in (din);
tr1->data_out (dout);

johnson_ctr* jc1 = new johnson_ctr ("johnson_ctr_jc1");
// Positional association:
*jc1 << clk << resetn << qout;
```

The include files in a testbench are used to specify the interface, that is, the header files for all modules that are instantiated in `sc_main()`.

A recommended style for ordering the constructs in a testbench is as follows. Signals and clocks can be declared first. This can be followed by all module instantiations. Then trace files can be opened and trace calls made. And finally simulation start and stop commands can be issued. Open trace files have to be closed after simulation is complete. Of course, in between, you can have any other SystemC or C++ code.

8.2 Simulation Control

SystemC provides the following constructs to aid in simulation.

i. sc_clock: Generate a clock signal.

ii. sc_trace: Dump trace information into a file in the specified format.

iii. sc_start: Run simulation for specified time.

iv. sc_stop: Stop simulation.

v. sc_time_stamp: Get current simulation time with time units.

vi. sc_simulation_time: Get current simulation time without time units.

vii. sc_cycle, sc_initialize: Use to perform cycle-level simulation.

viii. sc_time: Specify a time value.

8.2.1 sc_clock

The sc_clock type allows for the creation of a special clock object in SystemC that can contain a timing waveform. The clock declaration:

```
sc_clock rclk ("rclk", 10, SC_NS);
```

creates a clock waveform with a on-off period of 10ns and a default duty cycle of 50%, and the initial value by default is true (1); this is shown in Figure 8-2. The clock object is rclk.

Here is another clock declaration:

```
sc_clock mclk ("mclk", 10, SC_NS, 0.2, 5, SC_NS, false);
```

This declaration creates a clock mclk with a period of 10ns, duty cycle of 20%, the first edge occurs after 5ns and the initial value at the first edge is false(0). Figure 8-2 shows the waveform generated. The first argument is the clock name and must be specified. If no period is specified, the default is 1 default time unit. And a default time unit in SystemC is 1ns. So the following clock declaration:

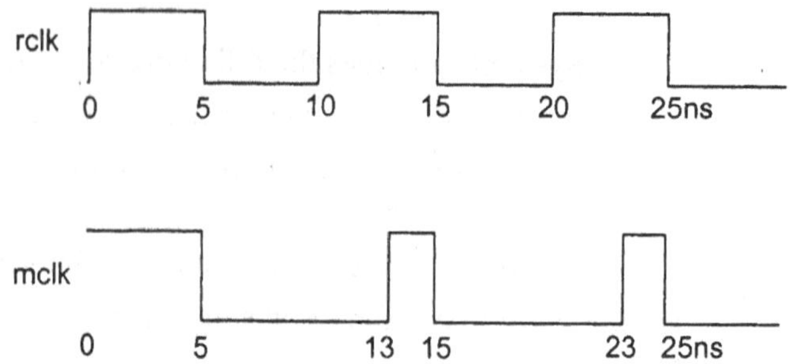

Figure 8-2 `sc_clock` clocks.

```
sc_clock clka ("clka");
```

declares a clock called `clka` with a period of 1ns, a duty cycle of 50% and with an initial value of `true` and the first edge at time 0.

8.2.2 sc_trace

SystemC supports three different formats in which simulation results can be saved. These are:

i. VCD (Value Change Dump)

ii. WIF (Waveform Interchange Format)

iii. ISDB (Integrated Signal Data Base)

To save values in one of these trace formats, first open a file using the appropriate function call.

i. For VCD, use `sc_create_vcd_trace_file()`. The `.vcd` extension is automatically added.

ii. For WIF, use `sc_create_wif_trace_file()`. The `.awif` extension is automatically added.

iii. For ISDB, use `sc_create_isdb_trace_file()`. The `.isdb` extension is automatically added.

The file handle is declared to be of type pointer to `sc_trace_file`. Here is an example.

```
sc_trace_file *tfile =
  sc_create_vcd_trace_file ("myvcddump");
```

This declaration creates a VCD trace file called `myvcddump.vcd`. The pointer to be used in the testbench is `tfile`.

By using the function `sc_trace()`, you can specify the signals whose values you want to save in the trace file. Here is an example of the function call `sc_trace()`.

```
sc_trace (tfile, signal_name, "signal_name");
```

This function logs the value of `signal_name` into the trace file `tfile`. The string value specifies the signal name that will appear in the trace file. Often it is best to keep it the same as the signal name.

Before exiting the testbench function `sc_main()`, close the trace file using one of the following functions as appropriate.

```
sc_close_vcd_trace_file (pointer_to_trace_file);
sc_close_isdb_trace_file (pointer_to_trace_file);
sc_close_wif_trace_file (pointer_to_trace_file);
```

The `sc_trace()` function calls must appear after the trace file is opened and after the traced signals are created.

The time unit of a VCD file can be set by using the `sc_set_vcd_time_unit()` method. For example,

```
sc_trace_file *trace_file =
  sc_create_vcd_trace_file ("ahb_trans.vcd");
((vcd_trace_file *) trace_file)->
  sc_set_vcd_time_unit(-6);
```

The argument to the method is a time unit that is specified as a power of 10. So an argument value of -6 specifies a unit of microsecond, an argument of -12 specifies a unit of picosecond, and so on. The default is -9 (nanoseconds).

It is possible to store delta cycle behavior in a VCD file - useful only with waveform viewers that offer this feature. The delta cycle trace can be enabled or disabled using the `delta_cycles()` method. A value of `true` turns on the tracing, and a value of `false` turns off the tracing.

```
trace_file->delta_cycles (true);
. . .
trace_file->delta_cycles (false);
. . .
trace_file->delta_cycles (true);
. . .
```

8.2.3 sc_start

This method tells the simulation kernel to start simulation. This method must be specified after all the instantiations and after all the trace calls. Here is an example of a `sc_start()` method call.

```
sc_start (100, SC_MS);
```

tells the simulation kernel to run simulation for 100ms. The method call:

```
sc_start(-1);
```

tells the simulator to run forever.

Correctly speaking, the `sc_start(time_value)` method continues simulation for another `time_value` time units. So it is possible to have multiple `sc_start()` calls. For example:

```
. . .
// First sc_start() call:
sc_start (100, SC_MS);
// Starts simulation and runs for 100ms.
. . .
// Second sc_start() call:
sc_start (20, SC_MS);
// Continues simulation for another 20ms.
. . .
// Third sc_start() call:
sc_start (15, SC_MS);
// Continues simulation for another 15ms.
```

To restart simulation, simply invoke the simulation executable again.

8.2.4 sc_stop

The method `sc_stop()` can be used in any process to stop simulation. It is of the form:

```
sc_stop();
```

and does not take any arguments. The `sc_start()` method cannot be called after an `sc_stop()` call.

8.2.5 sc_time_stamp

This method returns the current simulation time with its time units. For example,

```
cout << "Current time is " << sc_time_stamp() << endl;
```

would print, for example:

```
Current time is 25ns
```

8.2.6 sc_simulation_time

This method returns the current simulation time as an integer value of type double (without the time units) in terms of the default time unit. For example:

```
double curr_time = sc_simulation_time();
```

when executed, `curr_time` will have the current simulation time. So:

```
cout << "Time now is %f" << curr_time << endl;
```

will print:

```
Time now is 96
```

8.2.7 sc_cycle and sc_initialize

These two methods are used to perform cycle-level simulation. For example, if you want to evaluate your design every 10 time units, you would do a cycle-level simulation. In such a case, you would not use `sc_start()`, but use the methods `sc_initialize()` and `sc_cycle()`.

The method `sc_initialize()` initializes the simulation kernel. The method `sc_cycle()` executes all the processes that are ready to run, which could take a number of delta cycles, until no more processes are ready to run. It then traces the necessary signals before advancing the simulation time by the specified amount. So,

```
sc_cycle(10, SC_US); // 10 microseconds.
```

would simulate all the processes and then advance the simulation time by 10us.

8.2.8 sc_time

The `sc_time` declaration is used to specify a time value, such as 10ns, 20ps, etc. An `sc_time` object can then be used wherever a time specification is required, such as in `sc_clock` and `sc_start()`. Here are some examples.

```
sc_time t1 (100, SC_NS); // Specifies the value 100ns.
sc_time t2 (20, SC_PS);  // Specifies the value 20ps.

// Following two forms are equivalent:
sc_start (t1); // Run simulation for 100ns.
sc_start (100, SC_NS);

sc_cycle (t2);

sc_time period (10, SC_NS);
sc_time start_time (2, SC_NS);
sc_clock fclk ("fclk", period, 0.2, start_time, true);
```

The unit that can be used is one of: `SC_FS`, `SC_PS`, `SC_NS`, `SC_US`, `SC_MS`, and `SC_SEC`.

The default time resolution is 1ps. This can be overridden by using the method `sc_set_time_resolution()`, such as:

```
sc_set_time_resolution (100, SC_PS);
```

sets the time resolution to be 100ps. So if you specify:

```
sc_clock c1 ("c1", 20.26, SC_NS);
```

It is an error to specify the time resolution more than once or to specify it after a time value has been declared. The recommended strategy is to declare it right at the beginning of the `sc_main()` program.

will create a clock with a clock period of 20300ps. The time resolution specified can only be a power of 10, and it is usually specified only once at the very beginning of the `sc_main()` program.

There are a couple of methods available that can operate on a `sc_time` value. Here are some examples.

```
// sc_time_stamp() method returns an sc_time value:
sc_time curr_time = sc_time_stamp();

// Value in terms of time resolution:
cout << "As double:" << curr_time.to_double() << endl;

// Value in seconds:
cout << "In seconds:" << curr_time.to_seconds() << endl;

// Value in default time unit:
cout << "In default time unit:"
     << curr_time.to_default_time_units() << endl;

// Value as a string:
cout << "In string form:" << curr_time.to_string()
     << endl;

// Just to contrast with sc_simulation_time():
cout << "sc_simulation_time():" << sc_simulation_time()
     << endl;

// Just to contrast with default method:
cout << "sc_time_stamp():" << sc_time_stamp() << endl;
```

The output is:

```
As double:89000
In seconds:8.9e-08
In default time units:89
As string:89 ns
sc_simulation_time():89
sc_time_stamp():89 ns
```

The C `printf` and `fprintf` routines can also be used to print time values. For example, the following prints the current simulation time in seconds to a file:

The standard C `printf` and `fprintf` routines can also be used to print time values.

```
fprintf (file_ptr, "Simulation time is %5.12f\n",
  (float) sc_time_stamp().to_seconds());
```

After printing, the file would contain:

```
Simulation time is 0.000000089000
```

It is however recommended not to mix `printf` and `cout` as these can lead to ordering problems in messages that are written out.

8.3 Waveforms

Regular waveforms such as a clock can be generated by using the `sc_clock` declaration. Let us look at other ways of creating stimuli.

8.3.1 Arbitrary Waveform

How do you create an arbitrary waveform like the signal `reset` shown in Figure 8-3?

This can be done by using an SC_THREAD process in a module. The SC_THREAD process is the second kind of process that is supported in SystemC. Such a process can be suspended and restarted based on time or on the occurrence of certain events. (The SC_THREAD process is described in more detail in the next chapter). Here is a module with an SC_THREAD process that generates this arbitrary waveform.

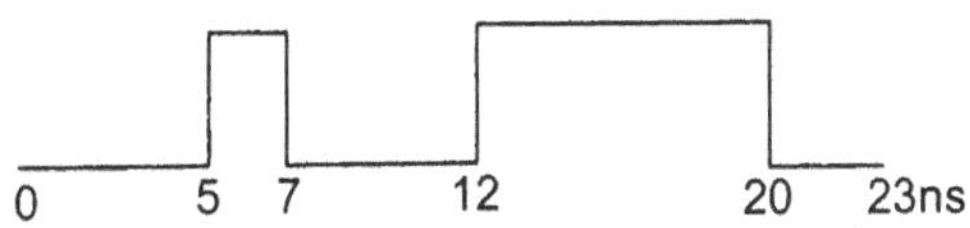

Figure 8-3 An arbitrary waveform.

```
// File: wave.h
#include "systemc.h"

SC_MODULE (wave) {
  sc_out<bool> sig_out;

  void prc_wave();

  SC_CTOR (wave) {
    SC_THREAD (prc_wave);
  }
};

// File: wave.cpp
#include "wave.h"

void wave::prc_wave() {
  sig_out = 0;
  wait (5, SC_NS);
  sig_out = 1;
  wait (2, SC_NS);
  sig_out = 0;
  wait (5, SC_NS);
  sig_out = 1;
  wait (8, SC_NS);
  sig_out = 0;
}
```

When does the SC_THREAD process `prc_wave` start execution? At initialization time. All processes (SC_METHOD and SC_THREAD) are executed once at initialization time, just before simulation starts. Upon process execution, output `sig_out` gets assigned 0. The subsequent wait statement causes the process `prc_wave` to suspend and wait for 5ns. Such a process suspension cannot occur in an SC_METHOD process. After 5ns, `sig_out` gets assigned 1 and the process suspends for 2ns, and so on.

8.3.2 Complex Repetitive Waveform

What if you want to repeat the above waveform every 100ns? This can be achieved by using a never-ending while loop in an SC_THREAD process. This is shown next.

```
// File: wave2.cpp
#include "wave.h"

void wave::prc_wave() {
  while (1) {
    sig_out = 0;
    wait (5, SC_NS);
    sig_out = 1;
    wait (2, SC_NS);
    sig_out = 0;
    wait (5, SC_NS);
    sig_out = 1;
    wait (8, SC_NS);
    sig_out = 0;
    wait (80, SC_NS);
  }
}
```

A clock can also be modeled in a similar manner. Here is one for completeness (you would rather use the predefined `sc_clock`). Figure 8-4 shows the generated clock for this example.

```
// File: myclock.h
#include "systemc.h"
const int START_VALUE = 0;
const int INITIAL_DELAY = 5;
const int FIRST_DELAY = 2;
const int SECOND_DELAY = 3;

SC_MODULE (myclock) {
  sc_out<bool> clk_out;
```

```
  void prc_myclock();

  SC_CTOR (myclock) {
    SC_THREAD (prc_myclock);
  }
};

// File: myclock.cpp
#include "myclock.h"

void myclock::prc_myclock() {
  clk_out = START_VALUE;
  wait (INITIAL_DELAY, SC_NS);

  while (1) {
    clk_out = ! clk_out;
    wait (FIRST_DELAY, SC_NS);
    clk_out = ! clk_out;
    wait (SECOND_DELAY, SC_NS);
  }
}
```

Figure 8-4 My own clock generator.

8.3.3 Generating a Derived Clock

Here is a model of a pulse generator. The generated pulses are synchronized to the main clock. Figure 8-5 shows the output produced.

```
// File: pulse.h
#include "systemc.h"
#define DELAY 2, SC_NS
#define ON_DURATION 1, SC_NS
```

```
SC_MODULE (pulse) {
  sc_in<bool> clk;
  sc_out<bool> pulse_out;

  void prc_pulse();

  SC_CTOR (pulse) {
    SC_THREAD (prc_pulse);
    sensitive_pos << clk;
  }
};

// File: pulse.cpp
#include "pulse.h"

void pulse::prc_pulse() {
  pulse_out = 0;

  while (true) {
    wait();           // Wait for positive edge of clock.
    wait (DELAY);
    pulse_out = 1;
    wait (ON_DURATION);
    pulse_out = 0;
  }
}

// File: pulse_main.cpp
#include "pulse.h"

int sc_main (int argc, char *argv[]) {
  sc_signal<bool> pout;
  sc_trace_file *tf;
  sc_clock clock ("master_clk", 5, SC_NS);

  // Instantiate the pulse module:
  pulse p1 ("pulse_p1");
  p1.clk (clock);
  p1.pulse_out (pout);

  // Specify trace file pulse.vcd and trace signals:
  tf = sc_create_vcd_trace_file ("pulse");
  sc_trace (tf, clock, "clock");
```

```
  sc_trace (tf, pout, "pulse_out");

  sc_start (100, SC_NS);
  sc_close_vcd_trace_file (tf);
  cout << "Finished at time " << sc_time_stamp() << endl;
  return 0;
}
```

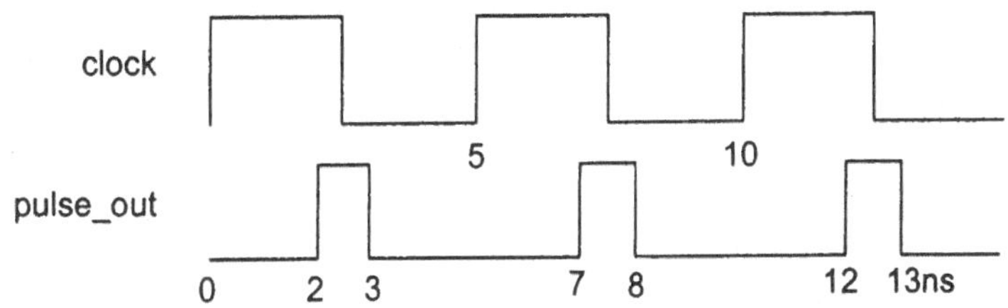

Figure 8-5 Clock synchronized pulse generation.

An SC_THREAD process can optionally have a sensitivity list; a wait statement in the process could wait for a signal in the sensitivity list to change. Such a wait statement `wait();` is specified as the first statement within the while loop. The other two wait statements wait only for the time elapsed and are not triggered by the sensitivity list.

8.3.4 Reading Stimuli from Files

It is possible to read the input stimulus from a file and apply it to a design under test. Here is such an example.

```
// File: read_vectors.h
#include <iostream.h>
#include <fstream.h>
#include "systemc.h"
#include "usr_define.h"

SC_MODULE (read_vectors) {
  sc_in<bool> read_clk;
  sc_out<sc_uint<SEL_WIDTH> > read_sel_op;
  sc_out<bool> read_clear, read_left_in, read_right_in;
  sc_out<sc_uint<WIDTH> > read_data_in, read_usr_out;
```

```
  void prc_read_vectors();
  ifstream infile;                          // Input file.

  SC_CTOR (read_vectors) {
    SC_METHOD (prc_read_vectors);
    sensitive_neg << read_clk;
    infile.open ("usr.in");

    if (!infile) {
      cerr << "**** ERROR: Unable to open input " <<
        "vector file, usr.in" << endl;
      sc_stop();                            // Stop simulation.
    }
  }
};
```

The endl is a C++ manipulator that inserts a newline character into the output stream and flushes the output stream.

hex, oct and dec are examples of other C++ output manipulators. For example, the hex manipulator causes the integer values to print in hexadecimal form.

```
// File: read_vectors.cpp
#include "read_vectors.h"
#include "usr.h"

void read_vectors::prc_read_vectors() {
  bool t_clr, t_lin, t_rin;
  int t_din, t_dout, t_sel;

  if (infile >> t_sel >> t_clr >> t_lin >>
      t_rin >> t_din >> t_dout) {
    cout << "Reading line(" << sc_time_stamp() <<
      "): sel=" << t_sel << "clr=" << t_clr << " lin=" <<
      t_lin << " rin=" << t_rin << " din=" << hex <<
      t_din << " dout=" << t_dout << endl;
    read_clear = t_clr;
    read_left_in = t_lin;
    read_right_in = t_rin;
    read_data_in = t_din;
    read_usr_out = t_dout;
    read_sel_op = t_sel;
  }
  else
    // Stop simulation when end of file reached:
    sc_stop();
}
```

```
// File: check_results.h
#include <iostream.h>
#include "systemc.h"
#include "usr_define.h"

SC_MODULE (check_results) {
  sc_in<bool> check_clk;
  sc_in<sc_uint<WIDTH> > expected_out, actual_out;

  void prc_check_results();

  SC_CTOR (check_results) {
    SC_METHOD (prc_check_results);
    sensitive_neg << check_clk;
  }
};

// File: check_results.cpp
#include "check_results.h"

void check_results::prc_check_results() {
  if (expected_out != actual_out)
    cout << "**** Mismatch results at time " <<
      sc_time_stamp() << " Expected:" <<
      expected_out.read() << " Actual:" <<
      actual_out.read() << endl;
  else
    cout << "Results match at time " << sc_time_stamp()
      << "Expected:" << expected_out.read() <<
      " Actual:" << actual_out.read() << endl;
}

// File: usr_main.cpp
#include "read_vectors.h"
#include "check_results.h"
#include "usr.h"

int sc_main (int argc, char *argv[]) {
  sc_signal<bool> clear, left_in, right_in;
  sc_signal<sc_uint<SEL_WIDTH> > sel_op;
  sc_signal<sc_uint<WIDTH> > data_in, usr_out,
    expected_usr_out;
```

```
// Generate clock:
sc_clock clock ("usr_clock", 2);

// Instantiate design under test
// before applying stimulus:
usr u1 ("usr_u1");
u1.clk (clock);
u1.clr (clear);
u1.lin (left_in);
u1.rin (right_in);
u1.select (sel_op);
u1.par_in (data_in);
u1.q(usr_out);

// Instantiate read vectors module:
read_vectors rv ("read_vectors_rv");
rv.read_clk (clock);
rv.read_clear(clear);
rv.read_left_in (left_in);
rv.read_right_in (right_in);
rv.read_sel_op (sel_op);
rv.read_data_in (data_in);
rv.read_usr_out (expected_usr_out);

// Instantiate checking module:
check_results cr1 ("check_results_cr1");
cr1.check_clk (clock);
cr1.expected_out (expected_usr_out);
cr1.actual_out (usr_out);

// Tracing:
sc_trace_file *tf =
  sc_create_wif_trace_file ("usrout");
sc_trace (tf, clock, "clock");
sc_trace (tf, clear, "clear");
sc_trace (tf, left_in, "left_in");
sc_trace (tf, right_in, "right_in");
sc_trace (tf, sel_op, "sel_op");
sc_trace (tf, data_in, "data_in");
sc_trace (tf, usr_out, "usr_out");

sc_start (-1); // Run forever. However simulation
// stops because of sc_stop() method in
```

```
  // module read_vectors.
  sc_close_wif_trace_file (tf);
  return (0);
}
```

The module read_vectors reads vectors from the file usr.in on every falling edge of a clock. Simulation stops when the end of file is reached. The vectors are applied to the design under test usr and the results are monitored using the module check_results which compares the expected value with the actual value and prints a message if a mismatch occurs. A WIF trace file is also created that saves the waveforms for the signals specified by the sc_trace() call. The simulation command sc_start() tells the simulator to run forever. However the sc_stop() method in the module read_vectors stops the simulation when all vectors in the input vector file have been read.

An alternate way of reading vectors from a file is by using an SC_THREAD process. Here is the read_vectors() module rewritten using this style.

```
// File: read_vectors2.h
#include <iostream.h>
#include <fstream.h>
#include "systemc.h"
#include "usr_define.h"

SC_MODULE (read_vectors) {
  sc_in<bool> read_clk;

  sc_out<sc_uint<SEL_WIDTH> > read_sel_op;
  sc_out<bool> read_clear, read_left_in, read_right_in;
  sc_out<sc_uint<WIDTH> > read_data_in, read_usr_out;

  void prc_read_vectors();

  // Member variable:
  ifstream infile;

  SC_CTOR (read_vectors) {
    SC_THREAD (prc_read_vectors);
    infile.open ("usr.in");
```

```
    if (!infile) {
      cerr << "**** ERROR: Unable to open input "
           << "vector file, usr.in" << endl;
      sc_stop();
    }
  }

  ~ read_vectors () {
    infile.close();
  }
};

// File: read_vectors2.cpp
#include "read_vectors2.h"

void read_vectors::prc_read_vectors() {
  bool t_clr, t_lin, t_rin;
  int t_din, t_dout, t_sel;

  while (infile >> t_sel >> t_clr >> t_lin >> t_rin
                >> t_din >> t_dout) {
    cout << "Reading line(" << sc_time_stamp()
         << "): sel=" << t_sel << "clr=" << t_clr
         << " lin=" << t_lin << " rin=" << t_rin
         << " din=" << hex << t_din << " dout="
         << t_dout << endl;
    read_clear = t_clr;
    read_left_in = t_lin;
    read_right_in = t_rin;
    read_data_in = t_din;
    read_usr_out = t_dout;
    read_sel_op = t_sel;

    wait (read_clk.negedge());
  }

  // Stop simulation:
  sc_stop();
}
```

8.3.5 Reactive Stimuli

In this type of stimulus generation, the next stimulus to be generated is based on the current state of the design under test, that is, the testbench is reactive based on the state of the design. This approach is useful if different stimulus need to be applied based on the state of the design. Consider the factorial design that computes the factorial of a number. Figure 8-6 shows the handshake mechanism between the design under test and the testbench model.

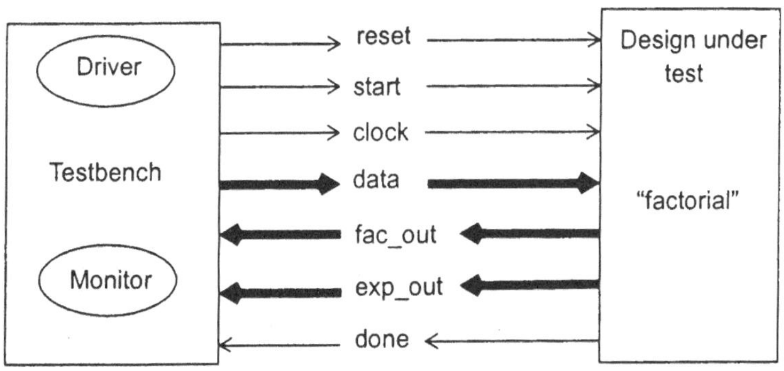

Figure 8-6 Handshake between the testbench and design under test.

The factorial model is described in Chapter 7. The input `reset` resets the factorial model to an initial state. The signal `start` is set after the input `data` is applied. When computation is complete, the output signal `done` asserts to indicate that the computed result appears on the outputs `fac_out` and `exp_out`. The resulting factorial value is $(fac\_out * 2^{exp\_out})$. The testbench model provides input on signal `data` starting from values 1 to 20 in increments of one. It applies the input data, sets the signal `start`, waits for the signal `done`, and then applies the next input data. Assertions are used to ensure that the values appearing at the output are correct. The testbench description follows.

```
// File: monitor.h
#include <math.h>
#include "systemc.h"
#include "fac.h"
```

```
SC_MODULE (monitor) {
  sc_in<bool> clk, done;
  sc_out<bool> reset, start;
  sc_out<sc_uint<DATA_SIZE> > data;
  sc_in<sc_uint<OUT_SIZE> > fac_out, exp_out;

  void prc_monitor();
  enum state_type {reset_state, start_state,
    apply_data_state, wait_result_state};
  sc_signal<state_type> next_state;

  SC_CTOR (monitor) {
    SC_THREAD(prc_monitor);
    sensitive_neg << clk;
    sensitive << done;
  }
};

// File: monitor.cpp
#include "monitor.h"
const int MAX_APPLY = 20;

void monitor::prc_monitor() {
  int num_applied;

  num_applied = 1;

  while (1) {
    wait();
    switch (next_state) {
      case reset_state :
        cout << "In reset state(" <<
          sc_time_stamp() << ") ...\n";
        reset = 1; start = 0;
        next_state = apply_data_state;
        wait();
        break;

      case apply_data_state:
        cout << "In apply_data state(" <<
          sc_time_stamp() << ") ...\n";
        data = num_applied;
        next_state = start_state;
```

```
        wait();
        break;
      case start_state:
        cout << "In start state(" << sc_time_stamp() <<
          ") with data:" << num_applied << " ...\n";
        start = 1;
        next_state = wait_result_state;
        wait();
        break;
      case wait_result_state:
        cout << "In wait result state(" <<
          sc_time_stamp() << ") ...\n";
        reset = 0;
        start = 0;

        while (! done)
          wait();

        cout << "Factorial of " << num_applied << " is " <<
          (int) fac_out.read() <<
          "*(2**" << (int) exp_out.read() << ")\n";
        num_applied = num_applied + 1;

        if (num_applied < MAX_APPLY)
          next_state = apply_data_state;
        else
          sc_stop();            // Done, stop simulation.
    }
  }
}

// File: main.cpp
#include "monitor.h"

int sc_main (int argc, char *argv[]) {
  sc_signal<bool> reset, start, finished;
  sc_signal<sc_uint<DATA_SIZE> > in_data;
  sc_signal<sc_uint<OUT_SIZE> > fout, eout;

  sc_clock clock ("clock", 10, SC_NS);

  // Instantiate the factorial model:
  fac f1 ("fac_f1");
```

```
f1.reset (reset);
f1.start (start);
f1.clk (clock);
f1.data (in_data);
f1.done (finished);
f1.fac_out (fout);
f1.exp_out (eout);

// Instantiate the reactive monitor:
monitor m1 ("monitor_m1");
m1.clk(clock);
m1.reset (reset);
m1.start (start);
m1.done (finished);
m1.data (in_data);
m1.fac_out(fout);
m1.exp_out (eout);

// Start simulation and run forever:
sc_start (-1);
return 0;
```

The output result of the factorial may not match exactly the mathematically computed value because of the normalization rounding performed during computation of the factorial. Here is the output produced on a simulation run.

```
In reset state(0 s) ...
In apply_data state(10 ns) ...
In start state(25 ns) with data:1 ...
In wait result state(45 ns) ...
Factorial of 1 is 1*(2**0)
In apply_data state(55 ns) ...
In start state(75 ns) with data:2 ...
In wait result state(85 ns) ...
Factorial of 2 is 2*(2**0)
In apply_data state(105 ns) ...
In start state(125 ns) with data:3 ...
In wait result state(135 ns) ...
Factorial of 3 is 6*(2**0)
In apply_data state(165 ns) ...
```

```
In start state(185 ns) with data:4 ...
In wait result state(195 ns) ...
Factorial of 4 is 24*(2**0)
. . .
```

8.4 Monitoring Behavior

In the reactive testbench described in the previous section, we saw how the testbench can monitor the behavior of the design under test and apply different patterns based on the state of the design. In this section, we look at how to automatically assert the right behavior when reading stimuli from a file and how to dump results into a text file for your own debugging and evaluation.

8.4.1 Asserting Valid Behavior

One common way of accomplishing this is to apply a vector, sample the output after a specific time, and then verify that the output response matches the expected value. Here is an example of such a testbench. The input and expected output vectors are stored as constants; alternately they could have been read in from an ASCII text file.

```
// File: apply_and_check.h
#include "systemc.h"
#include "usr_define.h"

SC_MODULE (apply_and_check) {
  sc_in<sc_uint<WIDTH> > actual_out;
  sc_out<bool> clear, left_in, right_in;
  sc_out<sc_uint<WIDTH> > data_in;
  sc_out<sc_uint<SEL_WIDTH> > sel_op;

  void behavior();

  SC_CTOR (apply_and_check) {
    SC_THREAD (behavior);
  }
};
```

```
// File: apply_and_check.cpp
#include "apply_and_check.h"
const int VECTOR_WIDTH = 13;
const int MAX_VECTORS = 3;

void apply_and_check::behavior() {
  sc_lv<VECTOR_WIDTH> in_vector [MAX_VECTORS];
  int index;
  sc_uint<WIDTH> expected;

  // The test vectors:
  in_vector[0] = "1100000111101";
  in_vector[1] = "1000010111001";
  in_vector[2] = "0100010000001";

  for (index = 0; index < MAX_VECTORS; index++) {
    // Apply the vector:
    clear = (sc_bit) in_vector[index][12];
    left_in = (sc_bit) in_vector[index][11];
    right_in = (sc_bit) in_vector[index][10];
    sel_op = (sc_bv<SEL_WIDTH>)
                 in_vector[index].range (9, 8);
    data_in = (sc_bv<WIDTH>)
                 in_vector[index].range (7, 4);
    expected = (sc_bv<WIDTH>)
                 in_vector[index].range (3, 0);

    // Wait for settle time:
    wait (5, SC_NS);

    // Check if output is correct:
    if (actual_out != expected)
      cout << "*** Mismatch at time " <<
        sc_time_stamp() << " with vector at index " <<
        index << endl;
  }

  sc_stop();                          // Done.
}
```

In this example, the application of test vectors is expressed in a single process. After a test vector is applied, the process waits for the clock edge, the edge on which the design under test is synchronized to, then the process behavior suspends for a settling time, samples the output, and then checks to see if the output is equal to the expected output vector. After this, the process continues and applies the next vector. Simulation stops when all vectors have been processed.

8.4.2 Dumping Results into a Text File

The output values of the design under test can be saved in a text file by using the file write (output stream) capabilities of the C++ language. The important point to note is that when the values are printed, the value is that of the signal at that current time. It may not be the one that has been scheduled to be assigned at the next delta.

Here is an example of the universal shift register testbench in which the results are dumped into a text file.

```
// File: dump_results.h
#include <iostream.h>
#include <fstream.h>
#include "systemc.h"
#include "usr_define.h"

SC_MODULE (dump_results) {
  sc_in<bool> clock, clear, left_in, right_in;
  sc_in<sc_uint<SEL_WIDTH> > sel_op;
  sc_in<sc_uint<WIDTH> > data_in, data_out;

  // Declare the output stream:
  ofstream outfile;
  void behavior_dump();

  SC_CTOR (dump_results) {
    SC_METHOD (behavior_dump);
    sensitive_neg << clock;
    // Open the output file "mydump.out":
    outfile.open ("mydump.out");
  }
};
```

```
// File: dump_results.cpp
#include "dump_results.h"

void dump_results::behavior_dump() {
  // Prints values of inputs and outputs at
  // every falling edge of clock.
  outfile << "At time " << sc_time_stamp() <<
    " clear = " << clear << "left_in = " << left_in <<
    "right_in = " << right_in << "sel_op = " << sel_op <<
    " data_in = " << data_in << " data_out = " <<
    data_out << endl;
}
```

The module dump_results prints out the values of all the inputs and the output at the falling edge of the clock; the output value should have stabilized by the falling edge of the clock since the shift register is synchronized on the rising edge of the clock.

8.5 More Examples

This section has a couple more examples on testbenches along with the descriptions of the design under test.

8.5.1 Flip-flop

Here is a model of a D-type flip-flop followed by a testbench. The testbench uses the wait() method to create a waveform on the input data. The wait() method suspends the process and waits for an event to occur on its static sensitivity list (the list described in SC_CTOR block); in this example it is the rising edge of the signal clk. The module check simply logs the output changes to the terminal output.

```
// File: ff_define.h
#ifndef FF_DEFINE_H
#define FF_DEFINE_H
const int SIZE = 8;
#endif
```

```
// File: ff.h
#include "systemc.h"
#include "ff_define.h"

SC_MODULE(ff) {
  sc_in<bool> clk;
  sc_in<bool> reset;
  sc_in<sc_uint<SIZE> > data;
  sc_out<sc_uint<SIZE> > data_out;

  void prc_ff();

  SC_CTOR (ff) {
    SC_METHOD (prc_ff);
    sensitive_pos << clk << reset;
  }
};

// File: ff.cpp
#include "ff.h"

void ff::prc_ff() {
  if (reset)
    data_out = 0;
  else
    data_out = data;
}
```

Testbench

```
// File: ff_tb.h
#include "systemc.h"
#include "ff_define.h"

SC_MODULE(ff_tb) {
  sc_in<bool> clk;
  sc_in<sc_uint<SIZE> > data_out;
  sc_out<bool> reset;
  sc_out<sc_uint<SIZE> > data;

  void test();
  void check();
```

```
  SC_CTOR(ff_tb) {
    SC_THREAD(test);
    sensitive_pos << clk;
    SC_METHOD(check);
    sensitive << data_out;
  }
};

// File: ff_tb.cpp
#include "ff_tb.h"

void ff_tb::test() {
  reset.write(1);
  wait();                      // For a rising clock edge.
  wait();
  reset.write(0);
  data.write(1);
  wait();
  wait();
  data.write(0);
  wait();
  wait();
  data.write(1);
  wait();
  wait();
  data.write(0);
  wait();
  wait();
  data.write(1);
  wait();
  wait();
  data.write(1);
  wait();
  sc_stop();
}

void ff_tb::check() {
  cout << "Output data is (@" << sc_time_stamp() <<
    "): " << data_out.read() << endl;
}
```

```
// File: main.cpp
#include "ff.h"
#include "ff_tb.h"

int sc_main(int argc, char *argv[]) {
  sc_clock clk("clk", 2, SC_NS);
  sc_signal<bool> reset;
  sc_signal<sc_uint<SIZE> > data, data_out;

  ff_tb tb("tb");
  tb.clk(clk);
  tb.reset(reset);
  tb.data_out(data_out);
  tb.data(data);

  ff f1 ("ff_f1");
  f1.clk(clk);
  f1.reset(reset);
  f1.data_out(data_out);
  f1.data(data);

  // Start simulation and run forever. Simulation stops
  // due to execution of sc_stop() in module ff_tb.
  sc_start(-1);
  return 0;
}
```

This is the output produced.

```
Output data is (@0ns): 0
Output data is (@4ns): 1
Output data is (@8ns): 0
Output data is (@12ns): 1
Output data is (@16ns): 0
Output data is (@20ns): 1
SystemC: simulation stopped by user.
```

Here is an example that shows the use of for-loops to describe repetitive connections. A generic N-bit register is built using a basic flop-flop. An array of `bool`s is used to model the input and output data.

```
// File: "dff.h"
#include "systemc.h"

SC_MODULE (dff) {
  sc_in<bool> d, clk, reset;
  sc_out<bool> q;

  void prc_dff();

  SC_CTOR (dff) {
    SC_METHOD (prc_dff);
    sensitive_pos << clk;          // Edge sensitivity.
    sensitive_neg << reset;
  }
};

// File: "dff.cpp"
#include "dff.h"
void dff::prc_dff () {
  if (!reset)
    q = 0;
  else
    q = d;
}

// File: "reg_spsr.h"
#include <string>
#include "systemc.h"
#include "dff.h"

#define REG_SIZE 8

SC_MODULE(reg_spsr) {
  sc_in<bool> clk;
  sc_in<bool> reset;
  sc_in<bool> d_in [REG_SIZE];

  sc_out<bool> d_out [REG_SIZE];

  dff *udff[REG_SIZE];
  int i;
  string ff_name;
```

```
  SC_CTOR (reg_spsr) {
    // Use for-loop to create all instances:
    for (i = 0; i < REG_SIZE; i++) {
      // Form name of flip-flop:
      ff_name = "udff" + i;
      // Create an instance:
      udff[i] = new dff (ff_name.c_str());
      // Connect it up:
      (*udff[i]) (clk, reset, d_in[i], d_out[i]);
    }
  }
};

// File: "reg_spsr_main.cpp"
#include "reg_spsr.h"

int sc_main(int argc, char *argv[]) {
  // Set the time value resolution:
  sc_set_time_resolution (1, SC_NS);
  sc_clock clk("clk", 2, SC_NS);

  sc_signal<bool> reg_in[REG_SIZE];
  sc_signal<bool> reg_out[REG_SIZE];
  sc_signal<bool> clear;

  reg_spsr ureg_spsr("ureg_spsr");
  ureg_spsr.clk(clk);
  ureg_spsr.reset(clear);

  // Use for-loop to connect all inputs and outputs:
  for (int j = 0; j < REG_SIZE; j++) {
    ureg_spsr.d_in[j](reg_in[j]);
    ureg_spsr.d_out[j] (reg_out[j]);
  }

  // Clear reg:
  clear = 1;
  sc_start(10, SC_NS);
  clear = 0;
  sc_start(10, SC_NS);
```

```
  // Check output:
  for (int j = 0; j < REG_SIZE; j++)
    if (reg_out[j] != 0)
      cerr << "Reg bit " << j << " not cleared." << endl;

  clear = 1;

  // Load value (all 1's):
  for (int j = 0; j < REG_SIZE; j++)
    reg_in[j] = 1;

  // Continue simulation for few clock cycles:
  sc_start(10, SC_NS);

  // Check output:
  for (int j = 0; j < REG_SIZE; j++)
    if (reg_out[j] != 1)
      cerr << "Reg bit " << j << " not set to 1 (it is "
           << reg_out[j] << ") at time "
           << sc_time_stamp() << endl;

  return 0;
}
```

8.5.2 Multiplexer with Synchronous Output

Here is a model of a 4-to-1 multiplexer with a latched output. The output is latched at the rising edge of the signal `clock`. A testbench to test the multiplexer follows. The module `driver` generates all possible input patterns and applies each one every 5ns. The module `monitor` prints the values of all inputs and outputs of the multiplexer whenever any of them change. The `sc_main()` function generates a VCD trace file and the simulation is run for 100ns.

```
// File: sync_mux41.h
#include "systemc.h"

SC_MODULE(sync_mux41) {
  sc_in<bool> clock, reset;
  sc_in<sc_uint<2> > sel;
  sc_in<sc_uint<4> > inp;
  sc_out<bool> out;
```

```
  void prc_sync_mux41();

  SC_CTOR(sync_mux41) {
    SC_METHOD(prc_sync_mux41);
    sensitive_pos << clock;
    sensitive_neg << reset;
  }
};

// File: sync_mux41.cpp
#include "sync_mux41.h"

void sync_mux41::prc_sync_mux41() {
  sc_uint<4> temp_inp;

  // Need to do this to access individual bits:
  temp_inp = inp.read();

  if (reset == 0)
    out = 0;
  else {
    if (sel.read() == 0)
      out = temp_inp[0];
    else if (sel.read() == 1)
      out = temp_inp[1];
    else if (sel.read() == 2)
      out = temp_inp[2];
    else
      out = temp_inp[3];
  }
}
```

Testbench

```
// File: sync_mux41_driver.h
#include "systemc.h"

SC_MODULE (driver) {
  sc_out<bool> d_reset;
  sc_out<sc_uint<2> > d_sel;
  sc_out<sc_uint<4> > d_inp;
```

```
  void prc_driver ();

  SC_CTOR (driver) {
    SC_THREAD (prc_driver);
  }
};

// File: sync_mux41_driver.cpp
#include "sync_mux41_driver.h"

void driver::prc_driver() {
  d_reset = 1;
  wait (7, SC_NS);
  d_reset = 0;

  for (int i = 0; i <= 20; i++) {
    d_inp = i;
    for (int j = 0; j <= 3; j++) {
      d_sel = j;
      wait (5, SC_NS);
    }
  }
}

// File: sync_mux41_monitor.h
#include "systemc.h"

SC_MODULE (monitor) {
  sc_in<bool> m_clock, m_reset;
  sc_in<sc_uint<2> > m_sel;
  sc_in<sc_uint<4> > m_inp;
  sc_in<bool> m_out;

  void prc_monitor ();

  SC_CTOR (monitor) {
    SC_METHOD (prc_monitor);
    sensitive << m_clock << m_reset <<
      m_sel << m_inp << m_out;
  }
};
```

```
// File: sync_mux41_monitor.cpp
#include "sync_mux41_monitor.h"


void monitor::prc_monitor() {
    cout << "At time " << sc_simulation_time() << "::";
    cout << "(clock, reset, sel, inp): ";
    cout << m_clock.read() << m_reset.read() <<
      m_sel.read() << m_inp.read();
    cout << "  out: " << m_out.read() << '\n';
}


// File: sync_mux41_main.cpp
#include "sync_mux41_driver.h"
#include "sync_mux41_monitor.h"
#include "sync_mux41.h"
const int CLOCK_PERIOD = 2;

int sc_main(int argc, char* argv[]) {
  sc_signal<bool> t_reset;
  sc_signal<sc_uint<4> > t_inp;
  sc_signal<sc_uint<2> > t_sel;
  sc_signal<bool> t_out;

  sc_clock t_clock("clock", CLOCK_PERIOD);
  // Since no time unit is specified for the clock
  // period, the default time unit of 1ns is used.

  // Instantiate the design under test:
  sync_mux41 m1 ("SyncMuxer4x1");
  m1.clock(t_clock);
  m1.reset(t_reset);
  m1.sel(t_sel);
  m1.inp(t_inp);
  m1.out(t_out);

  // Instantiate the driver:
  driver d1 ("GenerateWaveforms");
  d1.d_reset (t_reset);
  d1.d_sel (t_sel);
  d1.d_inp (t_inp);
```

```
    // Instantiate the monitor:
    monitor mo1 ("MonitorWaveforms");
    mo1.m_clock (t_clock);
    mo1.m_reset (t_reset);
    mo1.m_sel (t_sel);
    mo1.m_inp (t_inp);
    mo1.m_out (t_out);

    sc_trace_file *tf =
      sc_create_vcd_trace_file ("sync_mux41");
    sc_trace(tf, t_clock, "clock");
    sc_trace(tf, t_reset, "reset");
    sc_trace(tf, t_inp, "input");
    sc_trace(tf, t_sel, "select");
    sc_trace(tf, t_out, "output");

    // Run simulation for 100ns:
    sc_start(100, SC_NS);

    sc_close_vcd_trace_file (tf);
    return(0);
}
```

8.5.3 Full Adder

A full-adder module is described in Chapter 2. A testbench was also described in the same chapter. Here we describe another testbench for the same full-adder. This testbench reads the test stimuli from an input file and applies them one at a time with a delay of 5ns. The monitor process records the input and output values of the full-adder into an output file. A VCD trace file is also created.

Testbench

```
// File: full_adder_driver.h
#include <iostream.h>
#include <fstream.h>
#include "systemc.h"

SC_MODULE (driver) {
  sc_out<bool> d_a, d_b, d_cin;
  bool t_a, t_b, t_cin;
```

```
  ifstream infile;
  void driver_prc ();

  SC_CTOR (driver) {
    SC_THREAD (driver_prc);
    infile.open("full_adder.in");
    if (! infile) {
      cerr << "ERROR: Unable to open vector file," <<
          " fa_with_ha.in!\n";
      sc_stop();                  // Stop simulation.
    }
  }

  // Close the file in the destructor:
  ~ driver () {
    infile.close();
  }
};

// File: full_adder_driver.cpp
#include "full_adder_driver.h"

void driver::driver_prc() {
    sc_time apply_delay (5, SC_NS);
    // Read each line:
    while (infile >> t_a >> t_b >> t_cin) {
      d_a.write(t_a);
      d_b.write(t_b);
      d_cin.write(t_cin);
      wait (apply_delay);
    }
}
```

Note the use of sc_time declaration to specify a time value.

```
// File: full_adder_monitor.h
#include <fstream.h>
#include "systemc.h"

SC_MODULE (monitor) {
  sc_in<bool> m_a, m_b, m_cin, m_sum, m_cout;

  ofstream outfile;
  void monitor_prc ();
```

```
  SC_CTOR (monitor) {
    SC_METHOD (monitor_prc);
    sensitive << m_a << m_b << m_cin << m_sum << m_cout;
    outfile.open ("full_adder.out");
  }

  // Close the file in the destructor:
  ~ monitor () {
    outfile.close();
  }
};

// File: full_adder_monitor.cpp
#include "full_adder_monitor.h"

void monitor::monitor_prc() {
    outfile << "At time " << sc_time_stamp() << "::";
    outfile << "(a, b, carry_in): ";
    outfile << m_a << m_b << m_cin;
    outfile << "  (sum, carry_out): " << m_sum <<
      m_cout << '\n';
}

// File: full_adder_main.cpp
#include "full_adder_driver.h"
#include "full_adder_monitor.h"
#include "full_adder.h"

int sc_main(int argc, char* argv[]) {
  sc_signal<bool> t_a, t_b, t_cin, t_sum, t_cout;

  full_adder f1 ("FullAdderWithHalfAdder");
  // Positional association:
  f1 << t_a << t_b << t_cin << t_sum << t_cout;

  driver d1 ("GenerateWaveforms");
  d1 << t_a << t_b << t_cin;

  monitor mo1 ("MonitorWaveforms");
  mo1 << t_a << t_b << t_cin << t_sum << t_cout;
```

```
  if (! mo1.outfile) {
    cerr << "ERROR: Unable to open output file," <<
      " fa_with_ha.out!\n";

    return (-2);
  }

  sc_trace_file *tf =
    sc_create_vcd_trace_file ("full_adder");
  sc_trace(tf, t_a, "A");
  sc_trace(tf, t_b, "B");
  sc_trace(tf, t_cin, "CarryIn");
  sc_trace(tf, t_sum, "Sum");
  sc_trace(tf, t_cout, "CarryOut");

  sc_start(100, SC_NS);

  // The input and the output files are closed in the
  // destructors of the class to which they belong to.

  sc_close_vcd_trace_file (tf);
  return(0);
}
```

The input file `fa_with_ha.in` contains:

```
0 0 0
0 0 1
0 1 0
0 1 1
1 0 0
1 0 1
1 1 0
1 1 1
1 1 0
1 0 1
1 0 0
0 1 1
0 1 0
0 0 1
0 0 0
```

Here are the contents of the output file fa_with_ha.out after a simulation run.

```
At time 0ns::(a, b, carry_in): 000  (sum, carry_out): 00
At time 5ns::(a, b, carry_in): 001  (sum, carry_out): 00
At time 5ns::(a, b, carry_in): 001  (sum, carry_out): 10
At time 10ns::(a, b, carry_in): 010  (sum, carry_out): 10
At time 10ns::(a, b, carry_in): 010  (sum, carry_out): 00
At time 10ns::(a, b, carry_in): 010  (sum, carry_out): 10
At time 15ns::(a, b, carry_in): 011  (sum, carry_out): 10
At time 15ns::(a, b, carry_in): 011  (sum, carry_out): 00
At time 15ns::(a, b, carry_in): 011  (sum, carry_out): 01
At time 20ns::(a, b, carry_in): 100  (sum, carry_out): 01
At time 20ns::(a, b, carry_in): 100  (sum, carry_out): 11
. . .
```

8.5.4 Cycle-level Simulation

Here is a model of an and-or-invert logic gate and its testbench. The testbench shows how the methods sc_initialize() and sc_cycle() are used to perform cycle-level simulation. The sc_cycle() method simulates all the processes at the current time (which may take multiple delta cycles) and then advances the simulation time by the specified amount; in effect, it jumps to the time which is the current time plus the time argument specified in the method sc_cycle().

```
// File: aoi321.h
// And-Or-Invert 321 combinational logic gate.
#include "systemc.h"

SC_MODULE (aoi321) {
  sc_in<bool> a1, a2, a3, b1, b2, c;
  sc_out<bool> z;

  void aoi321_prc();

  SC_CTOR (aoi321) {
    SC_METHOD (aoi321_prc);
    sensitive << a1 << a2 << a3 << b1 << b2 << c;
  }
};
```

```
// File: aoi321.cpp
#include <iostream.h>
#include "aoi321.h"

void aoi321::aoi321_prc() {
  #ifdef DEBUG
    cout << "Debug: In aoi321_prc: " << endl;
    cout << a1 << a2 << a3 << endl;
  #endif

  z.write (!((a1 & a2 & a3) | (b1 & b2) | (c)));
}
```

Compiler directives, such as `#ifdef`, can be used for debugging purposes as shown.

```
// File: aoi321_main.cpp
#include "aoi321.h"

int sc_main (int argc, char *argv[]) {
  sc_signal<bool> aone, atwo, athree, bone, btwo,
    cee, zee;

  // Instantiate DUV before applying stimulus:
  aoi321 t1 ("aoi321");
  t1.a1 (aone);
  t1.a2 (atwo);
  t1.a3 (athree);
  t1.b1 (bone);
  t1.b2 (btwo);
  t1.c (cee);
  t1.z (zee);

// Tracing:
  sc_trace_file *tf =
    sc_create_vcd_trace_file ("aoi321out");
  sc_trace (tf, aone, "a1");
  sc_trace (tf, atwo, "a2");
  sc_trace (tf, athree, "a3");
  sc_trace (tf, bone, "b1");
  sc_trace (tf, btwo, "b2");
  sc_trace (tf, cee, "c");
  sc_trace (tf, zee, "z");
```

```
  // Generate waveform:
  sc_uint<6> ctr = 0;

  sc_initialize();

  for (int i = 0; i <= 100; i++) {
    ctr++;
    aone = ctr[0];
    atwo = ctr[1];
    athree = ctr[2];
    bone = ctr[3];
    btwo = ctr[4];
    cee = ctr[5];
    sc_cycle (2);
    cout << "At time " << sc_time_stamp() << ":: ";
    cout << "(a1, a2, a3, b1, b2, c): ";
    cout << aone << atwo << athree << bone << btwo << cee;
    cout << "   z: " << zee << endl;
    sc_cycle(1);
  }

  sc_close_vcd_trace_file (tf);
  return (0);
}
```

8.6 Statement Ordering within sc_main

SystemC is sensitive to the ordering of statements that appear within the function `sc_main()`. Basically the function is a sequential program, it executes sequentially, and so it expects certain things to be in sequence (even though module instantiations appear to be concurrent). All module instantiations and interconnections must appear before any trace calls. All trace calls should be set before simulation starts and after the trace file is opened.

No module instantiations can appear after a call to `sc_start()`.

If the default time resolution (of 1ps) is changed by using the method `sc_set_time_resolution()`, then the method must appear before any `sc_time` objects are created.

8.7 Tracing Aggregate Types

The `sc_trace()` methods are predefined for the SystemC types and other C++ scalar types. To trace an array or a structure type, you have to write your own overloaded `sc_trace()` method to trace values of its individual components.

Consider the following array declaration.

```
bool reg_file [NUM_BITS];
```

If you want to perform an `sc_trace()` function on the variable `reg_file`, you need to define an overloaded function of the following type.

```
const int MAXLEN = 8;

void sc_trace (sc_trace_file *tfile, bool *v,
               const sc_string& name, int arg_length) {
  char mybuf[MAXLEN];

  for (int j = 0; j < arg_length; j++) {
    sprintf (mybuf, "[%d]", j);
    sc_trace (tfile, v[j], name+mybuf);
  }
}
```

Having declared such a function, a trace call such as the following can be used.

```
sc_trace (tf, reg_file, "reg_file", NUM_BITS);
```

If you do not want to write a separate overloaded `sc_trace()` method, you could simply inline the above functionality into the `sc_main()` function itself instead of using the `sc_trace()` method on `reg_file`.

The `sc_trace()` function can be made generic to work on any array type by using a template. The following assumes that the element type of the array can be traced (using `sc_trace()`).

```
template <class T>
void sc_trace (sc_trace_file *tfile,
    const T array_var[], const sc_string &name,
    int arg_length) {
  for (int j = 0; j < arg_length; j++)
    sc_trace (tfile, array_var[j], name + "."
                + sc_string::to_string("%d", j));
}

// Examples of calls:
sc_signal<float> qms[4];
int mlef[8];

sc_trace (tfile, qms, "qms", 4);
sc_trace (tfile, mlef, "mlef", 8);
```

A structure can be traced similarly. Either write an overloaded `sc_trace()` method or simply write the `sc_trace()` calls on its individual members. If a signal is of a structure type, then an overloaded `sc_trace()` method along with other overloaded operators must be provided as explained in Section 3.12. Here we show what an overloaded `sc_trace()` function may look like for the following structure declaration.

```
// The structure:
struct packet {
  sc_uint<2> packet_id;
  bool packet_state;
};

// The overloaded sc_trace() method for type packet:
void sc_trace (sc_trace_file *tfile,
    const packet& v, const sc_string& name) {
  sc_trace (tfile, v.packet_id, name + ".packet_id");
  sc_trace (tfile, v.packet_state,
    name + ".packet_state");
}
```

With this function declaration, the following `sc_trace()` method call can be issued.

```
// An aggregate signal:
sc_signal <packet> saved;

sc_trace (tf, saved, "saved");
```

8.8 Tracing Enumeration Types

There is nothing special that SystemC provides to perform tracing of enumeration type values. Simply use C++ coding style. Here is one approach. For example, to trace an object of the following enumeration type:

```
enum fsm_state {IDLE, RESET, COUNT0,
                COUNT1, COUNT2, COUNT3};
```

create an array of strings representing each of the values in the enumeration type.

```
const char *fsm_state_strings[] = {"IDLE", "RESET",
  "COUNT0", "COUNT1", "COUNT2", "COUNT3"};
```

Note that the enumeration string names can be arbitrary, though it is recommended to keep these identical to the enumeration values so as to avoid confusion. The important correlation between the array of strings and the enumeration type is that there should be a positional correspondence, that is, the first enumeration value corresponds to the first string, the second value to the second string, and so on.

Note: Enumeration values are not standard values in a VCD file; your VCD viewer may or may not support viewing of such values.

Having defined these, now create an sc_trace() method.

```
void sc_trace (sc_trace_file *tfile,
    fsm_state curr_state, const sc_string &name,
    const char *fsm_state_strings[]) {
  sc_trace (tfile,
    fsm_state_strings[(unsigned int) curr_state],
    name);
}
```

Here is a call to this `sc_trace()` method.

```
fsm_state present_state;

sc_trace (tfile, present_state,
          "present_state", fsm_state_strings);
```

8.9 Exercises

1. Write a model for a N-by-M binary multiplier. Also write a testbench for the binary multiplier. Make it an interactive testbench by reading the operands from the keyboard and displaying the computed values to the output terminal.
2. Write a testbench for the pulse counter described in Section 5.8.
3. Write a Moore finite state machine model that detects a sequence "1101" on an input data stream. Write a testbench that tests this sequence detector.
4. Write a model for an up-down counter. The counter counts up by `UP` increments and counts down by `DOWN` increments. The counter also generates a parity output along with a carry/borrow bit.
5. Write a model for a BCD to seven segment decoder. Then write a testbench to test the model. Store the test input and expected output in a table within the testbench.
6. Write a testbench to test the 8-bit arithmetic logic unit described in Section 6.7.
7. Write a model for a stopwatch that displays hours, minutes and seconds. A reset button resets the watch to 0. Write a testbench to test the stopwatch.
8. Write a testbech for the UART transmitter block described in Section 7.9. Test the block to ensure that it works correctly. Use monitors and drivers and make it a self-testing testbench.

9. Write a model that generates a 6-tuple waveform. Each tuple is composed of a value and the number of clock cycles. The waveform is repeated optionally under the control of burst signal. You should be able to specify the waveform values at the time of instantiation of the model.

❑

CHAPTER

9

Modeling Beyond RTL

In the previous chapter, we saw many new features of modeling beyond SystemC RTL. In this chapter, we elaborate on some of these and describe additional new ones.

System designs require the modeling of communication and synchronization. This is provided in SystemC with concepts such as channels, interfaces and events that provide support for modeling of system design primitives such as queues, semaphores, memories and buses.

9.1 SC_THREAD Process

SystemC defines two[1] kinds of processes.

i. SC_METHOD, and

ii. SC_THREAD.

In previous chapters, we saw what an SC_METHOD process is and showed many examples of its usage. Basically, an SC_METHOD process has a sensitivity list associated with it and whenever an event occurs on a signal or a port in the sensitivity list, the process executes. In fact, it completes execution in the same time step (with no delays or waits) and returns control back to the simulation kernel. Thus such a process cannot suspend or contain an infinite loop. If the process were to contain an infinite loop, control would never be returned back to the simulation kernel. Figure 9-1 shows a more general view of a SystemC module. Notice that in addition to the two different kinds of processes, other methods are also allowed in a module as explained in Section 4.11.

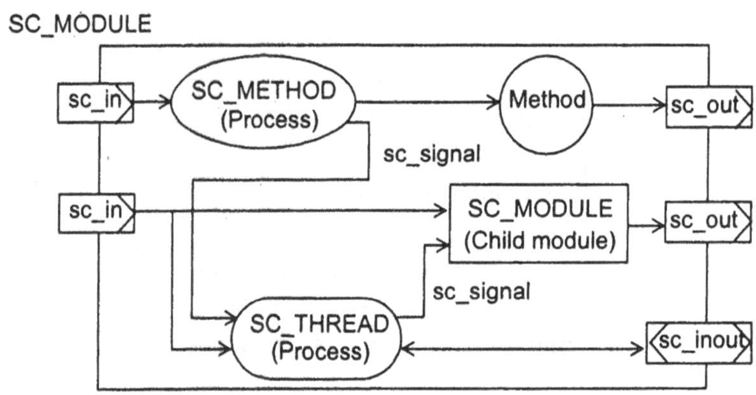

Figure 9-1 A SystemC module with SC_THREAD process.

1. In previous versions of SystemC, a third kind of process SC_CTHREAD also existed. It is a deprecated feature of the language and therefore is not described in this book.

Neither an SC_METHOD nor an SC_THREAD process can return a value.

We briefly introduced SC_THREAD processes in the previous chapter where it was used for specifying testbench behavior. An SC_THREAD process can be suspended and then made to resume execution based on a time delay or on a certain occurrence of an event. The `wait()` method is the primary mechanism used to suspend a process and can be used only in an SC_THREAD process. The `wait()` method causes the process to suspend, and the process reactivates from the statement where it was suspended and continues execution until the next `wait()` method. An SC_THREAD process can also have a sensitivity list, the list of events on which the `wait()` method triggers. The sensitivity list specification and the format and syntax of an SC_THREAD process is exactly the same as the SC_METHOD process except for the keyword SC_THREAD. Here is the format of an SC_THREAD process specification.

```
SC_THREAD (name_of_process);
sensitive << event_sensitivity_list;
sensitive_pos << edge_sensitivity_list;
sensitive_neg << edge_sensitivity_list;
```

We have already seen a number of examples of SC_THREAD process usage in the previous chapter on testbenches. Here is another example that has an SC_THREAD process. The process uses multiple `wait()` methods. The model increments or decrements a counter on every positive edge of `cp` depending on the control input `up`. Input `incr` specifies the amount to be incremented or decremented by.

```
// File: upc_wait.h
#include "systemc.h"
const int SIZE = 8;
const int INCR_SIZE = 3;

SC_MODULE (upc_wait) {
  sc_in<bool> cp, res, stop, up, ld;
  sc_in<sc_uint<SIZE> > din;
  sc_in<sc_uint<INCR_SIZE> > incr;
  sc_out<sc_uint<SIZE> > dout;

  void prc_upc_wait();
```

```
  SC_CTOR (upc_wait) {
    SC_THREAD (prc_upc_wait);
    sensitive_pos << cp;
  }
};

// File: upc_wait.cpp
#include "upc_wait.h"

void upc_wait::prc_upc_wait() {
  // Never gets out of the process:
  while (1) {
    wait();

    if (res)
      dout = 0;

    wait();

    if (ld)
      dout = din;

    while (! stop) {
      wait();

      if (up)
        dout = dout.read() + incr.read();
      else
        dout = dout.read() - incr.read();
    }
  }
}
```

At every `wait()` method, the process `prc_upc_wait` suspends and waits for a positive edge to occur on input `cp`.

Here is another example of an SC_THREAD process. The process computes the or-and-invert logic of the inputs and after a propagation delay assigns the value to the output.

```
// File: oai321.h
#include "systemc.h"
#define GATE_DELAY 5

SC_MODULE (oai321) {
  sc_in<bool> a1, a2, a3, b1, b2, c;
  sc_out<bool> z;

  void prc_oai321();

  SC_CTOR (oai321) {
    SC_THREAD(prc_oai321);
    sensitive << a1 << a2 << a3 << b1 << b2 << c;
  }
};

// File: oai321.cpp
#include "oai321.h"

void oai321::prc_oai321() {
  bool temp_z;

  while (true) {
    // Wait for an event in the sensitivity list.
    wait();
    temp_z = ~((a1 || a2 || a3) && (b1 || b2) && c);
    wait (GATE_DELAY, SC_NS);
    z = temp_z;
  }
}
```

The SC_THREAD process waits for an event to occur on any of the input ports specified in the sensitivity list. The required logic value is computed into a temporary variable `temp_z`. The process is suspended for the specified gate delay, in this case, 5ns. The temporary value is then assigned to the output `z`.

Before simulation starts, all SC_THREAD and SC_METHOD processes are executed once during the initialization phase.

An SC_THREAD process can only suspend and resume execution when it calls a `wait()` method. Such a process can never preempt when executing code between two `wait()` methods. Similarly, an

SC_METHOD process cannot be preempted. Once called, it completes execution and then returns control back to the simulator.

A typical SC_THREAD process has an infinite loop and at least one wait statement. This is because an SC_THREAD process is invoked only once and stays active until simulation completes. So if there is nothing to suspend the process, the process will terminate forever.

Consider the process `prc_oai321` of the or-and-invert logic described earlier. If the process is written without using any while loop and wait statement such as this:

```
void oai321::prc_oai321_1() {
  bool temp_z;

  temp_z = ~((a1 || a2 || a3) && (b1 || b2) && c);
  z = temp_z;
}
```

such an SC_THREAD process will execute all statements at beginning of simulation and then terminate forever. Subsequent events on the inputs do not cause any new change as the process is dead. If the process is changed to:

```
void oai321::prc_oai321_2() {
  bool temp_z;

  cout << a1 << a2 << a3 << b1 << b2 << c << endl;
  wait();
  temp_z = ~((a1 || a2 || a3) && (b1 || b2) && c);
  z = temp_z;
}
```

the process will execute the first statement upon start of simulation and then wait for an event to occur on a port that appears in its sensitivity list. When such an event occurs, the next two statements are executed and then the process terminates forever. Once again, subsequent changes on the inputs do not cause the process to execute as it has already been terminated. What is really required is a capability to loop back and wait again for a change on an input port. This is achieved by using an infinite wait loop.

Therefore, more often, the SC_THREAD process would have an infinite while loop, such as:

```
void oai321::prc_oai321_3() {
  bool temp_z;

  while (true) {
    wait ();
    temp_z = ~((a1 || a2 || a3) && (b1 || b2) && c);
    z = temp_z;
  }
}
```

So now at start of simulation, the SC_THREAD process waits for an event to occur on the process sensitivity list. It computes the output and then loops back to wait for an event to occur on the sensitivity list again; this really is the behavior of the logic.

9.2 Dynamic Sensitivity

Static sensitivity: the sensitivity of a process cannot be changed at runtime

In both kinds of processes that we have seen so far, the sensitivity list for the process is specified when the process is declared and the sensitivity list cannot be changed at runtime. This is called *static sensitivity* (specified using the `sensitive`, `sensitive_pos`, and `sensitive_neg` constructs).

Dynamic sensitivity can occur in SC_THREAD and SC_METHOD processes.

SystemC also supports *dynamic sensitivity*, that is, a process can be made to depend on events that are not specified in the sensitivity list. This is done using the more general form of the `wait()` method. In this way, the sensitivity of a process can be made dynamic, such as it could depend on a set of input values to occur, or a certain of set of signals to have events. Note that since we are talking about `wait()` methods, such methods can only be used with SC_THREAD processes.

Dynamic sensitivity can be achieved in an SC_METHOD process using the `next_trigger()` method. This is described in Section 9.6.4.

There are many different forms of the `wait()` method that are supported. These are listed next.

i. Wait for an event on static sensitivity list.

```
wait();
```

ii. Wait for an event.

```
wait (clk.posedge_event());
wait (reset.negedge_event());
// negedge_event() and posedge_event() methods can
// be applied to a signal or a port to identify the
// specific event.
```

iii. Wait for any event in a set of events.

```
wait (clk.posedge_event() |
      reset.negedge_event() |
      clear.value_changed_event());
// A value_changed_event() method is true when any
// value change occurs.
```

iv. Wait for events to occur on all set of events.

```
wait (clk.value_changed_event() &
      data.posedge_event() &
      ready.value_changed_event());
// The events can span over multiple simulation
// cycles. For example, if clk changes at 5ns,
// a positive edge on data occurs at 8ns and ready
// changes at 10ns, then the wait is triggered at
// time 10ns.
```

v. Wait for a certain time.

```
wait (20, SC_NS);
```

The events and the delays can be combined to form more complex `wait()` methods such as wait on an event for a specific time. An example follows.

```
wait (10, SC_NS, speed_ctrl.posedge_event());
// Waits for rising edge to occur on speed_ctrl
// for 10ns and then times out.
```

To wait for one delta, you can use one of:

```
wait (SC_ZERO_TIME);
wait (0, SC_NS);
```

The `posedge_event()` and `negedge_event()` methods can also be applied to a signal or a port of type `sc_logic`. A posedge event occurs when the value changes from a non-one to a one value. A negedge event occurs on a non-zero to zero transition.

```
sc_signal<sc_logic> sac;
sc_in<sc_logic> sync_reset;

// Wait for a positive transition on signal sac:
wait (sac.posedge_event());

// Wait for a negative transition on port sync_reset:
wait (sync_reset.negedge_event());
```

Use the `sc_event` type to explicitly declare an event.

An event can be declared explicitly by using the `sc_event` type. For example,

```
sc_event write_back;
```

declares an event called `write_back`. Having declared this, the event `write_back` can then be used with any wait statement or in any sensitivity list. For example,

```
// Event in sensitivity list:
sensitive << write_back;

// Event in a wait statement:
wait (write_back);
```

Such an explicit event can be triggered (event occurs) by using the `notify()` method (called *immediate event notification*). For example,

```
write_back.notify();
```

causes an event to occur on `write_back` immediately, that is, at the current simulation time (in the current delta cycle).

It is possible to delay the triggering of the event by specifying a delay value in the `notify()` method (called *delayed notification* or *timed event notification*). For example,

```
write_back.notify (20, SC_NS);
```

causes an event notification to be scheduled on `write_back` 20ns after the current simulation time.

To cause an event to occur in the next delta cycle, specify a zero delay explicitly. Note that signals and ports are always updated in the next delta cycle with their new values.

```
write_back.notify(SC_ZERO_TIME);
// Trigger event in next delta cycle.
```

An `sc_event` can have only one pending notification at any given time.

If multiple `notify()` methods are scheduled in the future (delayed notifications), only the `notify()` method with the smallest delay wins. A scheduled event, which has not yet occurred, can be cancelled by using the `cancel()` method.

```
write_back.cancel(); // Cancels a delayed notification.
```

An event is a fundamental synchronization primitive.

Events are the fundamental synchronization primitive in SystemC that do not have any type and do not transmit any value. An event transfers control from one process to another. An event notification causes sensitive processes to be resumed (a notification is treated as a change of value). Also an event notification can occur:

i. immediately, or

ii. a delta cycle later, or

iii. in a specific time in the future.

A `wait()` without any parameters is statically sensitive, while a `wait()` with arguments causes the static sensitivity to be temporarily overriden by the arguments of the `wait()` method. To combine both static and dynamic sensitivity in a `wait()`, include an event that identifies the static part as part of the `wait()` method. For example,

```
wait (timeout, clear.value_changed_event());
```

is statically sensitive to an event change on signal `clear`. If a `wait()` is statically sensitive to a large number of signals and if it is cumbersome to list all the signals in the `wait()` method, one approach would be to create a new event that gets notified every time there is an event on a signal in the static sensitivity list, and then use this new event in the `wait()` method. This is shown in the following example.

```
// File: large_static.h
#include "systemc.h"

SC_MODULE (large_static) {
  sc_in<bool> stat, bus1, ucint, adr_match;
  sc_in<bool> spi_clk, usb_rdy;

  void event_process();
  void another_process();

  sc_event static_list_event;

  SC_CTOR (large_static) {
    SC_METHOD (event_process);
    sensitive << stat << bus1 << ucint << adr_match;
    SC_THREAD (another_process);
    sensitive << spi_clk << usb_rdy;
  }
};

// File: large_satic.cpp
#include "large_static.h"

void large_static::event_process() {
  static_list_event.notify();
}
```

```
void large_static::another_process (){
  sc_time timeout (2, SC_MS);

  while (true) {
    wait (); // Wait for an event on spi_clk or usb_rdy.
    cout << "Found event on spi_clk or usb_rdy" << endl;

    wait (timeout); // Wait for timeout period (2ms).
    cout << "Waited for 2ms" << endl;

    wait (timeout, static_list_event); // Wait for
      // timeout or an event on stat, bus1, ucint or
      // adr_match.
    cout << "Either timed out or event occured on stat,",
         << " bus1, ucint or adr_match" << endl;
  }
}
```

9.3 Constructor Arguments

The SC_CTOR block is the constructor for the module.

The SC_CTOR macro does not accept any parameters other than the module name. This makes it inflexible when trying to model designs that need parameterized constructors. The parameterized constructor capability is provided in SystemC with a different macro, the SC_HAS_PROCESS macro.

In C++, a constructor is a method which has the same name as the class and can have any number of arguments.

When the SC_HAS_PROCESS macro is used, the macro and the constructor definition are specified separately. The name of the module is specified as an argument to the SC_HAS_PROCESS macro. The module constructor can have any number of arguments; however, one of the arguments to the constructor must be of type sc_module_name, and it is used to specify the module instance name. Here is the syntax.

```
SC_HAS_PROCESS (module_name);
// The constructor:
module_name (sc_module_name name_,
             <any number of other arguments>);
```

Here is an example of such usage. The example is rather simple but illustrates the usage of SC_HAS_PROCESS macro. The module is coded in a way to mimic the generate statement in VHDL.

Member initialization list is used to specify the name of the module.

```
// File: logic_gate.h
#include "systemc.h"
enum gate_type {AND_GATE, NAND_GATE, OR_GATE,
                NOR_GATE, XOR_GATE};

SC_MODULE (logic_gate) {
  sc_in<bool> a, b, c, d;
  sc_out<bool> z;

  void prc_and_gate();
  void prc_or_gate();
  void prc_nand_gate();
  void prc_nor_gate();
  void prc_xor_gate();

  SC_HAS_PROCESS (logic_gate);
  logic_gate (sc_module_name name, gate_type gate):
              sc_module(name) {
    switch (gate) {
      case AND_GATE:
        SC_METHOD (prc_and_gate);
        sensitive << a << b << c << d;
        break;
      case OR_GATE:
        SC_METHOD (prc_or_gate);
        sensitive <<a << b << c << d;
        break;
      case NAND_GATE:
        SC_METHOD (prc_nand_gate);
        sensitive <<a << b << c << d;
        break;
      case NOR_GATE:
        SC_METHOD (prc_nor_gate);
        sensitive <<a << b << c << d;
        break;
      case XOR_GATE:
        SC_METHOD (prc_xor_gate);
        sensitive <<a << b << c << d;
```

```
            break;
          }
        }
      };

      // File: logic_gate.cpp
      #include "logic_gate.h"

      void logic_gate::prc_and_gate() {
        z = a & b & c & d;
      }

      void logic_gate::prc_or_gate() {
        z = a | b | c | d;
      }

      void logic_gate::prc_nand_gate() {
        z = !(a & b & c & d);
      }

      void logic_gate::prc_nor_gate() {
        z = !(a | b | c | d);
      }

      void logic_gate::prc_xor_gate() {
        z = a ^ b ^ c ^ d;
      }
```

The module `logic_gate` can be instantiated in another module by passing various arguments during its construction, such as:

```
logic_gate *p1, *p2;
. . .
SC_CTOR (. . .) {
  p1 = new logic_gate ("p1", AND_GATE);
  p2 = new logic_gate ("p2", XOR_GATE);
  . . .
}
```

Module inheritance and derived modules.

Allowing a module constructor to have arbitrary arguments supports an important feature of SystemC, that of *module inheritance*. This is achieved by writing a derived module in the following fashion.

```
SC_MODULE (base_module) {
  . . .
  SC_CTOR (base_module) {
    . . .
  }
};
```

It is important to specify the access specifier `public`.

Member initialization list is used in the derived module constructor.

```
class derived_module: public base_module {
  public:
  . . .
  void prc_derived_module();
  SC_HAS_PROCESS (derived_module);

  // Declare member variables:
  <some_type> member_var1, member_var2;

  // New constructor with arguments:
  derived_module (sc_module_name name,
      <some_type> arg1, <some_type> arg2, . . .):
      base_module (name),
       member_var1 (arg1), member_var2 (arg2), . . . {
    SC_THREAD (prc_derived_module);
    . . .
  }
};
```

Member initialization list is used in the derived module constructor to specify the value of the member variables. Such initialization is useful for setting constant members and for passing parameters to the constructors of derived class member objects as well as to base class constructors.

Avoid multiple inheritance with `sc_module` class as it is not a virtual base class.

Here is an example of a `generic_alu` module from which a derived module `specific_alu` is written. The `specific_alu` module can be instantiated in another module or directly in a testbench; in this example, instantiation in the testbench function `sc_main()` is shown. The `generic_alu` module performs four functions: addition, subtraction, multiplication and division. The `enable_mask` member variable determines the functionality of the arithmetic logic unit. Each bit of the `enable_mask` variable controls one of the operations. For example, if the value of the enable_mask is 0x3, then the arithmetic logic unit does only addition and subtraction. If no bits of the enable_mask are set, the output contains all 'X' values.

```
// File: generic_alu.h
#include "systemc.h"
const int DATA_SIZE = 8;
const int NUM_OPS = 4;
enum op_type {add_op, sub_op, mul_op, div_op};

SC_MODULE (generic_alu) {
  sc_in<sc_uint<DATA_SIZE> > a, b;
  sc_in<op_type> select;
  // Output has to be of the logic vector type since it
  // can have the value 'X'.
  sc_out<sc_lv<DATA_SIZE> > z;

  // Member variable controls the kind of ALU:
  sc_uint<NUM_OPS> enable_mask;
  void prc_alu();

  SC_CTOR (generic_alu) {
    SC_METHOD (prc_alu);
    sensitive << a << b;
    enable_mask = 0xF;
  }
};

// File: generic_alu.cpp
#include "generic_alu.h"

void generic_alu::prc_alu() {
  sc_lv<DATA_SIZE> allxs (SC_LOGIC_X);

  switch (select) {
    case add_op:
      z = (enable_mask & 0x1) ? a.read() + b.read():
            allxs; break;
    case sub_op:
      z = (enable_mask & 0x2) ? a.read() - b.read():
            allxs; break;
```

```
    case mul_op:
      z = (enable_mask & 0x4) ? a.read() * b.read():
            allxs; break;
    case div_op:
      z = (enable_mask & 0x8) ? a.read() / b.read():
            allxs; break;
  }
}

// File: specific_alu.h
#include "generic_alu.h"

class specific_alu: public generic_alu {
  public:
    SC_HAS_PROCESS (specific_alu);
    specific_alu (sc_module_name nm,
          sc_uint<NUM_OPS> mask): generic_alu (nm) {
      enable_mask = mask;
    }
};

// File: main.cpp
#include "specific_alu.h"

int sc_main (int argc, char *argv[]) {
  // An ALU with all four operations:
  generic_alu g1 ("alu_g1");

  // An ALU with only addition and subtraction:
  specific_alu s1 ("alu_s1", 0x3);

  // An ALU with just multiplication:
  specific_alu s2 ("alu_s2", 0x8);
  . . .
  return 0;
}
```

9.4 More Examples

9.4.1 Greatest Common Divisor

Here is an example of an untimed functional model. No clock information is provided. The module computes the greatest common divisor of the two input values and returns the result any time the two input values change. The input `reset` causes it to reset the result value to 0.

```
// File: gcd.h
#include "systemc.h"
const int WIDTH = 16;

SC_MODULE (gcd) {
  sc_in<sc_uint<WIDTH> > first, second;
  sc_in<bool> reset;
  sc_out<sc_uint<WIDTH> > result;

  void prc_gcd();

  SC_CTOR (gcd) {
    SC_METHOD(prc_gcd);
    sensitive << first << second << reset;
  }
};

// File: gcd.cpp
#include "gcd.h"

void gcd::prc_gcd() {
  sc_uint<WIDTH> fopd, sopd;

  fopd = first.read();
  sopd = second.read();

  if ((fopd == 0) | (sopd == 0) | reset)
    result = 0;
  else {
    while (fopd != sopd)
      if (fopd > sopd)
        fopd = fopd - sopd;
```

```
        else
          sopd = sopd - fopd;

      result = fopd;
    }
  }
```

9.4.2 Filter

Here is a model of a filter that describes its cycle-accurate behavior. The behavior at each clock boundary is explicitly identified. So it takes seven clock cycles to compute the output.

```
// File: filter.h
#include "systemc.h"
const int PRECISION = 16;

SC_MODULE (filter) {
  sc_in<sc_uint<PRECISION> > xin, xd1, xd2, xd3;
  sc_in<bool> clk;
  sc_out<sc_uint<PRECISION> > yout;

  void prc_filter();

  SC_CTOR (filter) {
    SC_THREAD (prc_filter);
    sensitive_pos << clk;
  }
};

// File: filter.cpp
#include "filter.h"
const int k0 = 0x39;
const int k1 = 0x50;
const int k2 = 0x30;
const int k3 = 0x41;

void filter::prc_filter() {
  sc_uint<PRECISION> y1, y2, y3, y4;
```

```
    // Keep computing the output:
    while (1) {
      wait();
      y1 = k0 * xin.read();
      wait();
      y2 = k1 * xd1.read();
      wait();
      y3 = y1 + y2;
      wait ();
      y1 = k2 * xd2.read();
      wait();
      y2 = k3 * xd3.read();
      wait();
      y4 = y1 + y2;
      wait();
      yout = y3 + y4;
    }
  }
```

9.5 Ports, Interfaces and Channels

In SystemC RTL modeling, ports and signals were used and described in the form that apply within a hardware context. Such a hardware signal or port is not sufficient for modeling at the system level. There is a need to model architectures where several modules communicate using queues, or where several processes execute concurrently and share global data (shared variables) using mutexes. SystemC provides a more general behavior for ports and signals.

A signal is a form of a *channel*. To be precise, a signal is a primitive channel. Figure 9-2 shows the same figure as Figure 9-1 but shows the signals as channels. An instance port connects to a channel (signal), an SC_THREAD process reads the value of a channel and an output of a process is connected to a channel (signal). A port is able to read from and write to the channel (signal) using the `read()` and `write()` methods (the channel's interface).

In a generalized *port*, a port can be associated with an arbitrary number of access methods; the set of access methods is defined by an interface. A channel implements the interface. That is, the definitions of the

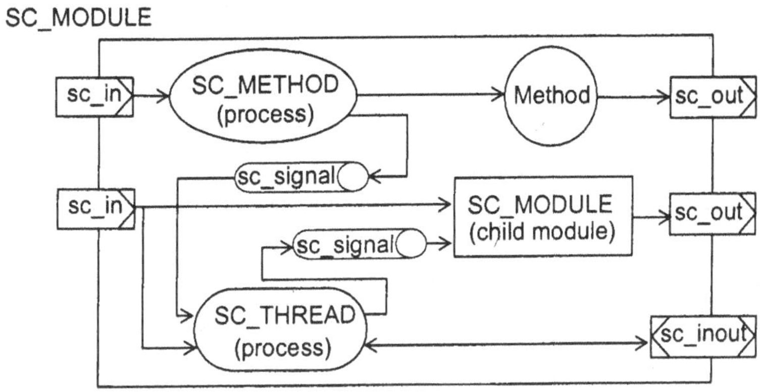

Figure 9-2 A SystemC module with channels.

methods declared in the interface is described in the channel. Figure 9-3 provides a generalized view of a port, its interface and its connection to a channel.

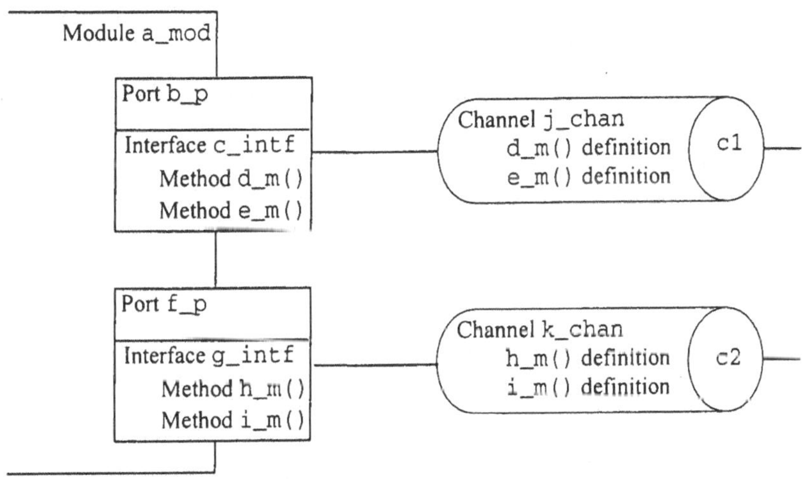

Figure 9-3 Ports, interfaces and channels.

Module `a_mod` has two ports `b_p` and `f_p`. Port `b_p` can only access methods `d_m()` and `e_m()` that are specified in the interface `c_intf` that port `b_p` is associated with. The interfaces `c_intf` and `g_intf` contain the declarations of these methods. The channels j_chan and k_chan contain the definitions of these methods. Here is a module declaration.

```
SC_MODULE (a_mod) {
  sc_port <c_intf<int> > b_p;
  sc_port <g_intf<bool> > f_p;
  sc_in <bool> clock;
  sc_out <sc_uint<4> > count;
  . . .
```

The module declaration contains four port declarations, two of these are the generalized port declarations and two are the built-in primitive ports. The port declaration for f_p specifies that the access methods defined by the interface g_intf is associated with it. In general, a port is declared using sc_port of a specific interface.

```
sc_port <interface_name> port_name;
```

port_name is a port that exhibits the interface behavior as specified by the interface name. That is, the port can access the methods specified by the interface and consequently can access the channel that is associated with that interface.

Accessing the methods is done using the -> operator, such as:

```
b_p->d_m()
f_p->i_m()
```

You can also define derived port types. Here is an example.

```
template <class T>
class z_port: public sc_port<c_intf<T> >
{
public:
  // Derived class methods here.
};
```

With this template definition, you can define a port of type z_port. For example:

```
z_port<bool> reset;
```

sc_port also provides a multi-port capability. The format of declaring such a multi-port is:

```
sc_port <interface_name, NUM_PORTS> port_name;
```

The size() method can be applied to a multi-port to determine the number of ports.

where NUM_PORTS is a positive integer constant indicating the number of sub ports in the multi-port. For example,

```
sc_port <c_intf<int>, 8> bit_map;
```

defines a 8-port multi-port called bit_map. Each sub port can be accessed by specifying its index, for example,

```
bit_map[2]->d_m()
```

In C++, a class containing or inheriting one or more virtual functions is called an *abstract base class*.

An *interface* is an abstract base class in C++ that inherits from the class sc_interface. An interface specifies a set of access methods without providing its definitions. The definitions are provided in the channel description. Here is how an interface can be specified.

```
template <class T>
class c_intf: public virtual sc_interface
  // c_intf is the name of interface.
{
public: // Specify virtual function declarations.
  virtual int d_m ( . . .) = 0;
  virtual bool e_m (. . .) = 0;
};
```

A *channel* is an object that serves as a container for communication and synchronization. A channel implements one or more interfaces. Here is how a channel definition may look like.

```
template <class T>
class k_chan:         // Name of channel.
  public sc_module,
  public g_intf       // Names of one or more interfaces
                      // that the channel is implementing.
{
public:
  virtual int h_m (. . .) {
    . . .
  }
  virtual bool i_m (. . .) {
    . . .
  }
  . . .
};
```

Multiple channels can implement the same interface.

A channel is declared much as a signal is declared.

```
j_chan<int> c1;          // Creates a channel called c1.
k_chan<bool> c2;         // Channel called c2.
```

Connecting channels to ports is just like connecting signals to ports.

```
a_mod.b_p (c1);
a_mod.f_p (c2);
```

There are two kinds of channels.

- *Primitive channels* are atomic in nature. They do not contain processes and cannot access other channels.
- *Hierarchical channels* are modules that implement interfaces. They can have ports and they can contain processes, module instances, and can access other channels.

The primitive channels are:

i. `sc_signal<T>`: The basic signal that is part of SystemC RTL.

ii. `sc_signal_rv<N>`: The resolved vector logic signal.

iii. `sc_signal_resolved`: The resolved scalar logic signal.

iv. `sc_fifo<T>`: Models a fifo (first-in, first-out) register.

v. `sc_mutex`: Used to model shared variables.

vi. sc_semaphore: Similar to sc_mutex.

vii. sc_buffer<T>: Same as sc_signal except that an event is generated even if the new value being assigned is identical to the previous value.

A hierarchical channel not only defines the interfaces, but it can also contain other channels and modules including shared data. A hierarchical channel is a module. Here is the syntax of a general template of a channel.

```
template <class T>
class channel_name :
  public sc_channel,
  public interface1,
  public interface2
{
public:
  // Data members
    // Can be ports, channels or variables.
  // Constructor:
    // Contains instantiation of other channels,
    // modules and processes.
  // Interface method definitions (interface1,
  // interface2)
private:
  // Data members
protected:
  // Data members
};
```

An example of a hierarchical channel is sc_clock. It has interfaces such as posedge_event() and negedge_event() that clock objects can access. In addition, it contains a process to generate the clock waveform.

9.6 Advanced Topics

9.6.1 Shared Data Members

Data member variables declared in a SC_MODULE class can be shared amongst more than one processes. Such data members represent storage for the module class.

```
SC_MODULE (members_only) {
  . . .
  // Examples of data members:
  int count;
  bool flag;
  sc_uint<5> bus_active;
  . . .
  SC_CTOR (members_only) {
    SC_METHOD (prc_a);
    . . .
    SC_THREAD (prc_b);
    . . .
    SC_THREAD (prc_c);
    . . .
  }
};
```

Care must be taken when there are multiple processes reading and writing to the data members. This is because of two reasons.

i. Assignment to a variable occurs instantaneously, that is, without a delay.

ii. The execution ordering of multiple processes is not defined.

For example, it could happen that process `prc_a` reads the variable `flag` before process `prc_b` writes to it, which is not what you may desire. A process execution order cannot be forced. What if two processes write to a variable and a third process reads it? What value would the third process see? Mechanisms such as semaphores can be used to ensure that shared variables are written to and read from in a well-defined manner. Of course, the simplest use of such variables is where only one process reads and writes to it and the variable holds it value between multiple invocations of that process.

9.6.2 Fixed Point Types

SystemC defines signed and unsigned fixed point types that can be used to model floating point literals at the hardware level. These fixed point types can be used in digital signal processing software and can be used to model fixed point hardware as well. The fixed point types support features such as modeling quantization and overflow behavior.

The four types are:

i. `sc_fixed`
ii. `sc_ufixed`
iii. `sc_fix`
iv. `sc_ufix`

Types `sc_fixed` and `sc_fix` are signed fixed point types, while types `sc_ufixed` and `sc_ufix` are unsigned fixed point types. For types `sc_fixed` and `sc_ufixed`, the size and functionality of such an object is known or can be determined at compile time. For types `sc_fix` and `sc_ufix`, the size can be specified using a variable and therefore is known only during simulation.

The above types can be of arbitrary precision. However, to achieve faster simulation time, it may be sufficient to model using limited precision fixed point types. SystemC provides four such limited precision types. These are:

i. `sc_fixed_fast`
ii. `sc_ufixed_fast`
iii. `sc_fix_fast`
iv. `sc_ufix_fast`

The usage of these types and the description of its arguments are beyond the scope of this book. More information on these can be obtained from [Bibliography - 20.].

9.6.3 Module

So far we have seen that a module can be written using the SC_MODULE macro, for example:

```
SC_MODULE (module_name) {
. . .
```

Alternately, a module can be written by explicitly declaring the derived class from the base class `sc_module`, such as:

The access specifier `public` must be used.

```
class module_name : public sc_module {
  public:
  . . .
```

A template class can be created of the form:

```
template <class T>
class module_name: public sc_module {
  public:
  . . .
```

9.6.4 Other Methods

Here are some of the other useful methods available in SystemC.

i. `end_of_elaboration()`: This method is allowed for modules, channels and ports. The body of this method is empty to begin with but can be defined by the user to perform whatever task he or she chooses. This method is called before simulation starts.

ii. `initialize()`: Applies to output ports (`sc_out` and `sc_inout`) only. It allows for unbound output ports to be initialized in the constructor.

```
SC_MODULE (mod_cpu) {
 // The output port:
 sc_out<int> out_a;

 void cpu_behavior () { . . . }

 SC_CTOR (mod_cpu) {
   // Initialize the port:
   out_a.initialize(0x56);
   SC_METHOD (cpu_behavior);
   . . .
 }
};
```

An alternate way to initialize an output port is to use the `end_of_elaboration()` method. If the module has an SC_THREAD process, then the outputs can be initialized prior to the while loop in the process or can appear as the very first statements in the process. Here is the above example rewritten assuming that `cpu_behavior` is an SC_THREAD process.

```
void mod_cpu::cpu_behavior () {
  out_a = 0x56;

  while (true) {
    . . .
  }
}
```

iii. `sc_get_time_resolution()`: This method returns a value of type `sc_time` with the current time resolution.

```
sc_time t_res;
t_res = sc_get_time_resolution();

cout << "The time resoltion is "
      << sc_get_time_resolution() << endl;
```

This method can be used to convert an `sc_time` value to a value of type `double`.

```
double time_in_dbl;
sc_time time_res = sc_get_time_resolution();
sc_time curr_time = sc_time_stamp();

time_in_dbl = curr_time / time_res;
cout << "Time as a double value is "
      << time_in_dbl << endl;
```

The same effect can be achieved by simply using the `sc_simulation_time()` method.

```
time_in_dbl = sc_simulation_time();
cout << "Time is " << time_in_dbl << endl;
```

iv. `sc_set_default_time_unit()`: The default time unit is 1ns. This method explicitly specifies a time unit. The value specified must be a power of ten and must be larger than the time resolution. This method if used, has to be specified prior to start of simulation.

```
sc_set_default_time_unit (100, SC_PS);

sc_set_default_time_unit (10, SC_NS);
```

v. `sc_get_default_time_unit()`: This method returns the current time unit as a `sc_time` value.

```
sc_time t_unit;
t_unit = sc_get_default_time_unit();
```

vi. `next_trigger()`: This method can be used in an SC_METHOD process to achieve dynamic sensitivity. The method takes the same arguments as those of the `wait()` method. It does not cause the process to suspend but schedules the next trigger of the process in the future. Only one `next_trigger()` is honored for a process even though multiple `next_trigger()` methods may be present and executed in a process; the last one executed is the one recognized. While a `next_trigger()` event is in effect, static sensitivity is turned off.

The `next_trigger()` method is non-blocking, that is, it does not stop the flow of execution but schedules the future process trigger.

```
// Wake up SC_METHOD process after 10ns:
next_trigger (10, SC_NS);

// Wake up SC_METHOD process on a rising edge
// of reset:
next_trigger (reset.posedge_event());
```

vii. `timed_out()`: This method can be used in conjunction with the `wait()` and `next_trigger()` methods to check if a time out occurred or not.

viii. `dont_initialize()`: All processes (SC_METHOD and SC_THREAD) are by default executed once before simulation starts. In some cases, you may not want to perform this initial execution of a process. This can be achieved quite easily for an SC_THREAD process by using an additional `wait();` statement as the very first statement in the process. The `dont_initialize()` method can be used to achieve the same effect in either an SC_METHOD or an SC_THREAD process. The method appears right after the SC_THREAD or SC_METHOD process declaration to which it applies.

```
SC_CTOR ( module_name ) {
  SC_METHOD (prc_a);
  sensitive << reset << stop;
  dont_initialize();

  SC_THREAD (prc_b);
  sensitive << start;
  dont_initialize();

  // Processes prc_a and prc_b do not execute
  // once before simulation starts.
  . . .
}
```

Be careful when using the `dont_initialize()` method with SC_THREAD processes. Make sure that the SC_THREAD process can be woken up due to some event; in the above example, an event on signal `start` will execute the process `prc_b`. Or else, the SC_THREAD process may never execute.

ix. `name()`: This method can be used to obtain the hierarchical name of any module. The `basename()` method can be used to obtain the base name of the module.

```
cout << "I am in module " << name() << endl;
// Would print, for example:
I am in module read_vectors_rv.read_blk
```

x. `kind()`: The `kind()` method can be applied to a port to find its direction.

```
cout << "First port is of kind " << read_clk.kind()
     << endl;
cout << "Second port is of kind " << clear.kind()
     << endl;
// Would print, for example:
First port is of kind sc_in
Second port is of kind sc_out
```

xi. `sc_get_curr_process_handle()`: Using this method, the hierarchical name of the currently executing process can be accessed.

```
#include "systemc/kernel/sc_simcontext.h"

cout << "I am in process "
  << sc_get_curr_process_handle()->name() << endl;
// Would print, for example:
I am in process read_vectors_rv.prc_read_vectors
```

xii. `simcontext()`: Using this method, the kind of process being executed can be determined.

```
#include "systemc/kernel/sc_simcontext.h"

switch (simcontext()->get_curr_proc_info()->kind)
{
  case SC_METHOD_PROC_ :
    cout << "Inside a SC_METHOD process" << endl;
    break;
  case SC_THREAD_PROC_ :
    cout << "Inside a SC_THREAD process" << endl;
    break;
  default :
    cout << "Not an SC_METHOD or SC_THREAD process"
          << endl; break;
}
```

9.7 Simulation Algorithm

Before describing the simulation algorithm, let us try to understand the timing model of SystemC. SystemC simulation is event-based, that is, all activities are triggered by events (for example, a change of value) which in turn cause additional events to occur. Also all events occur at certain times associated with a simulation time. Each simulation time is composed of a variable number of time steps, where each time step corresponds to a delta delay. This is shown in Figure 9-4. A delta delay is an infinitesimally small (zero) delay. It is not a real delay but an abstract delay used to model the "cause and effect" behavior of hardware logic. An activity (an execution of a process) at time 2ns for example, can cause additional events to occur at 2+1Δns, activity at 2+1Δns can cause additional events to occur at 2+2Δns, and so on. A number of such iterations (delta cycles) may be needed until the system reaches a stable state for that particular simulaion time. It is possible that there may be no events at certain times, for example at times 1ns and 3ns.

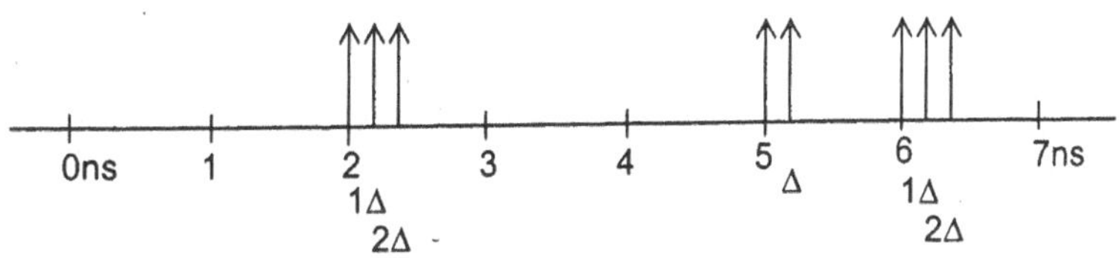

Figure 9-4 Simulation time and delta delays.

SystemC defines the following steps for simulation.

- *Step 1*: (Initialization phase) Execute all processes (SC_METHOD and SC_THREAD) in an arbitrary order. Each SC_METHOD process is executed once. Each SC_THREAD process is executed until it suspends.

The selection of a process is unspecified by the language and hence the order in which the processes are actually run in not known apriori.

- *Step 2*: (Evaluate phase) From the list of processes that are ready to run, select a process and resume its execution. This may cause immediate event notifications that may cause other processes to be ready to run in this same phase.
- *Step 3*: Repeat previous step for all processes that are ready to run.
- *Step 4*: (Update phase) Update signals or channels with the values that were assigned in Step 2.
- *Step 5*: If there are any pending delayed notifications for the current time, determine which processes are ready to run and go to Step 2.
- *Step 6*: If there are no more events in the future (or timed notifications), simulation is done.
- *Step 7*: Else, advance the current simulation time to the time of the next pending event.
- *Step 8*: Determine which processes are ready to run at the current time and go to Step 2.

Non-determinism is present in SystemC due to the random execution of the processes that are ready to run. Typically in a safe design, the behavior should be independent of the order in which the processes are executed.

9.8 Exercises

1. Write a model for a digital clock that has two seven segment LEDs for seconds, two for minutes and two for hours. The input to the digital clock is a clock with a time period of one second and a reset signal that resets all the digits to 0. First build an 8-bit counter that counts from 0 to 59 (mod 60). The lower four bits are for the unit digit and the upper four bits are for the tens digits. Hook up three 8-bit counters to model seconds, minutes and hours - output of the seconds counter drives the minutes counter - output of the minutes counter drives the hours counter. Attach a BCD decoder to the output of the counters to drive the seven segment LEDs. Write a testbench to test out the digital clock.
   For adventurous readers: Rig up a graphical user interface application

(for example, using Tcl/Tk) that displays the clock value and also has a reset button on it. Link it with the design and demonstrate that it works.

2. Write a model that computes an inverse of a matrix. The model has one input port though which the input matrix is passed and has one output port on which the computed result appears. A matrix is represented as a two-dimensional boolean array.
3. Write a model for a RAM memory using a parameterized constructor in which the size of the RAM is specified as constructor arguments.
4. Write a model for a logic unit that performs vector operations. The logic unit has two inputs which are pointers to the vectors with integer values. The result is passed back via a pointer to a vector. The length of the vectors is also passed in. The logic unit performs three operations based on a control signal: addition, subtraction and multiplication.
   For adventurous readers: Modify the model so that the logic unit can also work with vectors of float values.
5. Write a model for a FIFO as described in Section 5.8 but this time using a push clock and a pop clock, where both clocks are asynchronous to each other. Also extend the model to store elements of any class. Write a testbench to test this FIFO model.

❑

APPENDIX

A

Runtime Environment

This chapter describes how to install the SystemC software available at the `http://www.systemc.org` web site. In addition, it shows how to compile and simulate your design. The procedures described here are only for a machine running Solaris UNIX operating system. Equivalent commands can be issued on other host machines.

A.1 Software Installation

Here are the steps you can use to install a Solaris release.

i. Click on `"Download Now"`. Log into your account. If you do not have an account, click `"Create New Account"`.

ii. Under `"File List"`, save the file `systemc-2.0.1.tgz` into a directory.

iii. **cd** to the directory where the file is saved and **gunzip** `systemc-2.0.1.tgz`.

iv. **tar -xvf** `systemc-2.0.1.tar`
This will create the `system-2.0.1` directory with everything else below it.

v. Read the `README` file under the `systemc-2.0.1` directory.

vi. Read the `INSTALL` file under the `systemc-2.0.1` directory and follow instructions for installing on UNIX.

vii. See the instructions in the `INSTALL` file on how to run the pre-provided examples that come as part of the release and compile and simulate a couple of them.

viii. Read the RELEASENOTES file.

A.2 Compiling your Design

Here are the steps for compiling your design written in SystemC.

i. Create a directory and place your SystemC design files.

ii. Copy `Makefile.defs` from `<installed_dir>/systemc-2.0.1/examples/systemc` to your current directory. Set the `SYSTEMC` variable in `Makefile.defs` to point to the right location. It should be set to:

```
SYSTEMC=<installed_dir>/systemc-2.0.1
```

iii. Copy a make file `Makefile.gcc` from any of the examples in the `<installed_dir>/systemc-2.0.1/examples` directory (say the example `pipe` from the `<installed_dir>/systemc-2.0.1/examples/systemc/pipe` directory).

iv. Edit the make file `Makefile.gcc` to make sure that the path to `Makefile.defs` is set correctly - change it if it is not.

v. Specify the name of the executable in:

```
MODULE = <executable_name>
# The executable created is <executable_name>.x
```

vi. List all the cpp files under SRCS.

```
SRCS = fileA.cpp fileB.cpp fileC.cpp
```

vii. Use the appropriate CFLAGS depending on whether you want debug option to be set or not.

viii. To compile, type:

```
(bond-jbhasker): make -f Makefile.gcc
```

You will need C++ knowledge to debug any error messages reported by the C++ compiler. Here is the Makefile.gcc for the full_adder test-bench that is described in Chapter 2.

```
TARGET_ARCH = gccsparcOS5

CC     = g++
OPT    = -O3
DEBUG  = -g
OTHER  = -Wall
CFLAGS = $(OPT) $(OTHER)
# CFLAGS = $(DEBUG) $(OTHER)

MODULE = fa_with_ha.run
SRCS = half_adder.cpp full_adder.cpp driver.cpp \
       monitor.cpp main.cpp
OBJS = $(SRCS:.cpp=.o)

include ../Makefile.defs
```

Upon make, the executable created is fa_with_ha.run.x.

A.3 Simulating your Design

Simulating the design is done by simply invoking the executable produced by the make process. For example,

```
(bond-jbhasker): fa_with_ha.run.x
```

simulates the full_adder testbench. The amount of time that the simulation runs is dictated by the simulation commands in the testbench such as those specified by the methods sc_start() and sc_stop(). If any trace files are created and logged, these are also produced now.

A.4 Debugging

You can debug your SystemC design by first compiling them using the debug mode. Then using gdb (or your favorite C++ debugger), you can bring up a module in your design, set a breakpoint in a process (in one or more) and run the executable created by the make file. Try avoiding going into the SystemC kernel core as you might get lost if you are not familiar with the core.

You can also debug by printing messages to your screen, including variable values and simulation times (using method sc_time_stamp()), as shown in a number of examples in this book.

If you get an internal error, that is, an error in the SystemC code, for example,

```
/home/jbhasker/SYSTEMC/systemc-2.0.1/include/systemc/
communication/sc_port.h:248: failed assertion
'm_interface != 0'
Abort(coredump)
```

here is what you can do. Recompile your program with the debug option turned on (use the CLAGS with DEBUG). Run the executable under the debugger. When the debugger stops, the stack information in the debugger can help you identify the culprit or provide additional insight into the error message. Here is an example of a debug run (an assignment to an output was added in the constructor of the driver module to cause the error, such an output assignment in not allowed in SystemC).

```
(bond-jbhasker):gdb fa_with_ha.run.x
GNU gdb 4.18
. . .
(gdb) run
Starting program: /home/jbhasker/MYDIR/fa_with_ha/
fa_with_ha.run.x

/home/jbhasker/SYSTEMC/systemc-2.0.1/include/systemc/
communication/sc_port.h:248: failed assertion
'm_interface != 0'

Program received signal SIGABRT, Aborted.
0xff2981cc in _libc_kill () from /usr/lib/libc.so.1

(gdb) bt
#0  0xff2981cc in _libc_kill () from /usr/lib/libc.so.1
#1  0xff239450 in abort () from /usr/lib/libc.so.1
#2  0xac86c in Letext ()
#3  0xb1c94 in sc_port_b<sc_signal_inout_if<bool>
>::operator-> (
this=0xffbee288) at ../../../../src/systemc/communica-
tion/sc_port.h:248
#4  0xb1bb8 in sc_out<bool>::operator=
(this=0xffbee288, value_=@0xffbee064)
at /home/jbhasker/SYSTEMC/systemc-2.0.1/include/sys-
temc/communication/sc_signal_ports.h:1425
#5  0xb2d44 in driver::driver (this=0xffbee230) at
main.cpp:22
#6  0x52e0c in sc_main (argc=1, argv=0xffbeef24) at
main.cpp:49
#7  0x542d4 in main (argc=1, argv=0xffbeef24)
at ../../../../src/systemc/kernel/sc_main.cpp:69

(gdb)
```

The problem can be tracked to line 22 of `main.cpp`, which contains the culprit assignment in the module constructor.

```
SC_CTOR (driver) {
  SC_THREAD (prc_driver);
  d_a = 0;                          // Line 22, main.cpp.
}
```

In certain cases, it may be of some help to put a breakpoint at the function sc_stop_here(), which is a function within the simulation kernel, and check the stack backtrace information.

❑

APPENDIX

B

SystemC RTL: A Synthesizable Subset

To give an idea of what SystemC constructs are synthesizable, this appendix provides a listing of the synthesizable SystemC constructs. This subset may not be the same as that supported by currently available synthesis tools.

Constructs that have relevance only to simulation and not to synthesis, are identified as "ignored constructs" and constructs that are not synthesizable, such as those used for system modeling, are marked as "not supported". The constructs are categorized as follows:

i. *Supported*: Constructs that get synthesized into hardware.

ii. *Not supported*: Synthesis terminates when such a construct is present in the source design file.

iii. *Ignored*: Warning messages are issued during synthesis, except for declarations.

One way to mask off unsupported constructs for synthesis is to use the compiler directive `#ifndef` with the `SYNTHESIS` define as follows.

```
#ifndef SYNTHESIS
  <non-synthesizable code here>
#endif
```

This way the same model can be used for both verification and synthesis.

In the following tables, the first column specifies the SystemC or C++ feature, the second column indicates whether the feature is supported or not, and the third column is for comments and exceptions.

B.1 SystemC Features

Channels	Supported.	Only the predefined `sc_signal`, `sc_signal_resolved` and `sc_signal_rv` channels are supported.
Clock methods	Not supported.	
Data member variables	Supported.	As long as they are of the synthesizable types and not used in two or more processes.
Events	Not supported.	
Fixed point types	Not supported.	
Interfaces	Not supported.	
Methods	Supported.	As long as the method uses and returns synthesizable types.
Module constructors	Supported.	Only instantiations, method declarations and sensitivity list declarations supported.

Modules	Supported.	
Multiply driven signal	Supported.	Signals are shorted.
Ports	Supported.	Only the predefined ones, `sc_in`, `sc_out` and `sc_inout` are supported. The resolved ports `sc_out_rv`, `sc_inout_rv`, `sc_out_resolved` and `sc_inout_resolved` are also supported.
Processes	Only SC_METHOD process.	SC_THREAD process not supported.
SC_HAS_PROCESS	Supported.	To the extent that synthesizable types are used to pass in values.
sc_main()	Not supported.	
Sensitivity list	Supported.	Cannot mix edge-sensitive and level-sensitive events in one process.
Signals	Supported.	`sc_signal`, `sc_signal_resolved`, `sc_signal_rv`.
Simulation control	Not supported.	
Type sc_bit	Supported.	
Type sc_bv	Supported.	
Type sc_logic	Supported.	
Type sc_lv	Supported.	
Type sc_uint, sc_int	Supported.	
Types sc_bigint, sc_biguint	Supported.	
Waveform tracing	Not supported.	

B.2 C++ Features

Literals		
Character literal	Supported.	
Floating point literal	Not supported.	
Integer literal constants	Supported.	Decimal, octal and hexadecimal form.
NULL value	Not supported.	
String literal	Supported.	
Types		
Abstract data type	Supported.	
Array types	Supported.	Only for synthesizable element types.
Bool type	Supported.	
Class declaration	Not supported.	
Class types	Supported.	Equivalent of struct only supported. Only synthesizable types for member objects and synthesizable methods (functions) only. No constructors are supported. Destructors are ignored.
Enumeration type	Supported.	
Explicit user-defined type conversion	Supported.	Synthesizable types only.
Floating point type	Not supported.	
Integer types	Supported.	
Pointer type conversions	Not supported.	

Pointers	Supported.	To the extent that instantiate modules.
Const qualifier	Supported.	
Reference type	Not supported.	
Reference	Not supported.	
Struct type	Supported.	Members must all be of synthesizable data types.
Operators		
Address-of (&)	Not supported.	Except as for reference types.
Arithmetic if operator	Supported.	
Arithmetic operators	Supported.	
Assignment operator	Supported.	
Bitwise operators	Supported.	
Comma operator	Supported.	
Dereference operator	Not supported.	
Equality, relational & logical operators	Supported.	
Increment, decrement operators	Supported.	
Operators	Supported.	dot, arrow.
Scope operator	Supported.	Only to define functions in classes.
sizeof operator	Not supported.	
sizeof()	Not supported.	
Statements		
Break statement	Supported.	In a for statement only.
Compound statement and blocks	Supported.	

Continue statement	Supported.	In a for statement only.
Do while statement	Not supported.	
For loop statement	Supported.	The init statement and both the expressions must be compile time constants.
Goto statement	Not supported.	
If statement	Supported.	
Null statement	Supported.	
Switch statement	Supported.	`break` and `default` also supported.
While statement	Not supported.	
Functions		
C++ built-in functions	Not supported.	These include math library, input output library, file IO, etc.
C++ predefined libraries	Not supported.	These include stdio.h, iostream.h, string.h, fstream.h, etc.
Default initializers	Supported.	
Ellipses	Not supported.	
Function overloading	Not supported.	Except those defined by SystemC.
Functions	Supported.	Return type and argument types must be synthesizable types. Function may not return `void`. Recursion in functions with a static recursion bound is supported.
Global variables	Not supported.	
Inline functions	Supported.	Same restrictions on functions.

Pass by value	Supported.	Other forms not supported.
Pointer arguments	Not supported.	
Reference argument	Not supported.	
Miscellaneous		
Comments	Supported.	Both forms.
Derived classes	Supported.	Only those of SystemC modules and processes.
Dynamic memory allocation	Not supported.	
Exception handling	Not supported.	
extern keyword	Supported.	
Inheritance	Not supported.	Also multiple inheritance not supported.
Initialized variables	Supported.	Only variables declared in a method can be initialized - these are supported.
Member access specifiers (public, private, protected, friend)	Supported.	
Member variables	Supported.	Member variables accessed by two or more processes are not supported.
Operator overloading	Not supported.	Except those defined by the SystemC standard.
Preprocessor directives	Supported.	Included are `#define`, `#ifdef`, `#include`, etc.
Register local variables	Not supported.	
Static global variables	Not supported.	
Static local variables	Not supported.	
Static members	Not supported.	

This *pointer*	Not supported.	
Type casting, runtime	Not supported.	
Type conversion (implicit & explicit)	Supported.	Only between synthesizable types.
Type identification at runtime	Not supported.	
typedef	Supported.	
Unconditional branching	Not supported.	
Unions	Not supported.	
User-defined template class	Supported.	To the extent that only synthesizable types are used.
Using -> operator for struct members	Not supported.	Except for module instantiation.
Virtual functions	Not supported.	
*void * pointer*	Not supported.	
Volatile variable	Not supported.	

Bibliography

Here is a select list of suggested readings and books on SystemC and other related areas.

1. Alexander P. and D. Barton, *The Rosetta Functional Requirements Specification Domains*, Proceedings of the 9th International HDL Conference, March 2000.
2. Allara A., M. Bombana, P. Cavalloro and F. Ferrandi, *Requirements for Synthesis-oriented Modeling in SystemC*, Proceedings of FDL, September 2001.
3. Armstrong J.R. and Y. Ronen, *Modeling with SystemC: A Case Study*, Proceedings of the 10th International HDL Conference, March 2001.
4. Bhasker J., *A VHDL Primer, Third Edition*, Prentice Hall, 1999.
5. Bhasker J., *A VHDL Synthesis Primer, Second Edition*, Star Galaxy Publishing, 1998.
6. Bhasker J., *A Verilog HDL Primer, Second Edition*, Star Galaxy Publishing, 1999.
7. Bhasker J., *Verilog HDL Synthesis, A Practical Primer*, Star Galaxy Publishing, 1998.

8. Charest L., E.M. Aboulhamid and A. Tsikhanovich, *Designing with SystemC: Multi-Paradigm Modeling and Simulation Performance Evaluation*, Proceedings of the 11th International HDL Conference, March 2002.
9. *Describing Synthesizable RTL in SystemC*, http://www.synopsys.com/products/sld/rtl_systemc.pdf.
10. Economakos G., P. Oikonomakos and I. Poulakis, *Experiments with a C++ Synthesis Environment*, Proceedings of the 10th International HDL Conference, March 2001.
11. Einwich K., C. Clauss, G. Noessing, P. Schwartz and H. Zojer, *SystemC Extensions for Mixed-Signal System Design*, Proceedings of FDL, September 2001.
12. Embree P. and B. Kimble, *C Language Algorithms for Digital Signal Processing*, Prentice Hall, 1991.
13. *European SystemC Users Group Meetings*: http://www-ti.informatik.uni-tuebingen.de/~systemc.
14. Gajski D., J. Zhu, R. Domer, A. Gerstlauer and S. Zhao, *SpecC: Specification Language and Methodology*, Kluwer Academic Publishers, 2000.
15. Herrera F., C.I. Camargo and E. Villar, *Embedded System Design Methodology based on SystemC*, Proceedings of FDL, September 2001.
16. Lippman S.B. and J. Lajoie, *C++ Primer, Third Edition*, Addison Wesley, 1998.
17. Martin G. and B. Salefski, *System Level Design for SOCs: A Progress Report, Two Years On*, Proceedings of the 9th International HDL Conference, March 2000.
18. Narayan S. and J. Bhasker, *RTL Modeling using SystemC*, Proceedings of the 11th International HDL Conference, March 2002.
19. *SystemC web site*: http://www.systemc.org.
20. *SystemC Version 2.0 Users Guide.*
21. Thornberg B. and M. O'Nils, *Analysis of Modeling and Simulation Capabilities in SystemC and Ocapi using a Video Filter Design*, Proceedings of the FDL, September 2001.

❑

Index

❑